Believing in the Text

Religions and Discourse

Edited by James M. M. Francis

Volume 18

PETER LANG
Oxford · Bern · Berlin · Bruxelles · Frankfurt a.M. · New York · Wien

David Jasper & George Newlands
with Darlene Bird (eds)

Believing in the Text

Essays from the Centre for the Study of Literature, Theology and the Arts, University of Glasgow

PETER LANG
Oxford · Bern · Berlin · Bruxelles · Frankfurt a.M. · New York · Wien

Bibliographic information published by Die Deutsche Bibliothek
Die Deutsche Bibliothek lists this publication in the Deutsche Nationalbibliografie; detailed bibliographic data is available on the Internet at ‹http://dnb.ddb.de›.

British Library and Library of Congress Cataloguing-in-Publication Data: A catalogue record for this book is available from *The British Library*, Great Britain, and from *The Library of Congress*, USA

ISSN 1422-8998
ISBN 3-03910-076-9
US-ISBN 0-8204-6892-4

Hochfeldstrasse 32, Postfach 746, CH-3000 Bern 9, Switzerland
info@peterlang.com, www.peterlang.com, www.peterlang.net

Printed in Germany

Contents

DAVID JASPER AND GEORGE NEWLANDS
Introduction 7

DAVID JASPER
The Subject on Trial and Baudrillard's Nightmare 11

S. BRENT PLATE
T/here: Conversing and Traversing Julia Kristeva's Writings 25

J. STEPHEN FOUNTAIN
The Trace of the (M)other: Liminality and Maternity in *Dead Man Walking* 41

ANDREW W. HASS
Seeing Through a Glass Face to Face 57

ELIZABETH PHILPOT
Susanna: Indecent Attraction / Fatal Exposure 75

PETER STILES
To the Threshold: Window Scenes in Elizabeth Gaskell's *Ruth* 95

JEFFREY F. KEUSS
'Seeing' *Adam Bede* – An Iconographic Reading 115

CATHERINE RAINE
Sin and Theodicy – Victorian and Modern Style 135

DAVID E. KLEMM
Re-entering the Magic Theatre: The Trace of the Other in Hermann Hesse's *Steppenwolf* 145

DARREN J. N. MIDDLETON
Scratching the Barthian Itch: A Theological Reading of John Updike's *Roger's Version* 159

GEORGE NEWLANDS
Theology, Culture and the Arts 177

CHRISTOPHER BURDON
Christian Worship in the Third Millennium: Homage or Celebration? 199

ALISON JASPER
Word as Flesh: The Sign of Female Circumcision 219

KIYOSHI TSUCHIYA
A Response to Postmodern Theology 231

List of Contributors 247

DAVID JASPER AND GEORGE NEWLANDS

Introduction

All the contributors to this volume have been closely associated with the Centre for the Study of Literature, Theology and the Arts in the University of Glasgow, either as students, teachers or visiting fellows. Between them they represent the rich diversity of intellectual activity that has characterized the work of the Centre over the eleven years of its life in Glasgow, and before that for five years in the University of Durham, England. When it was founded the Centre was dedicated to the study of literature and theology, as was the journal of that title, with which the Centre has maintained close connections. In many ways life in those days was much simpler, and it was assumed that our work was at the identifiable face of, for example, the Bible and literature, or exploring the theological and religious themes (usually Christian) within the great works of literature. The theoretical basis within the humanities, and the political implications of such work remained very largely unexplored and even unacknowledged.

The rich diversity of the essays in this collection indicates the huge changes that have taken place over the past fifteen years. The debt to such scholars as Nathan A. Scott, Jr., Martin Jarrett-Kerr, F. W. Dillistone and John Coulson remains, although their work is too little read by the newer generations of scholars (with the exception, perhaps of that of Scott). However, we have deliberately not attempted to impose a strong and organizing editorial hand upon work which bursts with life and questions at the interface of the arts and religion. First of all there us an international diversity – of British, American, Canadian, Australian and Japanese background – which remains within the common conversation. Behind the differences between these scholars there lie literally thousands of hours of talk and debate, and it is significant that in the end they are all clear about their corporate aim and philosophy. What emerge are essays that range from the historical to the liturgical, to work on film, fiction, hermeneutics, cultural issues, theology, the fine arts, postmodern theory – the list is almost endless.

For, within the walls of a university, once the disciplinary barriers are challenged, interdisciplinarity quickly moves into multi-disciplinarity. Although theology and religious reflection remain very much at the heart of the Centre's concerns and the Centre continues to reside within the context of a Department of Theology and Religious Studies, most of us involved with it have found ourselves drawn into discussions within academic areas in which we have no formal training; yet questions of textuality and how we actually 'read' lead into ever-widening circles of debate and critique. In the end the most important questions addressed are not narrowly academic, but focus our attention upon fundamental issues of the nature of the self, society and philosophy. Indeed, as our 'subject' continues to grow and evade precise definition, we find ourselves challenging the very concept of what it means to be 'academic' or to pursue scholarship in any narrow sense. Yet in no way is this to diminish the scholarly claims of this book. Indeed, quite to the contrary – except that we have come to accept that scholarship, if it is really to matter, is to be 'lived' on the edge, or between boundaries. We set out to challenge and make people feel uncomfortable and to warn against established formulae or settling into the satisfaction (perhaps the self-satisfaction) of the 'expert'.

All this is not to say that these essays lack excellent credentials. They are intended to jostle together in diversity, coming from the pens of writers most of whom are teaching in universities or colleges world-wide. Some are very senior, established and distinguished scholars in their fields. One of the characteristics of the Centre has been its energetic hosting of conferences and seminars that have brought to it not simply academics, but also church-people, poets, novelists, artists, film makers – indeed all sorts and conditions of people have come prepared to talk across boundaries, stepping outside the safety zones of their specific expertise or confession. On one occasion, a retired Anglican bishop found common ground with a leading 'death of God' theologian; on another a distinguished novelist gave a lesson in theology to a room of theologians. Apart from the journal *Literature and Theology*, now edited by Professor Graham

Ward of the University of Manchester, books and articles have appeared in many continents through the medium of the Centre. Most of the essays in this book are, in a sense, by scholars of the 'third generation' of the study of theology and literature, and to those of us who learnt largely by trial and error, their writing has a sophistication and an ease with 'theory' that we can only admire from afar. But in the latter half of the twentieth century it was scholars like the late John Coulson of Bristol University who first bravely posed the questions for us, or, in the United States, the towering figure of Nathan Scott who set out in books like *The Wild Prayer of Longing* (1971) to relate poetry and the sacred and 'to suggest how powerfully the strategies of art invoke mysteries and meanings that might otherwise elude our grasp'. Other teachers followed, notably Robert Detweiler of Emory University, a figure directly connected with many of our contributors. These were great pioneers in the field of literature, religion and theology.

This collection appears appropriately in the series on Religions and Discourse. All our knowledge is linked to the rest of what we think we know. For theology this is understood as a gift which we are invited to explore and in which we are encouraged to participate. At a time when much contemporary theology is increasingly focused on its internal traditions and beliefs, these essays continue the task of seeking to build bridges and to initiate dialogue with other disciplines. In a transcultural perspective the dialogue with literature and art is understood not as a limiting but as an inclusive paradigm, as a particular example of an engagement which theology may undertake with the whole range of the humanities and the sciences. Theology is always done within the frameworks of cultural and political circumstances, and always involves a degree of integration, conscious or unconscious, with these frameworks. Counter-cultural theologies may turn out to be mirror images of the cultures they set out to critique, and theologies of mediation may lead to unthinking assimilation of dubious assumptions. The need for serious critical theology has perhaps never been greater, and the magnitude of the task is not to be underestimated. The book is a fragment, or rather a series of fragments, offered in encouragement, a stage on the way in the developing field of literary and religious studies. It is a celebration of the first ten years of the Centre in Glasgow, and, we hope, an indication of much more that is to come in future years.

Thanks are due to the skills and patience of many people in the preparation of this work for publication, but especially to Calum Shepherd of the University of Glasgow and J. Sage Elwell of the University of Iowa. We are grateful also to the Editor of *Literature and Theology* who provided us with a generous grant to assist with the costs of editing and preparing the manuscript.

The *Self-portrait as the Apostle Paulus* by Rembrandt is reproduced by kind permission of the Rijksmuseum, Amsterdam, The Netherlands. *The Slaughtered Ox*, also by Rembrandt, is reproduced courtesy of the Glasgow Museums and Art Galleries, Glasgow, Scotland. The drawing by C. F. Lindberg of the wall painting by the Risinge Master, *Susanna Bathing*, is reproduced by permission of the Antikvarisk-topografiska Arkivet, the National Heritage Board, Stockholm. *Susanna and the Elders* by Peter Paul Rubens is reproduced by permission of the Bayerische Staatsgemäldesammlungen, Alte Pinakothek, Munich. *Susanna and the Elders* by Guido Reni is reproduced by permission of the Nartional Gallery, London. *Susanna in the Bath* by Laurits Tuxen is reproduced by permission of the Ny Carlsberg Glyptotek, Copenhagen.

DAVID JASPER

The Subject on Trial and Baudrillard's Nightmare[1]

Part One

In February 1986, the French philosopher Jean-Luc Nancy was invited to undertake an enquiry based upon the question 'who comes after the subject?' The background to this question was explained in the following way:

> one of the major characteristics of contemporary thought is the putting into question of the instance of the 'subject', according to the structure, the meaning and the value subsumed under this term in modern thought, from Descartes to Hegel, if not to Husserl. (Cadava, 5)

Contributors to his enquiry included Maurice Blanchot, Gilles Deleuze, Jacques Derrida, Luce Irigaray, Emmanuel Levinas, Jean-François Lyotard – a star-studded cast of French postmodern thinking. Their placing of subjectivity 'on trial' seems initially a simple task, in essence involving a 'deconstruction' of the metaphysics which have largely undergirded Western thought and philosophical construction. This 'deconstruction' represents a shift from the claims of Enlightenment 'reason' and the apparent certainties of Descartes' *Meditations on First Philosophy* (1641), with its answer to the question, 'What then am I?', and an exposure to the ethical questions prompted by the move forward from the subject toward, in the words of Nancy's enquirer,

> someone – *some one* – else in its place (this last is obviously a mere convenience: the 'place' could not be the same). Who would it be? How would s/he present him/herself? (Cadava, 5)

1 An earlier version of this essay was published in William S. Haney II and Nicholas O. Pagan (eds.), *Ethics and Subjectivity in Literary and Cultural Studies*, (Peter Lang, 2002).

This shift from Enlightenment to post-Enlightenment thinking is easy to oversimplify and caricature. It involves a huge and complex move in philosophy, theology and ethics, not to say an encounter with scientific paradigm shifts which many of us – and I include myself in this number – are ill-equipped to appreciate fully.

Of course, in a brief essay I can barely even scratch the surface of these implications, and so my strategy will be to probe a number of 'pressure points' in order to test certain practical implications for ethics and culture. The concluding part of the paper will offer a meditation on what has gone before – a kind of visionary proposal with few, if any, scientific or philosophical pretensions – a response to the nightmare of the post-Enlightenment collapse of subjectivity: a possible verdict for the subject on trial (my title, it should be recognized, looks back gratefully to Ivan Klima's great novel from former Eastern Europe, *Judge on Trial* [1986]).

Martin Heidegger firmly locates the centrality of subjectivity in modernity (his term is *Neuzeit*) in Descartes, 'when the certainty of all being and all truth is founded on the self-consciousness of the single ego: *ego cogito ergo sum*'. Thence, in philosophy all is seen in terms of its relation to our consciousness, most notably in German Idealism and its attempt to prove subject and object identical, and the world itself and the way we think the world unified in one and the same process (see Bowie, 8–9). However, this neat Cartesian unity is already placed under severe strain in Kant's *Critique of Pure Reason* in its second edition of 1787 – a hugely important moment in the trial of the subject – where Kant adopts the term 'synthetic unity of self-consciousness' in opposition to Descartes' 'cogito', that is, the 'analytical unity of self-consciousness' which identifies the thinking and the being of the subject. Kant argues that the unity of self-consciousness is actually only a synthesis of different moments of consciousness allowing the subject to become 'self-aware', a synthesis dependent upon what Kant terms 'spontaneity'. That is, such synthetic unity is 'self-caused' and not caused by something else.

The consequences of this are immense and already shake the firm and simplified claims of Enlightenment thinking. Kant has a serious problem in adopting self-consciousness as the highest principle of his philosophy. It is also a huge problem for moral philosophy. This he returns to in the last of his large-scale works, *Religion within the Limits of Reason Alone* (1792), Kant's attempt to interpret Christianity solely in ethical terms and his notion of radical evil in human nature. And if freedom and freewill lie at the heart of Kant's enterprise, they remain, like Moses' God, hidden: as Kant acknowledges in the *Second Critique:*

> For we can explain nothing except what we can reduce to laws whose object is given in some possible experience. But freedom is a mere idea, whose objective reality cannot be shown either according to laws of nature and thus also not in any possible experience. (quoted in Bowie, 21)

The problem, we might conclude, for Kant, is that he is left with a moral philosophy in which the fundamental principle (not being the self) cannot be articulated in philosophy. This difficulty, with its narrowed options in religious terms, occupies the very heart of the present discussion.

Via the supreme idealism of Hegel's beautiful, and perverse, *Phenomenology of Spirit* (1807), surely the greatest of all candidates for Derrida's reading strategy of deconstruction as applied to Rousseau in *Of Grammatology*, there is a direct line between Kant's *First Critique* and Nietzsche's *The Genealogy of Morals* – works divided by almost exactly one hundred years of history (1791–1887). Notoriously, Alasdair MacIntyre in *After Virtue* (1981) opposes Nietzsche to Aristotle as the Father of Western Ethics, admitting Nietzsche's 'ruthless honesty', so that 'it would be easy in the contemporary world to be an intelligent Nietzschean' (MacIntyre, 238). Exactly – Nietzsche is, after all, the supreme rhetorician (celebrating the greatest of the four great classical tropes of rhetoric – irony); and does not Plato – through the other great rhetorician of the Western tradition, Socrates – warn us *against* rhetoric in the *Phaedrus*? In *The Genealogy of Morals*, Nietzsche draws Kant's arguments to a logical conclusion: if for Kant the self-consciousness of the subject fails as the highest principle of philosophy, for Nietzsche the 'devaluation of the highest values' is summarized in the death of God (see Vattimo, 20), and nihilism is the situation in which the human subject explicitly recognizes that the lack of foundation is a constitutive part of its condition. Rejoicing in the waning of Christianity, Nietzsche asks what values would replace Christian values as the guide for Western culture: quoting his own work *The Gay Science* at the very end of *The Genealogy*, Nietzsche triumphantly affirms:

> The Christian ethics with its key notion, ever more strictly applied, of truthfulness; the casuistic finesse of the Christian conscience, translated and sublimated into the scholarly conscience, into intellectual integrity to be maintained at all costs; the interpretation of nature as a proof of God's beneficent care; the interpretation of history to the glory of divine providence, as perpetual testimony of a moral order and moral ends; the interpretation of individual experience as preordained, purposely arranged for the salvation of the soul; – all these things are now of the past: they revolt our consciences as being indecent, dishonest, cowardly, effeminate. It is this rigor, if anything, that makes us good Europeans and the heirs of Europe's longest, most courageous, self-conquest. (Nietzsche, 297)

All great things, above all the 'subject', perish by an act of self-cancellation. In *The Genealogy*, Nietzsche triumphantly affirms what Heidegger was also, later, to realize, that the dominance of the subject is subverted (or deconstructed) because we articulate subjectivity in languages which we do not invent but by which alone self and world are articulated. In *Zein und Zeit* (1927), Heidegger struggles to recover an ontology in the nonidentification of Being and foundation, and as his philosophy wavers so he himself identifies culturally with that National Socialism which Nietzsche foresees and against which his rhetoric, with endless and, in the end, futile irony rages.

But this ontology Nietzsche consistently refuses, although admitting at the end of *The Genealogy* that 'man would sooner have the void for his purpose that be void of purpose' (299). *The Genealogy of Morals* is not about morals or morality – it begins in nothingness, without subject, admitting that the only moral position is to abandon 'morals'. Is this, in fact, a way back to a profound and neglected form of religious thinking and 'being', a way which abandons theological realism and Cartesian rationalism following in one sense – though it is not a simple return – the theology of Meister Eckhart in his boldest of all statements: 'Man's last and highest parting occurs when, for God's sake, he takes leave of God.' Nietzsche, the prophet who proclaims the death of God, would have recognized an echo of this in words of Jürgen Habermas, more familiar in tone to us, children of the Enlightenment, as obsessed with the subject as Eckhart's contemporaries were with Christian theology – words as applicable to Adorno's 'negative dialectics' and Derrida's 'deconstruction' as to Nietzsche on morals:

> The totalizing self-critique of reason gets caught in a performative contradiction since subject-centred reason can be convicted of being authoritarian in nature only by having recourse to its own tools [...] the only available means for uncovering their own insufficiency. (Habermas, 185)

But is this a way forward in linguistic celebration, beyond the subject – or simply an acknowledgement of the prison-house of language, and an entrapment of the subject in its own history? If it is the latter, then Nietzsche was wrong and all systems have won, and that being the case all we have is Baudrillard's nightmare in which the refusal to give up 'the real' (with all that that implies) consigns us to 'the desert of the real itself' (Baudrillard, 'Simulacra', 166). The fables of God and self persist until there is no possibility of distinguishing anything from simulacra and simulations. The refusal to let go to the point at which everything – God, Christ, truth, self – becomes merely a mirror image of what continues to be claimed, is the most profound of all moral failings and a realization of the horror whose shadow Kant saw: in the words of Andrew Bowie:

> The recurrence of the term 'spontaneity' is important, in that it links the problem of our free-will to the problem of describing the existence of our self-consciousness. It is as if Kant is in the position of Moses in Schönberg's *Moses und Äron*. The most fundamental part of his philosophy cannot be shown, just as Moses is faced with the unenviable task of persuading people to believe in a God they cannot see. (Bowie, 21)

As in the opera, there can be no true conclusion, but merely a sinking to the ground in despair with Moses who finally cries: 'O Wort, du Wort, das mir fehlt!' (O word, thou word, that I lack!).

Part Two

For a while, within Romantic thought, it all cohered. The affirmation of the rights of the individual, of the imagination and of feeling at least took the self beyond the Panglossian philosophy of work without arguing as the only way to make life bearable (Voltaire, 144), or beyond oversimplistic views of the human will. Kant's legacy of a noumenal rational agent was, at least, clear, if – as we have seen – at best fragile and fraught with future difficulties. For the great Romantics, the truth may be found *within*, from an inner voice heard in epiphanic moments, as in Wordsworth's *Tintern Abbey* (1798):

> [...] a sense sublime
> Of something far more deeply,
> whose dwelling is the light of setting suns,
> And the round ocean, and the living air,
> And the blue sky, and in the mind of man,
> A motion and a spirit, that impels
> All thinking things, all objects of all thought,
> And rolls through all things. (lines 96–103)

It is a voice heard in the poets – in Hölderlin's *Patmos* or Shelley's *Prometheus* – and also a moment of experience *seen* in the visual arts: Constable's most famous painting, now known as *The Hay Wain*, is an attempt to capture the experience of a moment of time – noon – exactly as seen and felt; while Turner endlessly tries to paint what it *feels* like to be, for example, on a ship in a storm, or to cross the Alps with Hannibal. Man is the creature who becomes aware and brings to expression that which Herder describes: 'See the whole of nature, behold the great analogy of creation. Everything feels itself and its like, life reverberates to life' (see Taylor, 369).

But the price was high. Upon the fragile subject Kant lays the categorical imperative, while Fichte writes in the Introduction to the *Wissenschaftslehre* of 1784:

> Attend to yourself: turn your attention away from everything that surrounds you and towards your inner life; this is the first demand that philosophy makes of its

> disciple. Our concern is not with anything that lies outside you, but only with yourself. (Fichte, 83)

As one of the few in England who were deeply read in German Idealist philosophy, Thomas Carlyle was profoundly aware, and morally so, that this intense self-consciousness was finally deeply diseased. The constructed subjectivity of modern man's self-consciousness has all but effaced, Carlyle argued, 'the memory of [Adam's] first state of freedom and paradisaic Unconsciousness'. For him (under the influence of Schiller) the birth of the modern 'subject' was a Fall into self-consciousness and a deviation from moral health. In *Sartor Resartus* (1833–4) Carlyle placed the mind's self-consciousness as a sort of frame around the narrative, which offers the possibility, in a kind of rhetorical striptease, of an inner 'meaning' held out to the reader but finally withdrawn – the truth which the framing subject seems to present turns out to be the truth that there is no truth. Subjectivity, then, merely frames, at best, a fiction – exemplified repeatedly in the poetic narratives of Robert Browning, a close friend of Carlyle.

But the tragedy was more than simply a literary game in the nineteenth century. Matthew Arnold, deeply aware of the Kantian legacy, simply could not sustain the demands made upon him by the categorical imperative, by the egotistical sublime or by the relentless pressure on the subject of Fichtean philosophy. For him it threatened a profound isolation in which 'we mortal millions live *alone*'. In this subjective isolation, 'God' himself is redefined so that only the emotive meaning of the word is retained (see Shaw, 142) – ethical ideas alone reside, for Arnold, in what remains of 'God', while his theology is reduced to the search for an abstract formula. When in 1852 Arnold published anonymously *Empedocles on Etna*, he looked back both to Shelley and to Wordsworth's *Prelude*, but now the images were reversed and ultimately dissolved. Arnold's Empedocles, you may recall, refers to the 'Living Clouds' round Etna echoed by 'the fainter sea below'. The image recalls the mist round Snowdon in *The Prelude* which echoes 'the real sea' below, and the same image is in Shelley's *Prometheus Unbound*. But Arnold reverses Wordsworth's priorities – in *The Prelude* the sea is 'real': for Empedocles it is 'fainter' than the 'living clouds', which are themselves the stronger 'sea' (see Jasper, 38). Where then lies reality – as a real or a fainter sea? In the airy, insubstantial clouds? The metaphor is fractured and the sea – that hugely important image in nineteenth-century imperial Britain – becomes the medium of our dissociation from self, of the finite from the infinite, and finally of our failure to articulate and communicate in words for which we can no longer bear the responsibility. Resistance to and a refusal to believe in this collapse of the self remains stubborn, though literature and art have been insistent that we continue to face it. As early as 1912, Thomas Hardy was reflecting on his portrayal of Sue Bridehead in *Jude the Obscure* (1895) as 'the intellectualized, emancipated bundle of nerves that modern conditions were producing', and on the critic whose regret it was 'that the portrait of the newcomer had been left to be drawn by a man, and was not done by one of her own sex, who would never have allowed her to break down at the end' (preface to the 1912 edition). Yet breakdown there is – dissociation – and crisis, both of self and of self-expression.

For the crisis in language – which emerged fully in the twentieth century, and not only in post-Saussurean literary theory but also in the *'krisis'* theology of Karl Barth's *Römerbrief*, written in blood shed in the trenches of Europe – is also the most profound crisis of the 'subject'. Charles Taylor, in his magisterial study *Sources of the Self* (1989), believes that there is no possibility of a return, no looking back. Is the alternative then that black pastiche of traditional Christian hope in Yeats's 'The Second Coming'?

> Things fall apart; the centre cannot hold;
> Mere anarchy is loosed upon the world [...]
> The darkness drops again; but now I know
> That twenty centuries of stony sleep
> Were vexed to nightmare by a rocking cradle,
> And what rough beast, its hour come round at last,
> Slouches towards Bethlehem to be born?

The excess of Christian hope has brought an excess of violence, and Christian theology, still feeding on the corpse of Hegelian philosophy, has become ever more bizarre across the range of the Western tradition from the Protestant Jürgen Moltmann to the Roman Catholic Hans Urs von Balthasar. And philosophy halts, with Heidegger's 'Origin of the Work of Art', in the Holocaust, the purest and most terrible work of art of the twentieth century.

In postmodern hyperlogic are we then left with only the option presented by Jean Baudrillard – the subject, while ethics drown in a deliberate mass suicide of pure consumerism, the only heir of Western Christendom:

> a system is abolished only by pushing it into hyperlogic, but forcing it into an excessive practice which is equivalent to a brutal amortization. 'You want us to consume – O.K., let's consume always more, and anything whatsoever; for any useless and absurd purpose.' (Baudrillard, *In the Shadow*, 46)

Part Three

In the concluding part of this essay, I want to expand a little further this notion of 'postmodern hyperlogic', and then offer a brief response to it.

In his 1993 book *Symbolic Exchange and Death*, Jean Baudrillard defines what he terms 'three orders of simulacra' responding to mutations of the law of value since the Renaissance. The first, of least relevance to us here, operates up to the Industrial Revolution, on the natural law of value, its dominant schema being that of the *counterfeit*. The copy 'counterfeits' the genuine original. The second, which is the true child of the Enlightenment, operates on the market law of value in terms of products and production. The third, into which the age of production inevitably falls, functions according to the structural law of value, our current code-governed phase in the nightmarish celebration of simulation.

In terms of what has been previously said, the nineteenth century was the great age of production, the flower of the Enlightenment, and the exposure of its agonizing placing of the subject on trial. Unlike the counterfeits of the Renaissance, the results of mass production no longer pose the problems of specificity and origin. The aim, rather, is the production of identical objects in celebration of equivalence and indifference. So-called 'quality control' guarantees infinite and indefinite reproducibility without origin. In human or rather inhuman terms the realization of the industrial simulacrum is found in Aldous Huxley's 1932 dystopia *Brave New World*, with its World State Motto set over the 'Central London Hatchery and Conditioning Centre', COMMUNITY, IDENTITY, STABILITY (Huxley, 15). Its irony recognizes, of course, that the achievement of the human production chain both realizes and negates precisely those three things. As Carlyle, Arnold and the rest of the nineteenth century after Kant knew full well, in the age of mechanical reproduction (or production) there can be no community, no identity and finally no stability.

Thus Walter Benjamin, in his great essay 'The Work of Art in the Age of Mechanical Reproduction' (1936) to which Baudrillard makes reference, shows how reproduction absorbs the process of production, changes its goals and alters the status of both product and producer – in short, redefines the notion of meaning and self-hood. For Benjamin (like Marshall McLuhan) recognized that production itself has no meaning, so that we find ourselves (and don't say we have not been warned) teetering on the brink of history, slipping into the postmodern abyss of *simulation*.

Baudrillard plays a game with Ferdinand de Saussure and his system of linguistics: take Saussure's structural laws to their extreme and what remains? The loss of determination, the loss of meaning – above all the loss of reference. In much the same way, Jacques Derrida picks up in Heidegger that which would have horrified Nietzsche. Take everything to its logical end (make no mistake, Baudrillard and Derrida are faithful, if grimly ironic, children of the Enlightenment), and where are we left at the implosion of the age of production – with the end of labour, of political economy, of the signifier/signified dialectic of the dialectics of value? Oh, Brave New World – from one hell we collapse into what Baudrillard terms 'the cool universe of digitality [which] absorbs the universe of metaphor and metonymy'.

In his Foreword to the 1946 edition of *Brave New World*, Huxley argued that the world he had projected was coming much faster than he had expected. What, then, of the year 2003? We have passed into a universe of structures and binary oppositions. There is, indeed, nothing outside the text, merely systems of interrelationship without grounding – the metaphysics of indeterminacy and the code. Values are merely strategic and tactical, and the subject identified only by DNA coding. Any finality, if that can be spoken of at all, is already inscribed in the code. All around us there is only cyberspace, since this cannot now be distinguished from 'real' space – or rather, as Nietzsche said, 'Down with all hypotheses that have allowed belief in a real world.'

Are ethics, like any vestigial claims of the subject, merely systems of defence to preserve the vicious circle of hyper-reality, simulacra and cyberspace? Are we in the nightmare of Baudrillard from which there can be no way out? The displacements and distortions of metaphor and metonymy which allowed reflection, the sense of the other, the aesthetic – have now been absorbed. There are no metaphors or metaphysics in cyberspace.

Or may we dare, at this point, to return to Plato's great allegory of the cave in *The Republic*? Have we now realized the condition of those confined and chained in the cave who see only their own shadows, or the shadows of one another – for whom, as Socrates puts it, 'the true would be literally nothing but the shadows of the images'? (Plato, 279). But Socrates does, in his conversation with Glaucon and 'according to his poor belief', suggest the possibility of the ascent of the soul even at the price of ridicule. What space remains after the terrible deconstructions of cyberspace? My conclusion, a return to Jean-Luc Nancy's project, is deliberately brief and, perhaps, naive. It is a return to art and to an image. It may be only a *place* to start again.

In an interview given in 1984, Baudrillard addresses the Descartes of the *Meditations*:

> In the Cartesian project there is at least the inauguration of a rational principle. It is from this rational principle that the whole question of doubt arises. This doubt comes from the subject – as subject of knowledge, as subject of discourse.
>
> Whether Descartes in fact succeeds in making the subject constitute itself, in its reality, in relation to a diabolical world which is full of superstitions and hallucinations and so on is a controversial matter. But the fact remains that

> Cartesian doubt is based on the promise of a world which can be confirmed only in terms of its own reality: there is doubt on the one hand and there is reality on the other hand; and here is the conflict between the two, which Descartes tries to resolve. (Baudrillard, *The Evil Demon of Images*, 43)

In response to this, Baudrillard returns to a moment anterior to Descartes, and a deep irrationality (compare Jung, or Stravinsky in *The Rite of Spring*) which dissolves the distinction between illusion and reality, making faith and doubt equally impossible in a world only of excess and distortion, overflowing with the demands of technology that generates the hyperlogic of ultimate destruction. Thus we are all King Lear on the blasted heath, without inside or outside, all inside and all outside.

But one of the contributors to Jean-Luc Nancy's enquiry offers a different note. Maurice Blanchot acknowledges the essential solitude to be found in the work of art and the literary text which *necessarily* becomes a space – the space of literature – in which language even and especially the language of an old theology, may be redeemed for the subject out of time, and for time. It is a solitude and a space which, outside the ethical, may grant a rebirth to morals in a new, tentative *koinonia*. Blanchot answers the question Who then comes after the subject? with an image of children playing in the garden: and only children (he says) can create a counting rhyme that opens up to impossibility, and only children can sing of it happily. 'So, let us be, even in the anguish and the heaviness of uncertainty, from time to time, these children' (Cadava, 60).

Bibliography

Baudrillard, Jean. 'Simulacra and Simulations', reprinted in Mark Poster (ed.), *Selected Writings*. Oxford: Polity Press, 1988.

—— *The Evil Demon of Images*. Sydney: Power Institute Publications No. 3,1988.

—— *In the Shadow of the Silent Majorities*. New York: Semiotext(e), 1983.

Bowie, Andrew. *Aesthetics and Subjectivity*. Manchester: Manchester UP, 1990.

Cadava, Eduardo, Peter Connor, and Jean-Luc Nancy (eds.). *Who Comes After the Subject?* New York: Routledge, 1991.

Detweiler, Robert. 'Literary Echoes of Postmodernism', *Journal of the American Academy of Religion,* Winter (1998).

Fichte, Johann G. *Wissenschaftslehre*, reprinted in R. Bubner (ed.), *German Idealist Philosophy*. Hamondsworth: Penguin, 1997.

Habermas, Jurgen. *The Philosophical Discourse of Modernity*. Cambridge: Polity Press, 1999.

Huxley, Aldous. *Brave New World*, reprinted Harmondsworth: Penguin, 1970.

Jasper, David. *The Sacred and Secular Canon in Romanticism*. London: Macmillan, 1999.

MacIntyre, Alasdair. *After Virtue*. London: Duckworth, 1982.

Nietzsche, Friedrich W. *The Geneology of Morals*, translated by Frances Golffry. New York: Doubleday, 1956.

Plato, *The Republic*, translated by H. D. P. Lee. Harmondsworth: Penguin, 1955.

Shaw, David. *The Lucid Veil*. London: Athlone Press, 1987.

Taylor, Charles. *Sources of the Self.* Cambridge: Harvard UP, 1989.

Vattimo, Gianni. *The End of Modernity*. Cambridge: Polity Press, 1988.

Voltaire, F-M. A. *Candide*. Harmondsworth: Penguin, 1947.

S. BRENT PLATE

T/here: Conversing and Traversing Julia Kristeva's Writings

> I do not know whence its origin, but I do know that innate desire to see new places and to change one's home. There is something truly pleasant, though demanding, about this curiosity for wandering through different regions, whereas those who remain in one place always experience a peculiar boredom in their repose. If anyone places the highest virtue not in the mind but in places, giving immobility the name of constancy, then sufferers from the gout must certainly appear constant, the dead must appear even more constant, while the mountains are the most constant of all. (Petrarch)

Since the dawn of literature the metaphor of the 'journey' has been used to write about the process of lived life, and there remains an implicit and sometimes explicit connection between travel and writing, journals and journeys. In a symposium in the New York Times Book Review aptly entitled 'Itchy Feet and Pencils', Russell Banks states: 'all good writing is travel writing. That is, it's an account of a journey' (Banks, 1). Along the same lines Robert Stone reflects: 'When one travels, I think one spends a lot of time imagining. To travel is also to judge. Writing is a similar procedure inasmuch as this constant judgment and imagination are taking place' (Banks, 25, emphasis added). From another angle and in a different context, Julia Kristeva states: 'Writing is impossible without some kind of exile' (Kristeva (1986), 298).

Journey is rupture. That is, it moves one away from home, wrests one from complacency. Likewise, the journey is also impossible without some kind of home; there must be a place from which one has been exiled, or from which one has travelled. These two elements – home and journey – have a necessary but tenuous relation, and in what follows i[1] will take a closer look at the metaphors and geographies of journey and home. Yet, rather than setting up a neat and clean dialectic between the two, through the writings of Kristeva i come to find an interesting and impossible liminal space, a perpetually situated place i am calling *T/here*. T/here is religious inasmuch as it connects with prophetic traditions as well as pilgrimage rituals found across religious traditions. Still, t/here enacts a pilgrimage without the guarantee of safety or promised lands. T/here is the event of being on the way, in process, becoming, the moments so radically *in* time and *in* space they provoke constantly new judgments and imaginations.

Contemporary travels and travails

T/here is, however, not self-evident. For even while the metaphor 'life is a journey' reigns throughout literature, it seems to hold little significance in contemporary western culture; it has lost its taste, become useless. The productive space of pilgrimage has given way to endless travel, to a Baudrillardian 'obscene' travel – a travel without a scene, where nothing is seen, but only captured in the image of the camera to be seen later. Technology has restructured our movements through time and has dislocated our concepts and contexts of space. As anthropologist Brad Shorre has commented: 'At one with modern telecommunications, modern air travel conveys a sense of total geographic simultaneity, of everywhere as nowhere special, of anyplace as everyplace' (Shorre, 147). With the ability to transcend widely diverse cultures in a matter of hours, we no longer know what it is to have the physical sensation of moving, but only perhaps of being 'elsewhere' which is 'nowhere special'. Such statements come as no surprise, for accompanying the endlessly moving contemporary life is a proliferation of books and articles telling us how restless and rootless we are.

1 As a rhetorical device that mimics the theme of this article, I use the lower-case for the first-person pronoun.

What we begin to long for then, in our binary mode of thinking, is an overly simplistic return to home. Opting for roots and staticity over movement and flux only binds us in a way that cannot be rebound. We foolishly desire the rest of stability and make an icon of home, thinking that, in the end, Dorothy's return to Kansas is a happy ending. However, as Salman Rushdie suggests of *The Wizard of Oz*, we are misreading that film if we come away from it thinking that it is speaking about the superior pleasures of home over the journey. We may remember the phrase, 'I want to go home', but Rushdie suggests that the power of the song 'Over the Rainbow' sheds the most emotion and cries out for life elsewhere. Rushdie claims: 'In its most potent emotional moment, this is unarguably a film about the joys of going away, of leaving the greyness and entering the colour, of making a new life in the "place where there isn't any trouble"' (Rushdie, 23). The naive assertion of home over journey is a Hollywood fantasy. But, then again, so are the pleasures of a journey without trouble.

So, while restlessness is certainly inherent in contemporary western life, the problem may be more complex than merely setting up a homestead. For we have not only lost the ability to be at home, but we have equally lost the ability to be on a journey, and these two dimensions impact each other. We do not know how to be away, or at home. What is needed is not just an assertion of 'staying put,' but a relearning of how to be on a journey, how to rediscover the strange(r). And this movement, this conversation, is a perpetually unsettling one, but one that nonetheless does not allow 'journey' to be prioritized. Somewhere in the turning point between home and journey, Kristeva finds the space of t/here.

L'Étrangère

Julia Kristeva is a stranger. She writes as one from the outside – outside of our time, our space, our language – she does not fit the pattern. Roland Barthes' early review of Kristeva's writings, entitled '*L'Étrangère*', suggests: 'Julia Kristeva changes the place of things.

She always destroys the latest preconception, the one we thought we could be comforted by' (Moi, 150). A French psychoanalytic theorist, born in Bulgaria, she is a self-described 'exile from socialism and Marxist rationality' (Kristeva (1986), 299) who entered a male-dominated French academic world (a world which, while radically changing after the political events of 1968, was still patriarchal enough for Luce Irigaray to be dismissed from her post at Jacques Lacan's Freudian School of Paris after the publication of her 1974 *Speculum of the Other Woman*). Writing and working against the continuing patriarchal structures, Kristeva and Irigaray, along with Cixous and others, gave rise to a new brand of feminism, influenced in part by Lacanian psychoanalysis (even when arguing against it) and movements in structuralist linguistics. Kristeva was particularly influenced by semiotics, but rearranged its categories; her 600-plus page doctoral thesis (later truncated and published in English as *Revolution in Poetic Language*) placed her firmly within respected circles of French academia. Still, she did not let go of her exile spirit but saw the need for critique within Parisian xenophobia.

Kristeva is interested in the possibilities of dissidence. She sees the dissident as 'a new type of intellectual', and exile as an essential element for survival, both individually and in society. Reminding us of our rootless lives, she nonetheless sees a vital role to be played within this rootlessness:

> Our present age is one of exile. How can one avoid sinking into the mire of common sense, if not by becoming a stranger to one's own country, language, sex and identity? [...] [I]f meaning exists in the state of exile, it nevertheless finds no incarnation, and is *ceaselessly produced and destroyed* in geographical or discursive transformations. Exile is a way of surviving in the face of the dead father, of gambling with death, which is the meaning of life, of stubbornly refusing to give in to the law of death. (Kristeva (1986), 298; emphasis added)

'Geographical transformations' are crucial to survival in the present age, living beyond God the Father. To 'live on' *(sur-vive)* means we must enter this liminal space in the wake of the 'dead father'. These transformations occur between one and another, without assurances of *telos* or *arche*. And meaning, even if it is continually produced and destroyed, comes about through the movement between the 'stranger' (prophet/artist) and society, a constant moving back and forth, bound and rebound, transforming self and other along the way.

The exile must be taken seriously, but there is fear. The exile (the foreigner, the stranger) is shied away from; she is different, strange, not familiar, a stranger and not family. The work of the exile is a relentless and tireless work, a 'gambling', a 'stubborn refusal' of giving in to death. It is a work of *faith* like Søren Kierkegaard's 'knight of faith'. Kristeva's exile is a *sujet en procès* ('subject-in-process/on-trial') while Kierkegaard's knight is the knight 'on trial' and 'under ordeal'.[2] Through a conflation of these two thinkers, one might come to a new religious understanding of the person of faith. Here it is not a person who can claim knowledge or can make a confession, but a person who suspends knowledge, who must shed pretensions of knowing. Such a suspension places the knight wandering in the desert. In other contexts, such a knight might be called a 'pilgrim', but for Kristeva (and, one could argue, for Kierkegaard as well) there is no Mecca or Santiago de Compostela, no *telos* at the end. The journey is undertaken without maps.

Kristeva's essay 'A New Type of Intellectual: The Dissident' spells out some implications of the exile's relation to society, while her later book *Strangers to Ourselves* provides further detail. The first section of the book is particularly intriguing in its poetic performance of the relation between foreigner and society. This section, entitled 'Toccata and Fugue for the Foreigner,' weaves the free-flowing poetic Toccata with the contrapuntal Fugue to recreate the experience of the foreigner.[3] And as Kristeva's writing is read, the reader feels the

2 Kristeva gives the label *sujet en procès* in her *Revolution in Poetic Language* (trans. Leon Roudiez [New York: Columbia University Press, 1984]). *En procès* is translated in the book as 'in process/on trial' and therefore connects well with Kierkegaard's knight who must endure 'trials' and 'ordeals'. On Kierkegaard's 'knight on trial' see especially 'Problema II' in *Fear and Trembling*, trans. Howard and Edna Hong (Princeton: Princeton University Press, 1983), pp. 66–81.

3 Besides the musical reference, 'fugue' is also a psychiatric term dealing with a person's amnesia during a period of time; a flight from reality. 'Toccata and Fugue' is also the title of a section in Lévi-Strauss's *The Raw and the Cooked*, the two elements corresponding to the vertical and horizontal aspects of myth.

unsettling and invigorating experience of being away from home. Her writing *is* a journey and the reader bccomes an exile and foreigner.

The two musical registers (Toccata and Fugue) correspond to Kristeva's two registers of the semiotic and the symbolic, respectively.[4] Significantly, between these two – the semiotic and symbolic – is the *thetic* phase. The thetic comes 'after' the semiotic and links the semiotic to the symbolic, becoming 'the threshold of language' and the true basis for all signification. Though it resides primarily on the side of the symbolic, it is also a connecting point *between* the semiotic and symbolic. The place of the thetic would be a 'safety zone' where the pulsating and disruptive drives of the semiotic meet the social constructs of the symbolic. The thetic is what is at stake in the unsettling elements of poetry that do not leave us with complete loss of identity: 'for us, this is precisely what distinguishes a text as *signifying practice* from the "drifting-into-non-sense" that characterizes neurotic discourse' (Lechte, 51). In the presence of the poetic, the subject is shaken as the semiotic bursts through the symbolic; yet the subject does not disappear, and meaning continues in a different form, 'ceaselessly produced and destroyed'. One might thus read Kristeva by describing the meeting between the foreigner and society as a meeting on the 'thetic' borderline. Only through this meeting can the conversational process occur. And thus only through this liminal meeting can subjectivity occur, defined as it is by Kristeva as *sujet en procès*.

The foreigner herself lives out this liminal life; the foreigner cannot remain in one position, but is driven to wandering by 'a secret wound.' Never content to settle in one place, as Kristeva notes in *Strangers to Ourselves*, the foreigner's happiness

> consists in maintaining that fleeing eternity or that perpetual transience [...] A devotee of solitude, even in the midst of a crowd, because he is faithful to a shadow [...] Not belonging to any place, any time, any love [...] the space of the foreigner is a moving train, a plane in flight, the very transition that precludes

4 For a good introduction to Kristeva and the terms 'Semiotic' and 'Symbolic', see John Lechte's *Julia Kristeva* (New York: Routledge, 1990). For more on Kristeva's ideas of exile, see *Julia Kristeva: Readings of Exile and Estrangement* (New York: St Martin's Press, 1996).

> stopping [...] Melancholy lover of a vanished space, he cannot in fact, get over his having abandoned a period of time. (Kristeva (1991), 4–10)

The space and time of the foreigner is a place of *between*, a place that is not no-place, but nonetheless it is hard to pinpoint where it is. She both belongs everywhere and nowhere. Time and space are interwoven and the foreigner, unsettled, moves in between both, linking as well as showing the differences.

There is a freedom entailed here on the part of the foreigner, but it is certainly of a strange sort. Just as meeting someone is 'a crossroad of two othernesses', a meeting that welcomes 'the foreigner without tying him down' (Kristeva (1991), 11), the ability to remain untied creates a paradoxical life. For when it comes to solitude, '[t]he paradox is that the foreigner wishes to be alone but with partners, and yet none is willing to join him in the torrid space of his uniqueness' (Kristeva (1991), 12). There is a love–hate relationship with the world, creating dynamic tensions and a 'secret wound' which keeps her moving. The foreigner struggles to be alone and to be with others, but both are unreachable.

Because of this tense and unsettling relation with the world, the foreigner has a unique ability to show difference. This difference, I suggest, is akin to the role of the prophet. Like the foreigner, the prophet holds up otherness, forces waking from dogmatic slumber: 'Confronting the foreigner whom I reject and with whom at the same time I identify, I lose my boundaries, I no longer have a container, the memory of experiences when I had been abandoned overwhelm me, I lose my composure. I feel "lost", "indistinct", "hazy"' (Kristeva (1991), 187). The foreigner is fought against (we are forever xenophobic) because the foreigner is something other, something to be pushed out and away. Unless one is unsettled, feels 'lost' and 'indistinct', ways are not changed; it all goes on as before, the same patterns are kept.

Making such bold claims for the 'prophetic' foreigner begs a few questions. These questions, in turn, point out how the sense of between that i have been describing herein is not a static and well-defined place. What must be acknowledged is that the 'losing of boundaries' that Kristeva esteems in the foreigner can slip into violence. There are perpetual and irreducible questions about what limits may be crossed, when it may or may not be 'appropriate', and who is involved in these transgressions. The limits of creation cannot be excised all too easily, and mystical unity is a dangerous myth. Furthermore, Kristeva herself in *Powers of Horror* shows how too much semiotic, boundless energy can manifest itself in destructive ends. Kristeva brings this point forward through examining the writings of the misogynist anti-Semite Céline. Céline's 'poetic language' exerted a great influence on French writing, but the influence is inseparable from certain 'powers of horror'.[5] Redrawing the boundaries in new ways is necessary for change and growth, for re-creation, yet aesthetics cannot be separated from ethics.

Therefore, in Kristeva's case, the strongest of points must be made for her assertion of the liminal 'thetic' phase. At this point of between, poetic language may gather the anarchic force of the semiotic realm (where the 'foreigner' may be said to stand) and link it with what could be called the 'ethical' force of limits in the symbolic realm. What must be articulated is just such a 'between' space where otherness can exist; indeed, a place where a division between self and other is created, but a place also where self and other may return

5 While some are troubled by Kristeva's use of this questionable figure (and rightly so), i believe that Kristeva may be employing a particular mode of ethical writing in *Powers of Horror*. While this is not the time and place to argue this out, i will suggest that by using Céline as an example of 'poetic language' she is ironically also pointing out the very limits of such language. Similar to Baudrillard, and not so far from certain works of Kierkegaard, her style is not a straightforward one of description, but of showing certain ends of our thinking, taking a particular thought to its extreme.

In this case, i disagree with Edith Wyschogrod's analysis of Kristeva in her *Saints and Postmodernism: Revisioning Moral Philosophy* (Chicago: University of Chicago Press, 1990). Overall, this is an excellent study, but on this particular point Wyschogrod does not take in the rhetorical element of *Powers of Horror*, and thinks Kristeva is almost condoning Céline. Again, i think there is more to it than that. Kristeva rather dismissively responds to Wyschogrod in 'The Speaking Subject is not Innocent' (*Freedom and Interpretation: The Oxford Amnesty Lectures, 1992*, Barbara Johnson, ed. [New York: Harper Collins, 1993], p. 166).

together and enter a conversation *à deux*, as two subjects-in-process, which pronounced otherwise is also a conversation *a-dieu*.

The other meets the other: two meet in a new space that is forged out of journey. But what is the end of exploring? What creates the 'secret wound?' Does the experience of being somewhere else not involve or point to some other thing? However it is looked at, it should be clear that this wandering, this longing, is bound up with desire. So, what is this desire? What is the other side of journey?

Home

> Home is where I wanna be, but I guess I'm already there. ('Home', The Talking Heads)

> Pilgrimages seem to be almost instinctive, or at least derived from behaviors now so ingrained in our species that it's difficult to distinguish between genetic and social origins. Of all the animals that migrate, we are surely among the most restless. But humans retain the influence of the geophysical habitat in which they pass their formative years. And often, it seems, we are drawn back to our childhood homes – if not physically, then mentally; if not out of love, then out of curiosity; if not by necessity, then by desire. Through such returnings we find out who we are. (Janovy)

'Home is where the heart is.' 'Home is where you hang your hat.' These clichés actually reveal more than they are given credit for. The first phrase gives the idea that home has to do with some sort of psychological attachment: 'where the heart is'. It may be a fixed place, but it may be with a group of people, a book, a soap opera. The second phrase locates home at a physical place, a place with a hook to hang your hat. But one could hang one's hat in many different places; it is not hard to find a hook. Keeping in mind the tension involved in these phrases between home as psychological space and home as physical space, i now turn to explore the element of 'home' in Kristeva's writing.

Recalling Kristeva's descriptions, we find within the foreigner 'a passion for another land, always a promised one, that of an occupation, a love, a child, a glory' (Kristeva (1991), 10). Wandering is a desire for someplace or something else. Kristeva's foreigner desires what is out in front of her: it is something she moves towards – or, it moves toward her. This is an inversion of the common conception of home (phrased in the question 'Where are you from?') which locates home as being somewhere behind, in the past. Kristeva's foreigner only locates home ahead of her, but not in the linear historical sense of 'future':

> His origin certainly haunts him, for better and for worse, but it is indeed *elsewhere* that he has set his hopes, that his struggles take place, that his life holds together today. *Elsewhere* versus the origin, and even *nowhere* versus the roots [...] He is from nowhere, from everywhere, citizen of the world, cosmopolitan. (Kristeva (1991), 31)

The foreigner has a unique ability in the world,

> for since he belongs to nothing the foreigner can feel as appertaining to everything, to the entire tradition, and that weightlessness in the infinity of cultures and legacies gives him the extravagant ease to innovate. (Kristeva (1991), 32)

The foreigner, being untied, can traverse various groups and create bonds. The foreigner becomes the generalist, able to move among disciplines and groups of people feeling at home in several. She may have several hats, but there are also several hooks to hang them on. Moving into a new space, the foreigner irradiates relationships.

While the foreigner repulses and scares, there is at the same time a fascination; there are new stories from abroad, those who have stayed behind are intrigued. It is this fascination that allows the foreigner to take on a peculiar position of 'authority'. The tension between this pushing away and pulling in – this *tremendum fascinosum* – is clarified by Kristeva via Freud's *Das Unheimlich.* This semantic study ('Unheimlich' is translated in *Strangers* as 'uncanny strangeness') shows the ambiguity of the term – 'familiar' and 'strange' both being contained in the etymology: 'that which is strangely uncanny would be that which *was* familiar and under certain conditions, emerges' (Kristeva (1991), 183). But ultimately Kristeva notes that Freud locates this 'strangeness' in the self: 'The other is my unconscious.' Perhaps then, the foreigner is at home with herself as much as the rest are 'strangers to ourselves'. Perhaps, after all, all are foreigners and all at home. But this does not turn all into the same.

Das Unheimlich has several ambiguous relationships with *home*. For one thing, 'heim' (the root of 'Unheimlich'), is a cognate with the English 'home', making 'Unheimlich' something which is not home – while at the same time retaining the trace of something familiar. In the notes to *Strangers*, Kristeva credits Yvon Bres with making a connection between Freud's and Heidegger's use of 'Unheimlich', and its connection with 'angst'. Heidegger states: "In der Angst ist einem "unheimlich"' (*Sein und Zeit*, 1927). 'Angst', for Heidegger, stems from our 'not being at home'. Angst then, is a journey. Elsewhere, Heidegger equates boredom with homesickness: 'Apparently this deep boredom – in the form of a search for spending time – is the hidden, inadmired, deflected yet still unavoidable attraction to our homeland: our hidden homesickness' (Heidegger, 237).[6]

But before 'angst' is quickly written off and run from, it must be recalled that Kierkegaard, who was such an influence on Heidegger, considered this anxiety to be an essential element of growth, and of faith: 'the persons whose souls do not know this depression are those whose souls have no presentiment of a metamorphosis' (Kierkegaard, 190). Kierkegaard also explicitly considers this anxiety to be produced from, among other things, one's 'not feeling at home in the world' (Kierkegaard, 190). Again, there is a necessary binding between home and journey. Angst is a time of journey, of unsettledness, but there is no 'metamorphosis', no change, without it. Most importantly here, there is also no home without it.

6 One may be skeptical of Heidegger here when one considers his past Nazi ties and the Nazi emphasis on the Fatherland (and the title of this essay, 'Homeland' is quite close), but this, i believe, helps support the point that home and journey must be seen together. Fascism rises out of fear of the other, and this fear is thought to be reduced only when there are no foreigners, others, and journeyers, i.e. no prophetic voice coming from a new place. Too much 'home' leads to destruction.

There is still a question of where home *is* to be found. Heidegger brings together the disparities between home being in our past ('Where are you from?') and home being at a point ahead of us:

> Therefore, in everything alien (even when hidden) the sought-out homeland comes towards us. Because it touches us in this form again and again, we must come towards it. But how? In the way that we are willing to preserve that from which we have come. There are signs of our origin all around us. (Heidegger, 237)

Home, then, is in the tension-filled space of between, coming towards us while retaining the place we have come from. Home is now and then, here and there. Home is t/here, the point one is continually confronted with. This still point of t/here is not passive, not something stumbled upon; rather, the home of t/here takes work, faith, and ordeals.

The doubly-bound space of t/here, the ground of home and the ground of journey, must be brought together within a critical reflection that understands home and journey, self and other as existing 'within' and 'without'. We are strangers to ourselves, we are other to our self. But this is not merely an individualistic enterprise of modern psychology designed for the edification of self. Kristeva speaks of the subject (in process), but her analysis is set within the context of a particular political situation in contemporary France, a France that faces struggles with otherness, with immigration and exile, and with the subsequent scapegoat myth of xenophobia. So, finally and paradoxically, it is only when one's own strangeness is confronted, the otherness in the unconscious, that it is realized home is with others, who are also foreigners. Here is a space where self is open to others, a space for love. Kristeva makes the political implications clear:

> It would involve a cosmopolitanism of a new sort that, cutting across governments, economies, and markets, might work for a mankind whose solidarity is founded on the consciousness of its unconscious – desiring, destructive, fearful, empty, impossible. (Kristeva (1991), 192)[7]

7 These words struck me as similar to Karl Barth's notion of fellowship: 'Genuine fellowship is grounded upon what men lack. Precisely when we

There is no other way of being with people, of being at home, than to recognize otherness. The journey of life must be an acknowledgement of strangeness and a resistance to any thought that tries to subsume home into journey, or vice versa.

Home is thus also the point for critical thought in which one stands over and against some other place and some other time. Home is always someplace, for there is no no-place (utopia) from which to criticize. There is no getting outside of a particular context; contexts are always t/here. Thus, t/here must run contrary to Paul Ricoeur's, and other's, attempts to establish utopia as a literary point of escape. In his *Lectures on Ideology and Utopia*, Ricoeur optimistically states: 'Utopia may provide a critical tool for undermining reality, but it is also a refuge against reality. In cases like these, when we cannot act, we write. The act of writing allows a certain flight which persists as one of the characteristics of literary utopias' (Ricoeur, 309). Writing is here bound to the sense of journey pointed out before, but it forgets that the journey does not lead to no-place ('u-topia'). And while there is not the space to do so here in any rigorous manner, i would argue that Ricoeur's notion fails because of its inability to understand its own t/hereness.

T/here is, rather, a point of critique akin to Foucault's 'heteropia' ('other-place') which stands in contrast to utopias: 'utopias permit fables and discourse: they run with the very grain of language and are part of the fundamental dimension of the *fabula*; heteropias dessicate speech, stop words in their tracks, contest the very possibility of grammar at its source; they dissolve our myths and sterilize the lyricism of our sentences' (Foucault, xviii). Utopian writing pretends that language can be separated from space and time; heteropian writing asserts the materiality and situatedness of language in a radical way. Through the heteropia Foucault brings in the unsettledness of the

recognize that we are sinners do we perceive that we are brothers' (*The Epistle to the Romans*, trans. Edwin C. Hoskyns, 6th edn. [London: Oxford University Press, 1968], p. 101). Yet, interestingly enough, Kristeva seems to anticipate this response and says that she is not arguing for a new form of brotherhood (and quotes Veuillot saying there must be a father to have brothers). Hers is an erotic relationship, between others, *à deux*; there are no hierarchies.

journey. T/here takes one's context and puts it on a journey realizing one's context is never one place only, but a myriad of places.

Home is a point (a still point of a turning world) where the tensions of time and space come to an interface, those times with the photograph album reminiscing on times past, perhaps with family (the familiar) rethinking and remembering. Hindsight is anything but 20/20, yet a new approach to meaning is made, a new home for the current time and place.

Home-in-journey/Journey-in-home

> The movies will always be one of my top all-time out activities. But to be honest, the peak moment for me is always being on the way to the movies. I love being on the way to the movies.
>
> We're in the car, trying to get there in time. Maybe you'll have good seats. Maybe it'll be a good movie. Maybe everything'll be good. You don't know, and when you're on the way it's still possible. I love that I'm definitely doing something and I haven't done it yet. That's a pure life moment. After you get a job and before you have to do it. Nothing beats that. Its the spaces between life that I like the most. (Jerry Seinfeld, 'Seinlanguage')

Kristeva is an exile. Her geographical excursions through lands other than that from which she came allowed her to experience herself as a foreigner. This movement through space (and time) brought her to a different understanding of home, a home no longer attached to a specific place. There had to be a way to be at home in different lands. Ultimately, home is within the self – just as the stranger is – while that self may be in a chapel in England, or on an airplane. The self is never dissociated from a particular space or time or other. The self is in a constant state of flux, being ruptured by every new moment and every new place, every new confrontation with (an)other. Space and time are inseparable, as are home and journey. One can never have a home without a journey and one can never be on journey without having a home. Kristeva's split and moving subjectivity, 'Subject-in-process', becomes 'Home-in-journey/Journey-in-home'.

Home is t/here. Within this calm tension one can never be nowhere (u-topia), but always already somewhere. Yet, one is never in one place only, but always already in movement away from something towards something else. 'To be' is to exist in space and time and all the tensions involved therein. 'To be' is to be on a journey. Prophetic/ poetic voices, rooted in space as much as time, point to new ways of living. To accept the strangeness within oneself means one may have to venture out into new space, be willing to be stared at, laughed at, mocked for one's accent. It is a risk to live well and every journey is 'gambling with death, which is the meaning of life' (Kristeva (1986), 298).

And in this is a mode of *in-vention*, the 'in-coming' of the other, a movement toward a religious aesthetics that centers on conversation, and thus also, on *love*. As novelist Jeanette Winterson declares, 'What you risk reveals what you value. In the presence of love, hearth and quest become one' (Winterson 81). Or Hélène Cixous:

> I look for a scene in which a type of exchange would be produced that would be different, a kind of desire that wouldn't be in collusion with the old story of death. This desire would invent Love, it alone would not use the word love to cover up its opposite: one would not land right back in a dialectical destiny, still unsatisfied by the debasement of one by the other. On the contrary, there would have to be a recognition of each other, and this grateful acknowledgement would come about thanks to the intense and passionate work of knowing. (Cixous, 78)

And Kristeva:

> The amorous and artistic experiences, as two interdependent aspects of the identificatory process, are our only way of preserving our psychic space as a 'living system', that is open to the other, capable of adaptation and change. (Kristeva (1984), 5).[8]

Perhaps here, t/here, we begin to come toward a religious space of between that is a space of love, a religious space for an aesthetics (not dissociable from an ethics) of between.

8 Quoted in John Lechte, *Julia Kristeva*, p. 184.

Bibliography

Banks, Russell et al. 'Itchy Feet and Pencils: A Symposium', in *New York Times Book Review*, 18 August 1991.

Cixous, Hélène. *The Newly Born Woman*, translated by Betsy Wing. Minneapolis: Minneapolis University Press, 1986.

Foucault, Michel. *The Order of Things*. New York: Vintage, 1973.

Heidegger, Martin. 'Homeland', *Listening*, 6.3 (1971).

Janovy Jr., *Vermilian Sea: A Naturalist's Journey in Baja California*. Boston: Houghton Mifflin, 1992.

Kierkegaard, Søren. *Either/Or II*, translated by Howard V. Hong and Edna H. Hong. Princeton: Princeton University Press, 1987.

Kristeva, Julia. 'Joyce, le retour d'Orphée', *L'Infini*, 8 (Autumn, 1984).

—— 'A New Type of Intellectual: The Dissident', in T. Moi (ed.), *The Kristeva Reader*. New York: Columbia University Press, 1986.

—— *Strangers to Ourselves*, translated by Leon Roudiez. New York: Columbia University Press, 1991.

Lechte, John. *Julia Kristeva: Readings of Exile and Estrangement*. New York: St Martin's Press, 1996.

Moi, Toril. *Sexual/Textual Politics*. London and New York: Routledge, 1985.

Petrarca, Francesco. *Letters on Familiar Matters*, vol. 2, translated by Aldo S. Bernado. Baltimore: Johns Hopkins University Press, 1982.

Ricoeur, Paul. *Ideology and Utopia*. New York: Columbia University Press, 1986.

Rushdie, Salman. *The Wizard of Oz*. London: BFI Publishing, 1992.

Shorre, Brad. *Culture in Mind*. New York: Oxford University Press, 1996.

Winterson, Jeanette. *Written on the Body*. London: Vintage, 1992.

J. STEPHEN FOUNTAIN

The Trace of the (M)other: Liminality and Maternity in *Dead Man Walking*[1]

> On close inspection, all literature is probably a version of the apocalypse that seems to me rooted, no matter what its socio-historical conditions might be, on the fragile border […] where identities (subject/object, etc.) do not exist or only barely so – double, fuzzy, heterogeneous, animal, metamorphosed, altered, abject. (Kristeva (1982), 207)

> 'The truth arrives disguised; therein the sorrow lies.' So wrote Jimmy Glass, executed by the state of Louisiana in 1987. (Prejean, 32)

When American audiences truly participate in the transformative rite of the cinematic experience, it is likely that Susan Sarandon guides them in their passage. Whether as the blossoming neophyte in the *Rocky Horror Picture Show*, as neighbourhood satanic cohort in *The Witches of Eastwick*, as mentor-groupie in *Bull Durham*, or as rebel with just cause/fugitive heading for the border in *Thelma and Louise*, Sarandon's characters often function as liminal entities, sacrificially effecting the cathartic transformations of others, including those in the audience. Nowhere does that aura of liminality burn as brightly as in her portrayal of Sister Helen Prejean in the film adaptation of Prejean's *Dead Man Walking*. Sarandon's portrayal of the 'spiritual adviser' Prejean works because the audience already implicitly recognizes and acknowledges Sarandon as such. It is in *Dead Man Walking*, however, that Sarandon most fully and directly performs her liminal role, dwelling in that region between death and life, sacred and profane, right and wrong, law and grace, heaven and earth, victim and victimizer…

1 This is a revised form of a paper presented at the Eighth Conference on Literature and Religion, Oxford, September 1996.

In a delightful work of biblical reinterpretation, Mark Ledbetter makes the observation that 'Western culture, its literature and art, comes from two traditions whose survival has depended on victimization; that is, either victimize or be victimized' (Ledbetter, 4). Those two traditions are of course the traditions associated with the Hebrew and Christian scriptures. Within the context of such passages as Mark 8 and Matthew 5, says Ledbetter, 'Jesus as victim, because he is victim, empowers his followers' *while victimizing them*, offering an ironic 'apotheosis' through which 'the victimizer does the victim a favor by *literally ushering him/her into the world of the religiously saved*' (4–5; emphases added). Following a creative critical treatment of two Biblical narratives of victimization (the rape of Dinah and the impregnation of Mary), Ledbetter challenges the critical community, stating that 'As responsible literary critics we can work hard not to abolish […] [the] longstanding master plots of position and power but to make sure that the entire story is told' (18). 'Remember,' says Ledbetter, 'reading and writing about victims is about the presentation of absence […] we must continue to listen for voices on the periphery […] and we must at every opportunity, tell and hold these marginal stories over against the master narrative' (18). Such an interpretive ethic is difficult to hold to at best, when the 'others' whose voices are silenced are easily redefined as innocent or noble victims, but if the other to whom voice is given is known as victimizer, radically offensive, repulsive, duplicitous and *abject*, one's motives and goals certainly come into question.

Within the shared conversations of literature and theology in the last few decades have been heard the shouts and whispers of a new awareness of our critical and ethical responsibilities as those who make and interpret the myths of our societies. We have become aware of the possibility of (as Robert Detweiler puts it) 'reading religiously', we have acknowledged (to borrow a phrase from Monty Python) 'the violence inherent in our systems', and we have attempted to remain, or to become, ethical, responsible, and even religious in the wake of the death of God. In short, we have begun to acknowledge that ours is a task carried out within the prison-house of language, and we have been advised of our obligation to choose whether we will be driven by hope or by despair. Just as the writings of post-structuralist, postcolonial and feminist thinkers have altered the context of critical discussion in general, the writings of such thinkers as Emanuel Levinas, Julia Kristeva and Luce Irigaray have contributed signify-cantly to my reflections upon Sister Helen Prejean's recent *Dead Man Walking*, her recollections of her experiences as spiritual adviser to death row inmates in Louisiana, and the film that it has become. I am still just beginning to grasp the relationships between these four writers, but there are certainly theoretical, critical and political concerns that are illuminated by their reflections.

Specifically, I am thinking of Levinas's placement of the category of 'the other' at the forefront of philosophical enquiry and the resultant priority of 'difference' and 'alterity' for ethical discourse, as well as the significance of 'the feminine', not merely as 'other', but as other to ontological discourse and system (Ainley, 56–7). As Alison Ainley points out, while 'bringing sexual difference into the arena of ontology and ethics', Levinas 'opens up the bias of language and the bias of metaphysical desire', moving toward 'an ethics based on community' (57). 'Ethics', for Levinas, does not simply entail the 'overcoming or abandonment of ontology, but rather the de-construction of the latter's limits and its comprehensive claims to mastery' (Critchley, 8). The notion of 'the feminine' provides Levinas with the foundation for a reconstruction of ethical relations, 'since it corresponds to the otherness established in terms of, for example, de Beauvoir's "woman as other"', but also endeavours to preclude 'the violence of the determining gaze' by stressing 'the *command*, or *address* of the other' rather than the *naming* of other as other (Ainley, 56). Levinas places the 'virility' of mere ontology under the conditions of 'the feminine', which is closely associated with, even identified as, ethics – ontology's other. The 'feminine' is for Levinas 'what is required in order to commune with oneself and to be capable of an ethical act' (Chalier, 122). The responsibility which is the result of such a capability is not the result of the 'choice' of a subject, but is rather 'a calling', a calling which enables the subect to know his/her 'uniqueness': thus the 'virile ego' is transformed into 'humanity in the service of the Other' (Chalier, 124).

The responsible subject is fully defined, according to Levinas, by the maternal body, 'with its anxiety for the one it protects', 'suffer(ing) for the Other', 'answer(ing) for the Other'. In short, 'a body of goodness that is devoted to the Other before being devoted to itself' (Chalier, 126). However, as Catherine Chalier has argued, Levinas does indeed seem to narrow the ethical possibilities of *real* females by suggesting maternity as 'the ultimate meaning of the feminine'; indeed, 'according to Levinas, ethics in feminine achievement means to be a mother and nothing else' (Chalier, 127). Chalier's critique of Levinas offers an understanding of the feminine as 'the disruption of being by goodness beyond maternity', which, she suggests, is the 'universal mission to interrupt the self-satisfaction of those beings who think that they are self-sufficient and reasonable' (128). This universal mission is, she says, 'the meaning of the feminine in the human being' (128). While, as Chalier argues, the maternal metaphor which Levinas applies to subjectivity is not '*only* a metaphor' (127; emphases added), it is also not the only metaphorical term employed by Levinas in order to illustrate the responsibility of the ethical subject. Elsewhere Levinas defines such responsibility as *liturgy*, which, in his original employment of the term, entails radical implications not only for philosophical discourse regarding the subject, but regarding God as well. In his seminal essay 'The Trace of the Other' Levinas writes:

> I should like to fix the work of the same as a movement without return of the same to the other with a Greek term which in its primary meaning indicates the exercise of an office that is not only completely gratuitous, but that requires, on the part of (the one) that exercises it, a *putting out of funds at a loss*. I would like to fix it with the term 'liturgy'. We must for the moment remove from this term every religious signification, *even if a certain idea of God should become visible, as a trace, at the end of our analysis. Liturgy, as an absolutely patient action, does not take its place as a cult alongside of works and of ethics. It is ethics itself.* (Levinas, 349–50; emphases added)

After the manner of Levinas's emphasis on the priority of the Other, Julia Kristeva's reformulation of the unitary subject into 'the subject in process/on trial' suspended between the realms of the symbolic and the semiotic, as well as her treatment of the 'abject', places the ethical subject 'within community and relationality', developing an ethics which, in Kristeva's words, is 'not the kind of "ethics" that consists in obedience to laws' (Ainley, 55). For Kristeva, the 'speaking subject' in the wake of the Freudian revolution must be understood as 'a divided subject, caught in the split between conscious and unconscious, between "bio-physiological processes" and "social constraints"' (Graybeal, 8). Thus suspended, Kristeva refers to the subject as *'le sujet en procès'*, *procès*, or process, referring to 'the ongoing, dynamic character of the subject', and avoiding any implication of staticity or unity in lieu of the subject's 'construction and reconstruction across time' (Graybeal, 8). Of course, Graybeal points out, *procès* suggests a legal connotation, as in the English 'due process', which has led to the translation of the term by others as 'subject in process/on trial', or 'subject in process/in question' in order to preserve the 'disruptive, troubling, even adversarial' aspects of the term (8). Kristeva's subject in process is not only suspended in the 'split between "bio-physiological processes" and "social constraints"' but also, more fundamentally, between the polarities of the 'semiotic' and the 'symbolic': two essentially distinct modalities operating within the 'discourse of the subject in process' (10). The unifying, orderly, lawful, rational symbolic dimension of language, of the discourse through which the subject exists, functions, in Kristeva's words, as the 'attribute of meaning, sign, and the signified object'; and corresponds, in a patriarchal system, to the role of the father-figure (12). The alterity, the 'something other', which opposes the symbolic is called by Kristeva 'the semiotic', and is operative 'through, despite, and in excess of' processes of signification, and does not itself refer to a 'signified object' in the subject's discursive existence (10). Controversially, but not incongruous with Levinas, Kristeva asserts that the drive-related semiotic facet of discourse is 'maternally connoted' (10). The symbolic (related to Lacan's *'le nom du pere'*, the name of the Father) 'demands adherence to social rules and regulations, as well as to laws of rational discourse' and, to reiterate, carries 'paternal' associations (11).

Now the relationship between the semiotic and the symbolic is founded upon the notion of 'abjection'. The function of the 'abject' in the development of the subject is to a certain extent analogous to the role of the 'Other' for Levinas. Not only does the semiotic realm appear as that which is 'abject' with regard to the symbolic, but it is that very abjection which is the condition for the existence of the symbolic and semiotic as such. 'Abjection' is characterized by Kristeva as 'a vortex of summons and repulsions'; the 'abject' is defined as 'what is radically excluded […] that which is violently and negatively chosen', and is further, 'that which I most clearly want not to be' (Graybeal, 26). Abjection recognizes 'the want on which any being, meaning, language, or desire is founded' (26) and thus *its* existence and recurrence, as well as that of the semiotic, *is* the Other which the Symbolic seeks to eradicate or deny. In a further similarity to Levinas, it is through Kristeva's treatment of the notion of maternity that Kristeva both stresses the importance of the contributions of previously marginalized discourse to the evolution of ethics and provides a metaphor for the discursive struggle of the writer. As she points out in her primary reflections on maternity, in *Stabat Mater*:

> if ethics is no longer to be seen as being the same as morality, if ethics amounts to not avoiding the embarrassing and inevitable problematics of the law but giving it flesh, language and jouissance – in that case its reformulation demands the contribution of women […] (quoted in Ainley, 59)

Such a reformulation calls not only for the contribution of women, but also a recognition of the maternal element upon which discourse (which is the mode of existence of the subject in process) rests. As Kristeva suggests in *Powers of Horror*:

> If 'something maternal' happens to bear upon the uncertainty that I call abjection, it illuminates the literary scription of the essential struggle that a writer (man or woman) has to engage in with what (s)he calls demonic only to call attention to it as the inseparable obverse of (her) very being, of the other (sex) that torments and posesses (her). Does one write under any other condition than being possessed by abjection, in an indefinite catharsis? […] In short, who, I ask you, would agree to call himself abject, subject of or subject to abjection? (Kristeva (1982), 208–9)

Kristeva foresees and calls for not only a reformulation of ethics, but a radical transformation of religious, moral, political, and verbal discourse (210). In an apocalyptic tone, Kristeva predicts that humanity possessed of 'an abject knowledge' is

> preparing to go through the first great demystification of Power (religious, moral, political and verbal) that (hu)mankind has ever witnessed; and it is necessarily taking place within that fulfillment of religion as sacred horror, which is Judeo-Christian monotheism. (210)

Reflections upon the necessity of the ethical contributions of women and the significance of regarding sexual difference are perhaps the most practical of Luce Irigaray's contributions to current philosophical dialogue, but just as crucial, and perhaps more fundamental is her examination of the pervasive influence of patriarchal myth and religion upon Western culture, especially in the eclipse of so-called 'pre-historic' gynocratic traditions. According to Irigaray, so much philosophical discourse, even that which includes a critique of the preceding religious tradition (such as Marx and Freud) 'remains bound to a patriarchal mythology which hardly ever questions itself as such' (Irigaray (1993), 23). Patriarchy and phallocracy, according to Irigaray, 'are in part myths which, because they don't stand back to question themselves, take themselves to be the only order possible' (23). Further, Irigaray points out that 'the disregard for what is termed, rather vaguely, Prehistory can be explained by the way in which Patriarchy is mistaken for the only History possible' (23–4). Irigaray, like Kristeva, is not hesitant to suggest the possibility of a new historical consciousness, as she submits that '[p]erhaps patriarchy has been a necessary stage in History', a stage which 'cannot mark the end of History if we can see its limitations and are able to interpret them' (27). 'Today,' she writes, 'this has become, or has once again become, possible' (27). Not only has such an exercise become *possible*, given Irigaray's assessment of our current ethical and social climate, it has become both *necessary* and *inevitable*. Irigaray observes:

> Instead of pursuing cultural development, the world is retreating to the minimum grounds for human definition. The consequences are that we no longer have any religion appropriate for our times, nor complete control of language as a tool of social exchange, or as a means to acquire or create knowledge. Our legislation is not adequate to regulate private, religious, national and international conflicts, *particularly when it comes to the protection of life*. Therefore we no longer have any God(s), any language, any familiar cultural landscape [...] (83; emphases added)

Certainly Irigaray, Kristeva and Levinas share a concern that human definition be informed by more than the 'minimum grounds', and all three find an oppressive drive toward unity and stasis within the systems they criticize. It is not simply 'other' which is intolerable to a system of 'the same', but 'other' which cannot be assimilated, integrated or annihilated. The patriarchal, ontological, symbolic system is founded upon the either/or, and cannot tolerate the both/and of difference: multiple genealogies, multiple discourses, multiple identities – the both/and of which the multiplicity of 'the immeasurable, unconfinable maternal body' (Kristeva (1986), 177) is a consummate image. As Kristeva observes of this image, '[She] lives on that border, [a] crossroads being, [a] crucified being […] A mother is a continuous separation, a division of the very flesh. And consequently a division of language' (178). Continual division is of course unbearable, unreasonable to the system; Kristeva clearly establishes the maternal body as a site of abjection by defining the cause of abjection as that which 'disturbs identity, system, order. What does not respect borders, positions, rules. The in-between, the ambiguous, the composite' (Kristeva (1982), 4). Once-marginalized voices can be heard calling from this site, this borderland, this crossroads, voices calling for reconstruction, duplicitous voices such as that of Sister Helen Prejean, who speaks from within the 'institution' (both Church and prison, though marginalized, insider and outsider in both cases), calling within the body of her text for the recognition of the dual nature of society's most radically abject and dehumanized, the condemned, as criminal *and* person. Kristeva draws a fitting portrait of the paradoxical personality of Sister Helen when she describes the opposing possibilities open to woman:

> When, striving for access to the word and time, she identifies with the father, she becomes a support for transcendence. But when she is inspired by that which the symbolic order represses, isn't a woman also the most radical atheist, the most committed anarchist? (Kristeva (1986), 158)

When asked in a recent interview whether she had written 'the *true* story' or simply '[her] impressions', Sister Helen Prejean responded by saying 'I wasn't writing this book to be a journalist […]

That wasn't the scope of my book. My book was to take it through the prism of my experience of accompanying people to their death, [and] the victims involved in the case' (*Frontline*, 9). Sister Helen's account of her experiences with death-row inmates in Louisiana has since given rise to an academy-award-winning film, a nationally televised documentary, numerous articles both in print and on the Web, and her public appearances have sparked renewed interest in the multifaceted debates surrounding capital punishment. Prejean's work has effectively opened up a space for public conversation, resulting not only from the nature of her subject, but, perhaps even more directly, from her style. While Sister Helen neither writes nor speaks with the cold objectivity of the journalist, she also shuns a self-assured philosophical or theological tone. There is certainly an instructive rhetoric in Prejean's work, but it is a self-subversive rhetoric which is critical of authority while not itself authoritarian, which struggles toward community and not toward singularity. Prejean writes neither Theology nor History; she writes narrative autobiography, reminiscences of conversation, traces of others, remembrances of silenced voices which are not made present, but whose absence is presented in writing, fiction, liturgy – preserving, in fact emphasizing, the fictive element within her work (and by the term 'work' I am not referring simply to her book but also to her 'absolutely patient action', her *liturgical* response to the command of the other which refuses to reduce identities to simple unities, consistently emphasizing the multiplicity of the subject).

Prejean admits that she was thrown unexpectedly into her first relationship with a death-row inmate, when Patrick Sonnier, who had been described to her as 'a loner [...] (who) doesn't write', answered the letter she had written as a favour to a representative from the Prison Coalition (Prejean xi.3). In the screenplay, when asked why she would waste her time helping a condemned criminal, Prejean replies, 'Because he asked me.' That is, she (and perhaps the same might be said of Sonnier) responded to the call, the command, of another, another who was not simply disadvantaged or displaced, but another who had been radically removed from society. In Prejean's own words, 'Execution is the opposite of baptism into a community [...] [it is] removing a person from the human family step by step, saying [...]

"You are not human, like we are, so we can terminate you"' (*Frontline*, 1). The title of Prejean's work, *Dead Man Walking*, is not simply an ironic proclamation announcing the condemned prisoner's last walk from cell to execution chamber, it is a designation which is affixed to the prisoner's existence as condemned. The condemned is no longer 'yet to become a corpse', as are all other subjects, all other citizens of a given society, the condemned is necessarily characterized as 'dead', but, paradoxically, not without the chance for life, should the system see fit. The condemned prisoner therefore presents a unique opportunity to exert control over that most chaotic of abject realms, death itself. Kristeva describes the corpse as evocative of abjection in the extreme: 'the most sickening of wastes, [it] is a border that has encroached upon everything' (Kristeva (1982), 3). The condemned is an abject object, a corpse, whose 'abjection' may be controlled because its qualification as corpse, unlike the truly dead body, may be revoked. The 'Dead Man Walking' is an abject object all the more abject because of its duplicitous existence on the border between death and life.

It is worth noting that the single condemned prisoner with whom Prejean dialogues in the screenplay is a composite character, another example of multiple identities within the single subject. Real-life individuals Patrick Sonnier and the second inmate to whom Prejean was spiritual adviser, Robert Lee Willie, are edited and consolidated to form the cinematic character 'Matthew Poncelet'. As Christopher Buchanan puts it, the film 'captures Sonnier's crime and Willie's character'. Of the resulting Matthew Poncelet character Prejean observes: 'he is worse than any single person I've ever encountered. He was harder and I concurred with Tim [Robbins, who directed the film] when he said we cannot make him sympathetic at all because the moral issue is not whether we can kill sympathetic people, but the Matthew Poncelets of the world' (*Frontline*, 2). Matthew Poncelet is the abject personified, especially as Prejean refuses to deny his humanity. Recall the cause of abjection that Kristeva offers:

> It is thus not lack of cleanliness or health that causes abjection but what disturbs identity, system, order. What does not respect borders, positions, rules. The in-between, the ambiguous, the composite. The traitor, the liar, the criminal with a

> good conscience, the shameless rapist, the killer who claims he is a saviour […] any crime, because it draws attention to the fragility of the law, is abject, but premeditated crime, cunning murder […] are even more so because they heighten the display of that fragility […] Abjection […] is immoral, sinister, scheming, and shady: a terror that dissembles, a hatred that smiles […] (Kristeva (1982), 4)

Of course, to say that the condemned is representative of the abject, the uncontrollable, the chaotic, in short, the maternal semiotic element which is repressed by the propriety, the control, the order, of the paternal symbolic is not to say that rape and murder are somehow necessarily associated with the semiotic. Rape and murder may very well arise as a result of a subject's failure to recognize another as other, reducing them to the status of object, an object which becomes the site of defilement; and murder is the result of the repression, the attempt to negate the other and the crime (the defilement, the transgression, the chaos) entirely (by murdering the victims). Perhaps within the paternal legal system, this reduction of other to object is only the right of the transcendent Father, which finds representation in the Law itself, those who enforce it, the State, and God. However, *Dead Man Walking*, especially the film, with its haunting juxta-position of the scenes of the crime and the execution, clearly associates the victimization of both Poncelet's victims and Poncelet himself. Further, Poncelet is further identified as victim, and the recurrence, the remembrance of victims is enacted as the images of Poncelet's victims are reflected upon the window through which the viewers have witnessed his death. The body of the condemned becomes an anamnestic site through which the innocent victims are memorialized. Unsurprisingly then, it is as 'victim' that Poncelet most adamantly refuses to be identified: 'I can't stand peple that act like victims. That why I don't much like niggers […] chinks and spics' (Prejean, 150; these words are spoken by Sonnier, but preserved in the screenplay). Upon Prejean's suggestion that there might be similarities between himself and those whom he hates, Poncelet quickly retorts, 'But I ain't no victim – can we talk about somethin' else?' However, just as the murder of Poncelet's victims is an act of dominance and control, the victimization of the condemned is deemed necessary in order to replace lawlessness with justice. This scheme is played out not only in the penal code applied to the condemned, but in Patrick Sonnier's theology as well. Prejean notes that unlike her, Sonnier (whose personality is here reflected in Matthew Poncelet) adheres to a theology of atonement based on victimization, suffering and fear. She writes:

> He admits that he never 'got much religion', when he was growing up, but says he believes that Jesus died for him on the cross and will 'take care' of him when he appears before the judgment seat of God.
>
> I recognize the theology of 'atonement' that he uses: Jesus, by suffering and dying on the cross, 'appeased' an angry God's demand for 'justice'. I know the theology because it once shaped my belief, but I had shed it when I discovered that its driving force was fear that made love impossible. What kind of God demands 'payment' in human suffering? (Prejean, 150)

There is more than a simple similarity between theological victimization, the practical victimization of the condemned and the repression and disposal of philosophical 'alterity'. A motivating factor in the disposition of the condemned person is the identification of the condemned not only as feminine, but as maternal.

Irigaray, in her discussion of the gender designation of objects, observes that within the patriarchal linguistic system, not only is it true that 'what has value must be masculine', but also that 'living beings, the animate and cultured, become masculine; objects that are lifeless, the inanimate and uncultured, become feminine' (Irigaray (1993), 70). The condemned, the 'dead man walking', is, as we have said, understood as one who has already passed on, but whose designation as corpse may be controlled. Now, not only is the condemned multiple in this respect, but – and this is crucial – the violent, incorrigible body of the condemned is also understood to be the mortal bearer of an immortal soul. This is the motivation behind the state-sanctioned activity of the 'spiritual adviser' (the only visitor who may stay with condemned prisoners until their executions). As Prejean's superior, the 'old school, pre-Vatican Catholic' chaplain of the prison (25), points out to her, 'prisoners are the scum of the earth', and the role of a spiritual adviser is solely to help save the soul of the condemned by ensuring that the sacraments of the Church are received before death – nothing more, nothing less. Unlike any other citizen, the condemned prisoner has a representative recognized as connected to both the Church and the State working to guarantee that his death is not in vain, that a regenerated soul is delivered to heaven free from its profane attachments. This typically phallocratic gesture thereby receives a return in the next life (where it really matters) on the losses society has inflicted in this life. By 'impregnating' the condemned, bringing the soul to life, a profit is gained from expenditure (the *capital* of capital punishment). Thereby the letter killeth but the spirit gives life, as the body of the condemned is consigned to mother earth (and in the case of Matthew Poncelet, alongside the bodies of Sister Helen's departed sisters) and the soul is delivered to heaven (a delivery which occurs as a result of 'lethal injection'). As Irigaray observes, 'The patriarchal order is based upon worlds of the beyond: worlds of before birth and especially of the afterlife [...] It doesn't appreciate the real value of the world we have and draws up its often bankrupt blueprints on the basis of hypothetical worlds' (Irigaray (1993), 27). One might suggest, following thinkers such as Mary Daly, that the patriarchal society, misunderstanding its own role in the creation/continuation of life, responds to its apparent impotence in light of feminine creativity by negatively usurping bio-power and renaming death 'birth', not to mention the Church's employment of Prejean as an agent of that transaction.

Having been instructed that her sole purpose is to save the soul of Matthew Poncelet (Sonnier and Willie), Prejean seemingly makes no mention of recommending the sacraments to the condemned in her work, but stresses the need for them to 'take responsibility for what they've done' and proceeds (and continues even now) to make every effort to save the *life* of the condemned individual as well.[2] As Irigaray asks, '[W]hat do spirituality and heavenliness mean without ethics?' (Irigaray (1993), 27). Such a question was apparently

2 Ironically, Prejean's efforts against the death penalty are, while contrary to the stated beliefs of the majority of Catholics in America, in virtual agreement with the US Catholic Conference's declaration opposition and Pope John Paul II's 1995 statement that cases in which capital punishment is necessary are 'very rare, if not practically non-existent', (*Frontline*: 'US Catholic Bishops Statement', 1; 'The Pope's Statement', 1).

irrelevant to the chaplain of the prison who would make further efforts to 'bar (Prejean) and other women from serving as spiritual advisers to death-row inmates' (Prejean, 25). It seems that the chaplain feared not only that Prejean was ill equipped to fulfill her paternal role, but also that Prejean's choice not to wear the habit (as did all the sisters in her order) amounted to a 'flouting of authority' which might encourage the inmates to do the same. According to the chaplain, 'the inmates know that the Pope has requested nuns to wear the habit.' This is an observation about which Prejean has her doubts, though she understands that 'seeing (nuns) dressed like regular people had been very upsetting for many Catholics, who said that when they saw us in our long, flowing robes, dressed like angels, it had made them think of God' (25). Not only nuns, but as Irigaray observes, 'most women's experience tells them, on a cultural level, that they are first and foremost asexual or neuter, apart from which they are subjected to the norms of the sexual arena in the strict sense and to family stereotypes' (Irigaray (1993), 21). Without angelic attire, constrained to the earth, no longer transparent, no longer a symbol eclipsed by the Other to which it points, Prejean will be noticed, put under the determining gaze, but she will also be free to find her own voice.

Perhaps the most memorable scene in *Dead Man Walking* depicts Prejean and Poncelet in their second dialogue, during which Poncelet's tone becomes more and more seductive. He asks, 'Don't you miss having a man? Bein' married, havin' sex?' 'You don't have to be married to have intimacy,' she replies. 'We got intimacy right now, don't we?' he says. 'I went to see your mother,' she responds. 'I like bein' alone with you,' he remarks slyly, 'you lookin' real good to me.' 'I'm not here for your amusement […] show some respect!' she retorts. 'Why should I repect you, 'cuz you a nun?!' 'Because I'm a person; every person needs respect.' Nun or object, nun and object, heavenly or earthly, heavenly and earthly: as Irigaray observes, 'women find it so difficult to speak and to be heard as women. They are excluded and denied by the patriarchal linguistic order. They cannot be women and speak in a sensible, coherent manner' (Irigaray (1993), 20). In order to speak *as woman, as person*, Prejean's voice is necessarily duplicitous, multiple. It is a voice with which Prejean can respond to Poncelet's comparison of himself and Christ, both rebels, with 'No, you're nothing like Jesus', and at the same time declare to Poncelet that he is 'a son of God'. It is a voice which can speak (with/for) the silenced voices of both the condemned and the victims of his crime. Pat Sonnier would describe Prejean to his brother like this: 'She's a nun, but she talks natural and doesn't quote the Bible all the time' (Prejean, 32).

To 'talk natural' is to allow herself to speak, with multiple voices, through a text the body of which holds and preserves and delivers the discourses of the abject. If we cannot in our writings and our readings prevent victimization, the silencing of the abject voice, perhaps we can ensure as Prejean does that silenced voices may 'be for a time that is after them' (Levinas, 349). For writers such as Prejean, this means that the challenge offered by Hélène Cixous will be met, to 'Write [one's] self. [One's] body must be heard' (Smith, 261). Prejean's experience, Prejean's text, answers that challenge by offering the possibility that by confronting the humanity, the identity, and the personhood, of the condemned, that most radically and obviously Abject/Other, we might move toward an acknowledgement of other inadequacies in our cultural myths. 'Of course, it is impossible for each individual to recreate the whole of History,' as Irigaray cautions; but as Irigaray suggests:

> any individual, a woman or a man, can and must recreate her or his own personal and collective history. For this to be accomplished, everyone's body and opinions must be respected. *Everyone should be aware of her or his obligations* [...] (Irigaray (1993), 28; emphases added)

Bibliography

Ainley, Alison. 'The Ethics of Sexual Difference', in Fletcher and Benjamin, 53–62.

Bernasconi, Robert, and Simon Critchley (eds.). *Re-Reading Levinas*. Bloomington: Indiana UP, 1990.

Chalier, Catherine. 'Ethics and the Feminine', in Bernasconi and Critchley, 119–29.

Chanter, Tina. 'Female Temporality and the Future of Feminism', in Fletcher and Benjamin, 63–79.
Dead Man Walking (film, directed by Tim Robbins; Polygram, 1995).
Fletcher, John, and Andrew Benjamin, (eds.). *Abjection, Melancholia, and Love: The Work of Julia Kristeva*. London: Routledge, 1990.
Foucault, Michel. *Discipline and Punish: The Birth of the Prison*, translated by Alan Sheridan. New York: Random House Vintage, 1977.
—— *The History of Sexuality*, vol. 1, translated by Robert Hurley. New York: Random House Vintage, 1990.
Frontline (PBS). WGBH Educational Foundation, www.wgbh.org
Graybeal, Jean. *Language and the Feminine in Nietzsche and Heidegger*. Bloomington: Indiana UP, 1990.
Gross, Elizabeth. 'The Body of Signification', in Fletcher and Benjamin, 80–103.
Irigaray, Luce. *Je, Tu, Nous: Toward a Culture of Difference*, translated by Alison Martin. New York: Routledge, 1993.
—— 'Questions to Emmanuel Levinas: On the Divinity of Love', in Bernasconi and Critchley, 109–18.
Kristeva, Julia. *Black Sun*, translated by Leon Roudiez. New York: Columbia University Press, 1989.
—— *The Kristeva Reader*, edited by Toril Moi. Oxford: Blackwell, 1986.
—— *Powers of Horror*, translated by Leon Roudiez. New York: Columbia University Press, 1982.
Ledbetter, Mark. 'The More Things Change, The More They Remain the Same' (unpublished essay, 1995).
Levinas, Emmanuel. 'The Trace of the Other', in Taylor (1986), 345–59.
Prejean, Helen. *Dead Man Walking*. New York: Random House Vintage, 1994.
Smith, Johanna. 'Feminist Criticism and *Frankenstein*', in J. Smith (ed.), *Frankenstein*. Boston: Bedford St Martin's, 1992.
Taylor, Mark C. *Alterity*. Chicago: University of Chicago Press, 1987.
—— (ed.) *Deconstruction in Context*. Chicago: University of Chicago Press, 1986.

Andrew W. Hass

Seeing Through a Glass Face to Face

Art galleries are always, to me, places of reflection. That is, I find myself in reflection. I mean this in two senses: that I find myself reflecting *on* what I encounter there, and that I find myself reflected *in* what I encounter there. The first sense we can comprehend easily, for who does not become reflective, pondering, ruminative, before the great masters of canvas and paint, or of bronze and clay? The second sense, however, though an extension of the first, is far more complex. When I say I see myself reflected in the works on display, I am saying something that involves much more than a simple notion of mental stimulation or observational provocation. I am resituating what it means to encounter a work of art by, in effect, expunging the gap that separates us. I am saying that the work of art, to some lesser or greater degree, is *me*. This is no simple claim.

Thus, in the summer of 1999 when I encountered an exhibition of Rembrandt self-portraits at the National Gallery in London, I found myself in an odd position. One could say I found myself in many odd positions, as many as the variegated expressions and postures depicted by Rembrandt of himself. But the one that caught me most off guard, the one that, you might say, *dislocated* me, was a self-portrait that was both a self-portrait and not a self-portrait. It was a self-portrait depicting another: Rembrandt, that is, depicting himself as the Apostle Paul (see Fig. 1). It was not simply the unusualness of the conceit which struck me – Rembrandt using his own face for the portrait of a saintly figure – but the complexity of the implications which, the longer I stared at it, became more apparent. These implications arise in relation to the reflexivity of the artistic experience I have just mentioned. For if I can claim I find myself reflected in a work that I observe, it seems more credible that an artist himself or herself can make that claim, and with even greater justification or veracity, since

Fig. 1. Rembrandt van Rijn, *Self Portrait as the Apostle Paul*, 1661. Rijksmuseum, Amsterdam.

the evidence is that much more to hand, so to speak. But when an artist paints *himself*, paints himself *consciously* and *literally*, and then paints himself as *another*, the dislocations that result lead us down all sorts of intricate paths, as many and as intricate as the pencil lines or brush strokes that made up this fascinating exhibition. Furthermore, at risk of dislocating the reader also, I want to venture down some of what I think are the most important of these paths. For they lead us, I want to contend, into some of the greatest crises of this so very young twenty-first century.

Let us take our starting point from the notion of *fracture* inherent in this painting of Rembrandt as the Apostle Paul. There are two obvious fractures at work within this picture. The first is the fracture between Rembrandt the artist and Rembrandt the subject. The one who actually applied paint to this canvas is, ontologically, different from the one which (who?) the commingling of paints comes to depict. This fact is patently obvious. But this sets up a fracture akin to our own experience every time we look in the mirror in the morning. What we see on the other side of the sink is, phenomenally or ontologically, not *us*. It is light reflecting off the back of the quicksilver behind the glass of the mirror. We never stop to consider this reality because, practically, it is of little or no importance or consequence. We need to get on with our day; nor are many of us sharp enough first thing in the morning to think about, much less care about, the ontology of our being. But what if the image in the mirror were at any time to freeze itself, so that no matter how much we moved our face or our body, or how much time elapsed, the initial image would not change? Such an occurrence would be very disconcerting, for issues of ontology would quickly break upon us like an icy shower. And yet this is precisely what any self-portraitist does: they look at themselves in a mirror, and freeze the image they see by transferring it to paint on a canvas. I am convinced that self-portraitists are more aware of the fractures within what we call the 'self' than any of us, having to endure them for at least as long as it takes to paint their picture.

Of all people, Oscar Wilde, creator of the revelant Dorian Gray, knew of the divisions of self. 'Man is least himself when he talks in his own person,' he once wrote; 'Give him a mask, and he will tell you the truth' (Wilde, 45). But here with Rembrandt we have someone who divides himself even further, who not only 'masks' himself (that is, makes a mask of himself) in paint, but who masks the mask with the supposed figure of St Paul. Here, then, lies the second fracture within the work.

But is Rembrandt really breaking himself, or breaking with himself, in this move? Does he sever himself, or does he break himself in the same sense of breaking a one-dollar bill, whereby constitutionally he has not changed, though he has now become 'change', coinage with which to purchase or give away? In his defence, we might think of it in yet other terms, and say he simply 'lends himself' to the Apostle. But does the schema of lending and borrowing really hold? I do not think so, for there is much more going on in this 'transaction' besides a simple temporary exchange or giving-over of goods, however personal the goods may be. A great price comes with this bargain, a fee of interest, we might say, an interest that accrues upon the self. *Self-interest*, let us call it. And let us not forget the Latin derivation of this word 'interest': literally a 'being between'.

One way we could calculate this interest of the self or of the self-portrait is to trace it back to the principal. The principal in this case is held within a philosophical or theological framework of the sign, a framework which occupies the attention of so much critical theory today, insofar as the 'sign' is taken in its more elemental form of semiotics, the form of language, written or otherwise (but especially written). There are great fractures within the sign, we are told, and these fractures work their way down to the very core of our being, since our being and our language can no longer be held apart. In fact, in this post-Heideggerean world, they constitute one another. But rather than starting from these present-day theories, let us start from a more distant theory, one nonetheless hugely influential, handed down to us by another sainted theologian, who was as intimate with St Paul as Rembrandt leads us to believe *he* was, though on a much different level. Here I mean St Augustine.

In Books II and III of his *De Doctrina Christiana*, Augustine offers the first attempt at a comprehensive theory of signs. He offers it, of course, in relation to a hermeneutics of Scripture: 'There are some rules for dealing with the scriptures', he opens in the Prologue of the work, 'which I consider can be not inappropriately passed on to students, enabling them to make progress not only by reading others who have opened up the hidden secrets of the divine literature, but also by themselves opening them up to yet others again' (Augustine (1996), 101). In Book I he begins these rules by setting out the difference between 'things' and 'signs', 'things' being 'those that are not mentioned in order to signify something, such as wood, a stone, an animal, and other things like that,' and 'signs' those things 'which are used in order to signify something else' (106–7). These distinctions are set up to help the student of Scripture distinguish between what should be read as a literal thing, and what should be read as a sign, something pointing beyond itself to another signification. Augustine introduces them, then, in support of his allegorical strategies of reading, by which the figurative can be discerned from the literal. Hence his imaginative, and not wholly surprising, interpretation later in Book II of a passage from Song of Solomon: 'Your teeth are like a flock of shorn ewes coming up from the washing, which all give birth to twins, and there is not one among them that is barren' (Song of Solomon, 4:2). To Augustine, who naturally could never read anything from Song of Solomon at face value, this verse refers to the saints as 'the Church's teeth that cut people off from their errors, and after softening up their hardness by biting them off and chewing them transfer them into its body'. Now if such rumination is not enough, Augustine goes on to equate the second half of the Hebrew simile with 'faithful and true servants of God': 'I also get enormous pleasure', he continues, 'from recognizing who the shorn ewes are, the burdens of the world laid aside like their fleeces, as they come up from the wash, that is from baptism, and all give birth to twins, that is to the two commandments of love, and from seeing that none of them is barren and lacking this holy fertility' (Augustine (1996), 131–2). The pleasures of the body here are safely transferred to the fertile pleasures of the spiritual realm, where the saint Augustine can happily find an 'enormous pleasure' as he experiences the impregnation of the literal that brings forth the figural. Augustine's is an elaborate reading of an elaborate simile, and one that allows him a certain ecstatic moment – 'And yet I don't know how it is, but I find it more delightful to contemplate the saints when I see them as […]' (131), while he stands outside of himself (he, the future saint) to delight in the saintly faithful and their offspring.

I am not suggesting here that Augustine is painting his own self-portrait with this reading, either wittingly or unwittingly. But I am suggesting that the fractures of the self are evident even here at this level of language, as the separating out of the figurative from the literal implicates the one who does the separating, here in (or with) a certain kind of ecstasy, which we know means literally to stand outside of oneself. But let us consider another example of Augustine's, one less elaborate, which implicates yet another beside himself, the Apostle Paul. A few pages later in Book II he writes:

> Now there are two reasons why texts are not understood: if they are veiled in signs that are either unknown or ambiguous. Signs, for their part, can be either proper or metaphorical. They are said to be proper when they are introduced to signify the things they were originally intended for, as when we say 'ox' to signify the animal which everyone who shares the English [*sic* – 'Latin' in original] language with us calls by this name. They are metaphorical when the very things which we signify with their proper words are made use of to signify something else, as when we say 'ox', and by this syllable understand the evangelist, whom scripture itself signified, according to the apostle's interpretation of *You shall not muzzle the ox that threshes the corn* (1 Corinthians 9:9; Deuteronomy 25:4). (135)

Now exactly what 'evangelist' Augustine intends to refer to here is unknown. One commentator offers the possibility that Augustine refers to Luke the Evangelist, since supposedly by Augustine's time the ox had become an accepted symbol of Luke's gospel, as we see in much medieval depiction. But how Augustine could make the link to Luke in the context of 1 Corinthians is still a mystery. Paul in this Corinthian passage is defending himself against those who question his right as an apostle, and particularly those who question whether he should demand financial support as such an apostle. 'Who tends the flock without getting some of the milk?' Paul retorts (1 Corinthians 9:7 (Revised Standard Version)). His metaphor here seems relatively straightforward, especially in comparison to Augustine's shorn ewes. He certainly has the right to at least food and drink as a worker of God. So he continues:

> Do I say this on human authority? Does not the law say the same? For it is written in the law of Moses, 'You shall not muzzle an ox when it is treading out the grain.' Is it for oxen that God is concerned? Does he not speak entirely for our sake? It was written for our sake, because the plowman should plow in hope and the thresher should thresh in hope of a share in the crop. If we have sown spiritual good among you, is it too much if we reap your material benefits? (1 Corinthians 9:9–12 (RSV))

According to Paul, then, adopting Augustine's distinction between the proper and the metaphorical, this law was written for *his*, *Paul's*, sake, so that the 'ox' proper refers to himself metaphorically. This he seems to state in unequivocal terms. How then could Augustine maintain that by 'ox' we must understand the 'evangelist', in contradistinction to the 'apostle'? Was Paul doing what Rembrandt later did to him – painting a picture of himself, only then to label it 'the evangelist', whether Luke, or some other? According to Augustine, this is indeed what he must have done. In that dangerous gap between the thing and the sign, the literal and the figurative, the proper and the metaphorical, something, or someone, is getting lost, or loses identity, or conversely, gains identity. The ox becomes Paul, but in Augustine's hands, Paul in turn becomes the 'evangelist', or we could say Paul is dropped out altogether, without much explanation why, or who exactly replaces him. The ox then becomes a dangerous animal – certainly for Paul, who, just as he is not paid his due by the Corinthian church, is muzzled out of the picture by Augustine. And if we cast ourselves forward to Rembrandt's two paintings of the slaughtered ox which hangs upside down in the uncomfortable but richly suggestive form of a crucifix (see Fig. 2), even the ox proper does not escape the terrible dangers of being gutted and transformed into something other. The figurative, or the figural, is a costly creature.

Too costly for some. Martin Luther, that great Augustinian monk, thought the figure was too high for such allegorical readings of Scripture. In his polemic of 1521 concerning 'the letter and the Spirit' he says: 'The fact that a painted picture signifies a living man without any words or writing should not cause you to say the little word "picture" has two meanings, a literal one, signifying the picture, and a spiritual one, signifying the living man' (Luther, 79). For Luther, the leap from the literal to the figural exposed too many great perils, so

Fig. 2. Rembrandt, *The Slaughtered Ox*, c. 1638. Glasgow Museums and Art Galleries, Glasgow, Scotland.

that one could lose oneself all too easily in meanings that are simply not there. Granting that the things described in Scripture do indeed mean something further, Luther does not however believe that Scripture has what he calls a 'twofold meaning': that there is one thing a word refers to ('ox' referring to a four-legged beast, let us say), and then yet another thing behind that first reference ('the evangelist', for example). 'It is much more certain and much safer to stay with the words and the simple meaning,' he claims, 'for this is the true pasture and home of all the spirits' (79).

The 'true pasture and home of all the spirits'? Luther's own language betrays him, of course. There is never merely 'one meaning to which the words refer' (79). The metaphor is always in the literal, as his own words just prove. Paul's words 'You shall not muzzle an ox when it is treading out the grain' do not simply have one meaning, even for Luther. What Luther would call literal here is already metaphorical. Luther wants to keep the word 'picture' as simply the picture. He wants to say the living man is not part of the meaning of 'picture'. But were he to look at Rembrandt's painting of St Paul and 'read' the work, his 'simple meaning' would collapse in upon itself. What would the sign of St Paul, the face of St Paul, refer to? Literally, it is Rembrandt. Figuratively, it is St Paul. Metaphorically, you could say it is both. Where is Luther's 'true pasture and home' in this painting? On what could he ruminate? How would his teeth cut through the implications of this self-portrait? It seems he would have to leave his two greatest influences, Paul and Augustine, behind. *He*, Luther, would not come up from the washing and give birth to these sainted twins; rather, he would stand barren. 'The letter kills but the Spirit gives life,' wrote Paul (2 Corinthians 3:6). And here, then, in Rembrandt, is Paul, standing with a letter in his hand – the Letter to the Ephesians, it can be surmised from the Hebrew (?) letters on top of the page – standing with the sword at his side, the sword of the Spirit, the word of God, ready to run in poor Luther who will not let the picture signify the living man. The letter kills indeed, as Rembrandt himself very well knows. This we are about to see more clearly.

What I am contending here, of course, is that the difficulties inherent in the shift from the 'thing' to the 'sign' in Augustine's theory of signs are the same difficulties one encounters when trying to negotiate the referentiality of Rembrandt's painting. We get far more than we bargained for. Furthermore we, the bargaining ones, pay the price, just as Luther would pay his price, and Rembrandt paid his. No one today has explored these matters of interest, these accruing matters, more than the great interdisciplinary theorist Paul Ricoeur. In his challenging work of a decade ago *Soi-même comme un autre* (1990), he cuts to the very heart of the issues at stake here – the issues of selfhood. And we see his work's relevance most forcefully in the English translation of the title: *Oneself as Another*. Working within both the Anglo-American tradition of analytic philosophy and the Continental tradition, especially of twentieth-century European thought, Ricoeur sets out to rediscover the 'self' amid the increasing difficulties posed by analytic language theory and postmodern discourse. He wants, as he says repeatedly, to rescue the 'who' from both the 'what' and the 'why' in any relations of signification, whether they be speech acts, written texts, or any other kind of signifying gesture. The question 'who?', he claims, has continually given way to the 'what?'–'why?' axis of semantic investigation, to the point where the 'who?', which in Heidegger's existentialist terms shares all affinity with the problematic of the self, is completely obscured or concealed within the referential framework of a predicative structure. The question 'what?' can predicate even the thinking self into a purely detached entity, as indeed Descartes' *Cogito* did, Ricoeur explains. But the self as an acting, participating existential self begs to resurface, and it is Ricoeur's intention to show how it might resurface vis-à-vis the concept of 'other', or 'another'. It is in this spirit of Ricoeur, then, that I approach Rembrandt's self-portrait. I have not been concerned with the questions 'What does this painting mean or refer to?', or 'Why did Rembrandt paint the picture the way he did?' This is not to negate the importance of such questions. Indeed, we could pursue this line of questioning towards all kinds of fascinating and fruitful ends, asking, for example, 'What in fact is the manuscript in Paul's hand?', or 'How does the manuscript relate to the figure being represented, whether Paul or Rembrandt himself?', or 'What does the sword signify?', or 'Why did Rembrandt choose this figure upon whom to superimpose his face?', or 'Does Rembrandt feel some psychological affiliation with Paul?', or 'Does

Rembrandt, as an artist of biblical scenes and lessons, see himself sharing a similar mission to Paul's teaching amongst the Gentiles, as suggested by some?'(White and Buvelot, 214), or 'Was he simply following a tradition or vogue in which people commissioned themselves to be portrayed as biblical or mythological characters?' All these questions, interesting though they may be, I have put aside for the more self-interested question of 'who?'. Who, I ask, stands not only behind this painting, but in front of it? *Who is this painting?*

Ricoeur's series of studies, which set the problematic of the self within the modalities of 'discourse, action, narrative, and ethical commitment' (Ricoeur, 335), are far too involved to summarize adequately here. Nor are they in their entirety germane to our specific concerns. But I want to isolate one idea that Ricoeur puts forward which I think does pertain well to this painting. He writes, in reference to speech acts, that 'every advance made in the direction of the selfhood of the speaker or the agent has as its counterpart a comparable advance in the otherness of the partner' (44). By this he wants to say, and indeed goes on to work out with typically rigorous philosophical analysis, that the determination of selfhood is 'by way of its dialectic with otherness' (297). This may not seem like such a radical concept, for indeed, our understanding of ourselves has always, we might say, been conceived in relation to those around us on some level. But Ricoeur here is not simply talking about an understanding of ourselves as individuals who carry certain characteristics and traits in differentiation from others. He is talking about the very constitution of the 'self', the self *qua* self, which is predicated necessarily on the other in a determination that will carry with it ethical and moral imputations for the self. We are selves not in some Cartesian sense, holed up in our enclave of pure interiority, only after which we then emerge to encounter and reconstruct the world around us. Rather, we are selves only as we admit the other, in what we might call an a-priori gesture, as our '*counterpart*, that is, someone who, *like* me, says "I"', according to Ricoeur (335). Hence the title, oneself *as* another. This is a movement that Ricoeur calls, drawing from Husserl's phenomenology, an 'analogical transfer' (335). It is in this 'transfer' where the 'who' is recovered, and recovered both ways: the 'who' of the self, and the 'who' of the other. Or in relation to

Rembrandt's painting: the 'who' *standing in* and the 'who' *standing in for*. To this I would want to add the 'who' *standing in front of*.

Granted, we have come a long way from the visuals of the self-portrait. And I will be the first to admit that introducing the likes of Ricoeur in such a truncated manner runs great risks, not the least of which is to do great disservice to Ricoeur himself. But if we reconceive Rembrandt's picture in terms of an 'analogical transfer', even without all the intricacies of Ricoeur's argument, not only do we gain an apt description which functions at almost any level of critical assessment, but in addition we gain the field of view which most interests Ricoeur, and which I have been suggesting is at the core of this second fracture in this painting – the field where the 'who' of the self is struggling to emerge from the 'what' of the representation. It is this struggle, I maintain, which perhaps best defines our contemporary critical, and indeed we should stress *existential* and *spiritual*, dilemma, that dilemma which has been called in that celebrated phrase of Lyotard's our 'postmodern condition'. For are we not all struggling in some sense to emerge from the prison (and prism) of representations?

Thinkers of a more postmodern bent have had much to say about the phenomenon of the portrait/self-portrait. I find Hélène Cixous's recounting of an Edgar Allen Poe story in her *Three Steps on the Ladder of Writing* particularly significant here (Cixous, 27–9). Poe's story, called 'The Oval Portrait', is told to us by a narrator, who, being fatally wounded, is forced to enter a old chateau for shelter, where he encounters an oval portrait which absolutely captivates him. The portrait is of a woman with an extraordinary personal history. The narrator then begins in turn to recount this history to us, which soon overtakes the story of the narrator himself. The woman's story involves her husband, a brilliant painter, who was so taken with his new bride that he set out with a feverish passion to paint her portrait in the turret of this chateau. After many weeks of intense obsession, his bride posing at his side the whole time, her smile constant but her spirits fading, he arrives at the completion of his masterwork. Upon the last brush stroke ('one tint upon the eye'), the artist husband stands entranced before the canvas, and with a brooding Gothic energy that is typical of Poe, cries out 'This is indeed Life itself!' Whereupon he suddenly turns to gaze at his beloved, only to find her dead. With this startling, yet not totally surprising, revelation (we cannot help but think of Wilde's Dorian Gray), the story abruptly ends. *Poe*'s story ends, that is, the one entitled 'The Oval Portrait'. What interests Cixous is that we the readers have become so caught up in the story of the woman in the portrait, we forget the narrator who is retelling her story. And rightly so, as Poe never reintroduces him back into the narrative before bringing this narrative, i.e. the original overall narrative, to an end. 'This is Poe's genius,' writes Cixous:

> It is a kind of allegory for what happens in creation. It is mythical, it might also be considered a cliché. It is not, because in the course of reading we have ourselves become the painter. We too have followed and started painting and forgetting and erasing the narrator in particular, which is very strange. And I suspect we may come out of the turret or the tale without realizing what we have done. (28–9)

What have we done? We have in effect killed off the narrator, the one who was wounded in the first place. And in doing so, we have become just like the husband painter in the story within the story. 'We the murderer-painter,' Cixous calls us. 'This is the art of Edgar Allen Poe: he makes *us* carry out what is done in the text (here, by the painter)' (30).

What concerns Cixous here is the aspect of death in any act of creation. 'To begin (writing, living) we must have death,' she states (7). And having begun, in the midst of the act, there will always be a certain blindness. Hence the painter in the story only ever sees 'Life' upon the completion of his portrait, blind as he has been to his dying wife. And 'death' will soon follow upon his momentary insight, as he looks back upon his lifeless bride.

What concerns us is our complicity in the event. It does not take much to translate this story into our painting of Rembrandt. If we change the medium of the written word to the painted picture, we see a direct superimposition: Rembrandt the painter (Poe) has painted a representation of himself (the wounded narrator) who, in representing yet someone other to himself (the husband painter), effectively kills off the middleman. In doing so he has implicated us, the viewer, for as we stand before the painting, we are put in a position of having to divest or bury one or the other. Is this a self-portrait of Rembrandt, or is it a portrait of St Paul who happens to look an awful lot like Rembrandt? Like Augustine, we bring to life one at the expense of the life of the other. Do we kill off Paul to allow for Rembrandt (or if we are Augustine, 'the Evangelist')? Or do we kill off Rembrandt, to allow for Paul? Rembrandt, as much as he sacrifices himself in the 'analogical transfer' of the portrait, makes us complicit. His 'self' of the portrait depends on another. And that other in this case is us, or you, or me – the viewer. We decide if this is a *self*-portrait. We settle the question of *'Who?'*

The question remains: Can we reverse this self-interest, this arbitration between the selves, so that the portrait helps decide *our* self?

In aid of some provisional answer to this question, let me conclude my ruminations with the visual insight of Jacques Derrida in his *Memoires of the Blind* (1993). This meditation on the self-portraits in the Louvre (among other things) was written in the same year as Cixous's meditation on writing (1990), and shares a kinship with that work – beyond its compatriotism – in its notion of blindness. Derrida carries his meditation much further, however, and brings us into a very theological space. He concludes his thoughts with commentary on both St Paul and St Augustine, bringing us full circle.

Derrida refers to three very striking pictures of Paul's blinding conversion on the road to Damascus, among them Caravaggio's deeply moving rendition. In his commentary, Derrida points us to Paul's own two accounts in Acts of his extraordinary divine encounter, what Derrida calls two versions of a self-portrait, 'the self-portrait of a convert' (Derrida, 116). In wonderfully descriptive language, Derrida remarks upon the second version of this self-portrait, with Paul before King Agrippa and Festus:

> Sunflower blindness, a conversion that twists the light and turns it upon itself to the point of dizziness, the blacking out of the one bedazzled, who sees himself go from brightness and clarity to even more clarity, perhaps to too much sun. This clairvoyance of the all-too-evident is Paul's madness. And one blames it on books, in other words, on the visibility of the invisible word: Festus cries 'You are out of your mind, Paul! Too much learning [*grammata*] is driving you

> mad!' One can bet that Paul's confession, the self-portrait of this mad light, will have come to represent the model of the self-portrait [...] (117)

What might Derrida mean by this last suggestion? Derrida has his own answer in relation to the ruins of blindness. But we can answer in our own way, by referring to the ending of the account which Derrida does not quote:

> And Agrippa said to Paul, 'In a short time you think to make me a Christian!' And Paul said, 'Whether short or long, I would to God that not only you but also all who hear me this day might become such as I am – except for these chains.' (Acts 26:28–9)

Could we say that this is exactly what Rembrandt has done: become such as Paul is, literally, figuratively, in a conversion? And does Paul not thus represent the *model* of the self-portrait insofar as he models the quintessential self-portrait to us, that we in turn should model ourselves after him, as Rembrandt has done, literally, figuratively, for us to model in our own conversion? And can this conversion move us, like Paul's, from a necessary killing of the other to a reconstitution of our own self through the other?

Derrida moves us immediately from Paul to Augustine, and particularly the Augustine of the *Confessions*. 'In Christian culture there is no self-portrait without confession,' writes Derrida. For indeed, the *Confessions* are Augustine's great self-portrait (and one might say the first ever drawn to such an elaborate degree). Derrida then points us to that passage in Book X where Augustine denounces works of art, and in particular paintings and their painters:

> They make them on a far more lavish scale than is required to satisfy their own modest needs or to express their devotion. And all these things are additional temptations to the eye that men follow outwardly, inwardly forsaking the one by whom they were made, ruining what he made of them. (*Confessions,* X.34, quoted in Derrida, 119)

Derrida then asks:

> Would Saint Augustine thus condemn the temptations of *all* Christian painting? Not at all, just so long as a conversion saves it. A sort of allegory makes

> corporeal vision conform to divine vision. In this case, allegory would not exclude analogy. (119)

Painting is saved by a conversion from the 'thing' (the 'corporeal vision') to the 'sign' (the 'divine vision'), by gazing upon the Beauty of the divine eye. For as Augustine writes: 'the beauty which flows through men's minds into their skilful hands comes from that Beauty which is above their souls and for which my soul sighs day and night [...] If only they [these painters] could see it, they would not depart from it' (Augustine, (1961), 241). But perhaps they *do* see it. Perhaps Rembrandt sees it in his conversion of himself to St Paul, in an allegory that 'would not exclude analogy', whereby he saves himself and his painting through what Derrida calls 'this exchange of glances' (Derrida, 119), the self-beholding the gaze of the other, the self *becoming* the gaze of the other.

This conversion, we might say, is an 'analogical transfer', and this returns us to Ricoeur. Where Derrida leads us to a specular blindness from which we see the possibility, if not the necessity, to believe, we, along with Ricoeur, may find ourselves at a place now where our self *as* self finds its 'who' through a kind of conversion to another. Oneself *as* another. And not only Rembrandt as St Paul, but we in an exchange of glances with both figures, we who, as in any self-portrait, take the place of the mirror into which the self-portraitist gazes, we who become the eye of the self-portraitist, internalizing the light of his or her gaze within us, our counterpart, someone who, *like* me, as me, says 'I'. This then might constitute our dialectic with otherness, our recovery of 'who', existentially and confessionally.

I began by saying that, in reflection, a work of art to some degree is me. Through the fractures and dislocations of one sense of myself, perhaps this highly invested language of conversion allows me to re-invest myself in now a higher rate of exchange. For conversion is not just a change, but an exchange, as 'conversion' shares the same etymological root as 'conversation', a turning around. Perhaps as all these glances of Rembrandt's painting turn around each other, as we all come face to face with each other in conversation: I am my *self* only as I stand in front of, and as I stand in for, Rembrandt, or Paul, or Luther, or Augustine, or, as Paul tells us, Christ, or as Derrida obliquely informs us, the wholly Other. 'Now we see in a mirror dimly, but then face to face' (1 Corinthians 13:12). We have been taught to think the greater the art, the greater the polish of the mirror. If this be so, then Rembrandt here, as in so many of his works, shows his great theological polish.

Bibliography

Augustine. *Confessions*, translated by R. S. Pine-Coffin. London: Penguin, 1961.

—— *Teaching Christianity (De Doctrina Christiana)*, ed. John E. Rotelle, translated by Edmund Hill. Hyde Park, NY: New York City Press, 1996.

Cixous, Hélène. *Three Steps on the Ladder of Writing*, translated by Savah Cornell and Susan Sellers. New York: Columbia UP, 1993.

Derrida, Jacques. *Memories of the Blind*, translated by Pascal-Anne Brault and Michael Naás. Chicago: Chicago UP, 1993.

Luther, Martin. '"Concerning The Letter and The Spirit" from Answer to the Hyperchristian, Hyperspiritual, and Hyperlearned Book by Goaf Emser in Leipzig (1521)', in T. F. Lull (ed.), *Basic Theological Writings*. Minneapolis: Fortress Press, 1989.

Ricoeur, Paul. *Oneself as Another*, translated by Kathleen Blamey. Chicago: Chicago UP, 1992.

White, Christopher, and Quentin Buvelot (eds.). *Rembrandt by Himself* London: National Gallery Publications; The Hague: Royal Cabinet of Paintings Mawitshuis, 1999.

Wilde, Oscar. 'The Critic as an Artist', in *Plays, Prose Writings and Poems*. London: Dent, 1975.

ELIZABETH PHILPOT

Susanna: Indecent Attraction / Fatal Exposure

The stimulating story of Susanna and the Elders, which was written between the years 165 and 100 BCE, is one of the three accounts in the Apocrypha dealing with the life of Daniel. The narrative of Susanna[1] is short and is contained within the entire sixty-four verses of the Book of Susanna.

It can be summarised as follows: Susanna, the wife of Joachim, a prosperous Jew exiled in Babylon, is sexually desired by two lusty Elders who spy on her while she bathes in the garden. As soon as her maids leave to fetch 'olive oil and ointments' (verse 17) they leap out from their hiding place and solicit her to submit to their amorous advances; and when she refuses to 'lie with' them, they seek their revenge and wrongfully accuse her of having committed adultery with a young man. Tried and condemned to death without her side of the story being heard, it is only through the intervention of Daniel, who skilfully questions them individually in court, that the truth emerges. Susanna is saved and the wrongdoers are put to death. This therefore is an erotically charged story of danger, lust, voyeurism, fear, provocation, the power of men over women, false accusations and finally justice.

Most of the main elements of this story are to be found in the painting of 1517 by the Venetian artist Lorenzo Lotto (*c.*1480–1556/7) in the Galleria Uffizi in Florence. As Peter Humfrey (Humphrey, 62 and fig. 70) suggests, this work was probably commissioned by a Venetian magistrate or someone, like Daniel, who administered justice. Several events from the story are shown together. We can see the two maids returning to the house (here shown as a rather grand castle), while Susanna walks demurely fully clothed in the garden,

1 The story and all quotations in this paper are taken from *The Holy Bible*, New Revised Standard Version.

oblivious of the two Elders skulking in the bushes. We are witnesses to the dramatic scene taking place in the foreground where the 'people in the house' (verse 26), who have heard the commotion, rush in through the side door to discover Susanna naked with the Elders. Lotto has concentrated on the moral of the story made clear by the words spoken by Susanna and one of the Elders written on old-fashioned scrolls with Latin inscriptions. The one over the Elder reads as follows: 'Vidimus eam cum iuvene commisceri Ni nobis assenties testimonio nostro peribis' (We saw her consort with a young man. If you do not submit to us you will perish from our testimony), while the inscription behind Susanna says: 'Satius duco mori quam peccare. Heu me.' ('I would rather die than sin. Alas!')

Susanna's reputation in both art and biblical history grew to represent chasteness, innocence and vulnerability and yet many artists prefer to depict the more feminine and sensual aspects of her, as we shall see. However, before we look at further images of Susanna bathing and have any preconceived ideas, we should ask ourselves what do we actually learn from the Apocryphal text about Susanna? The first three verses tell us that she was the daughter of Hilkiah and the wife of Joakim, a rich and well-respected man living in Babylon, whose house had a fine adjoining garden where Susanna went every day just after noon to walk. We also read that she had been raised by her righteous parents according to the Law of Moses and that she had children and other relatives (verse 30). Susanna is described as a 'woman of great refinement and beautiful in appearance' (verse 31) and in this she was not alone among biblical women to be described as 'beautiful'. Rachel (Genesis 29:17) is 'graceful and beautiful', Sarai (Genesis 12:11) is 'a woman beautiful in appearance' (although she was said to be in her eighties), Esther (Esther 2:7) is 'fair and beautiful', Sarah, the daughter of Raguel (Tobit 6:12) is 'sensible, brave and very beautiful' and Judith is 'beautiful in appearance, and was very lovely to behold' (Judith 8:7). Like Judith, who also found herself in a dangerous situation, Susanna too has an unshakeable faith in God, because we are also informed in verse 2 that 'she feared the Lord' and later in verse 35 that 'her heart trusted in the Lord.' At her trial she turns to God and cries out:

> O eternal God, you know what is secret and are aware of all things before they come to be; you know that these men have given false evidence against me. And now I am to die, though I have done none of the wicked things that they have charged against me!

The chaste Susanna is usually regarded as the real hero of this story with Daniel playing only a minor role as the judge who rescues her from the false testimony of the two wicked Elders. Painters, sculptors and other artisans recognize this and generally only include Daniel when their work forms part of a history cycle, as for example, on the carved door panels of a Dutch oak cabinet dating from about 1630–50 in the Rijksmuseum, Amsterdam.[2] Appropriately, this cabinet illustrated with scenes from the story of Susanna and other virtuous subjects was probably given as a wedding present as a suitable warning and reminder of the state of chastity.[3]

Having said that, artists prefer to concentrate on the more thrilling and provocative aspects of the narrative where Susanna is bathing in the garden. She is occasionally shown seated by a sunken bath or fountain clothed, where the painter can demonstrate his skills in the depiction of different textures, which is less common and the least popular representation among patrons. Jacopo da Empoli (1554–1640) gives full justice to the materials of the sumptuously dressed Susanna in his painting of her in the Kunsthistorisches Museum in Vienna. However, it is the more voyeuristic interpretation, where Susanna appears nude or partially naked, which appealed to artists and patrons alike. The majority of painters expose Susanna's body to the viewer's gaze, but usually create a sense of decency by covering the more intimate area of her body. In these cases the exposure can in no way be described as indecent as, for example, in the eighteenth-century painting entitled *Susanna Bathing* by the Swedish artist Georg Engelhard Schröder (1684–1750) in the Nationalmuseum in Stockholm where the drapery falls in delicate folds between her legs. Peter Paul

2 Other well-known history cycles of Susanna are the fourth-century sarcophagus in San Feliú, Gerona; the Crystal of Lothair, 9th century, British Museum, London and the Susanna cycle by H. Aldegrever BVIII 371.30.33 of 1555.

3 The other subjects depicted are St George defeating the dragon and Marcus Curtius, the Roman hero.

Rubens (1577–1640), on the other hand, in his first extant version of this subject, now in the Galleria Borghese in Rome of *c.*1607 paints Susanna completely nude, like the Venetian painters of the sixteenth century whom he admired, and makes no attempt whatsoever to hide her genitalia. In this instance, the exposure becomes more erotic and slightly indecent. In fact, he does his utmost to accentuate her naked beauty by giving her soft pink flesh, erotically erect nipples and material which slips off her shoulder revealing even more of her body to the onlooker. We know that Rubens is not interested in presenting Susanna as the chaste maiden of the Apocrypha, but rather as a sensuous mature woman. He himself called this type of picture a *'galanteria'* meaning that it was 'neither sacred nor profane, although taken from the Holy Writ'. This desire for sensual religious heroines by patrons is borne out by the letter written by Sir Dudley Carleton, British Ambassador to The Hague, to Rubens on 22 May 1618 concerning a painting of Susanna which he had commissioned from the artist, where he says that he hopes that 'la Susanna hà da esser bella per inamorar anco li Vecchij'[4] ('the Susanna would be beautiful enough to enamour even old men'); (Rooses and Ruelens, II. 165). At other times, painters will adhere to the biblical story by showing Susanna bathing alone before the Elders appear on the scene. Jean-Jacques Henner (1829–1905) makes us the voyeur in his painting entitled *The Chaste Susanna*, 1864 (Musée d'Orsay, Paris) where it is our response which can be said to be indecent because Susanna, whose face is turned away from us, is unaware that we are admiring and possibly being sexually aroused by the glowing portrayal of her skin.

In other examples, Susanna is being besieged by the two lecherous Elders leaning over trying to touch, silence, or menace her. In these works where she bathes she still manages to play the traditional female role of chastity to perfection. She is good, meek, vulnerable, innocent, mild, timid and always ultra-feminine and yet

4 Even more indecent are those images where Susanna is depicted displaying her pubic hair, as for instance, in more contemporary images e.g. *Susanna and the Elders* by the American artist, Thomas Hart Benton (1889–1975), now in the Fine Arts Museum, San Francisco.

also voluptuously and provocatively displaying her nakedness. Gill Saunders (Saunders, 9) sets out the four types of nudity as defined by the medieval theologians, in her book on the nude. Susanna is the epitome of the third category of nakedness – that of *nuditas virtualis* – meaning 'a state of nakedness intended to symbolise innocence, purity and truth'.[5]

Susanna was not always depicted in an overtly sexual manner. In the very earliest images of her in the catacombs in Rome dating from the second and third centuries CE she is shown standing in an attitude of prayer *(orans)*, dressed in a long robe,[6] while in the fourth-century fresco of her in the Catacomb of Praetextatus in Rome, she is represented as a white innocent lamb with the letters SUSANNA inscribed above her, flanked by two threatening-looking wolves. This sets the scene for all future portrayals of her as the powerless and innocent maiden and the Elders as the wicked perpetrators of lust because even in this early image there is already a sense of evil foreboding. The bravery, innocence and symbolism of the story of Susanna was soon recognized by early Christian writers; Tertullian, Ambrose[7] and Augustine all wrote commentaries about her.

It was not long before this virtuous Susanna, who could not be blamed for her predicament, was regarded 'as an exemplar, or emblem even, of the virtuous soul saved from the clutches of the Devil' (Murray (1996), 510). Her chastity too was soon regarded as synonymous with the Virgin Mary. She represents sublime purity, even though she was a married woman and therefore no longer a virgin in the Marian sense of the word. Even her name Susanna means 'lily' (emblem of the Virgin). Often the garden is represented as a

5 The three other types of symbolic nude are: (i) nuditas naturalis (The natural state of man as born into the world as represented by Adam and Eve before the Fall); (ii) nuditas temporalis (the renunciation of all worldly good, like St Francis); (iii) nuditas criminalis (symbolizing lust, vanity and self-indulgent sin).

6 For example in the Catacomb of St Peter and St Marcellinus, Chamber XIII, arcosolium lunette (Rome, late third or early fourth century CE).

7 St Ambrose wrote that Susanna 'did well to pour forth her soul, so that the fires of the body and the fears of death and the desires of life could not evaporate into it' (Ambrose, 320–1).

kind of *hortus conclusus* – another reference to the Virgin – and occasionally containing some of her other symbols such as the rose and the fountain. In the decorous 1526 painting by Albrecht Altdorfer (*c*.1480–1538) in the Alte Pinakothek in Munich of *Susanna and the Elders*, better known for its architectural extravaganza and exercise in perspective, Susanna sits richly attired, oblivious of the two Elders lurking in the long grass waiting impatiently for her maids to depart. She bathes (here reduced to a washing of the feet), while a maid carries a large lily and a pitcher – an obvious reference to her analogous position with the Virgin Mary. At other times, especially in the fifteenth and sixteenth centuries, artists recognized her importance and elevated her to sainthood by depicting her with a halo.[8]

In these works there can be no suggestion of indecent attraction through nudity. The narrator describes how the two Elders would watch her walking about in her husband's garden and how individually they were 'overwhelmed with passion for her' (verse 10). Certainly in their case viewing stimulated their sexual urges in spite of her being dressed and her nakedness covered. However, later in the story we learn that on another day when she went into the garden to walk she decided to take a bath because it was a hot day. The narrative does not say that she removed her clothes but this would have been understood and artists and others choose to present her in this way. Does Susanna, like Judith, set out consciously to be seductive? The answer is, I believe, irrevocably, no. Why is Susanna the Pious shown in the nude? She bathes in all innocence, not knowing that the Elders are already concealed in the garden. She thinks she is alone and feels safe because all the doors to the garden are shut. There is no prearranged meeting with these men, but imagine their added delight when she decided to bathe.

Fifteenth-century artists would sometimes show Susanna in the nude but it was not until the sixteenth century that they portrayed her in the bath setting, giving rise to the more lascivious images of her with bare breasts. This more erotic type of representation became particularly popular, not only in Venice with Tintoretto (1518–94) and

8 For example, fresco cycle from 1494 of *Susanna and the Elders* by Bernardino Pinturicchio (*c*.1454–1513) in the Borgia Apartments in the Vatican, Rome.

Veronese (*c.*1528–88) but also in northern Europe with artists such as Jan Massys (1509–75). A follower of this Flemish artist copies the type of seminude biblical heroine initiated by Massys in the panel of *Susanna and the Elders* (Musées Royaux des Beaux-Arts de Belgique, Brussels) where a radiant Susanna recoils from the touch of the white-bearded Elder. Religious representations were gradually becoming too lewd, emotions were stirred and the Roman Catholic Church instigated reforms.

The last session of the Council of Trent in December 1563 laid down the new rules for the Arts. Artists who painted religious imagery had to follow rules of decorum, especially when it came to portraying the nude. The Council forbade the depiction of 'licentious nudes' and artists had to disguise nudity under the veil of biblical or historical narratives. It became perfectly in order to show nudity as long as it was done in a decent manner under the auspices of the Bible. So one can say that the biblical text becomes a pre-text, a means to explore powerful themes of sexuality under the protection of scriptural sanction. During the Renaissance and Baroque periods, it became commonplace for artists to portray a naked Susanna as alluringly, seductively and beautifully as possible. Not only did they paint the lovely Susanna, but we can also instance Esther, Judith, Potiphar's wife, Lot and his Daughters, Bathsheba, Delilah and Penitent Magdalenes were also shown in various states of *déshabillé.* It meant that during this period, artists could concentrate on the more subtle aspects of depicting the female nude for the titillation and sexual pleasure of their patrons.

Decency is upheld in the small painting on copper of *Susanna and the Elders*, attributed to the Circle of Adam Elsheimer (Murray (1980), 57) possibly by the artist Johann Koenig (1586–1620), executed in about 1607 and now in the Dulwich Picture Gallery. Set in a lush garden, it depicts an almost completely nude defenceless Susanna with only the lower part of her torso draped. She is a potential rape victim, one Elder is physically exceedingly close to her. Susanna knows that she is doomed and is powerless to put up much of a fight, but by her outstretched hand repulsing the Elder, she manages to convey to us that she is not a willing participant. The two men together have the upper hand; they have complete power over her and she has no witnesses to corroborate her version of events. This artist also enhances the sexual mood by including an erotic fountain with dolphins and small naked putti, one of which spouts water from a little penis. Koenig concentrates, as did so many of the painters from the sixteenth to the eighteenth centuries, on the sexual and erotic aspects of the story.

Artemisia Gentileschi (1593–*c.*1652), who moves away from the traditional garden scene presents Susanna, almost naked with voluptuous curves and soft breasts in her canvas in the Schönborn Collection, Schloss Weissenstein, Pommersfelden, dated 1610 and entitled *Susanna and the Elders*.[9] It is interesting that as a female artist, Artemisia, unlike Rubens, does not show Susanna with erect nipples indicating a state of sexual arousal. This young innocent girl bathing on her own is frightened; her natural reaction is to twist her body away and to raise her arms in a gesture of rejection. The main point of the picture is not just her nudity but her virtue which is under threat as she resists the lecherous advances of the two villains. Susanna is correctly shown alone because she had sent her maids away. She appears completely vulnerable beset by these smarmy old men who hover over her like a dark threatening cloud; the red of the cloak adding to the sexual intent of the scene. Her only defence is the wall, behind which they have sneaked up aggressively. It has been said that as a woman painter, Artemisia was able to show the inner conflict and fear of Susanna. The painting becomes erotic because, not only are the Elders sexually aroused and bent on rape or seduction, but the seventeenth-century viewer, most likely being male, would have felt excited by the image in front of him. Unlike Denis Diderot, the French eighteenth-century critic, who maintained in his *Pensées détachées sur la peinture* (1776) that only the Elders were voyeurs and not the spectators, Mary D. Garrard (Garrard, ch. 3) has pointed

9 There are four other paintings recorded by Artemisia on this subject. These include the picture which was in Charles I's collection and is mentioned in the Van de Doort Inventory – see *Walpole Society*, vol. 37, 1960, p.177. The seventeenth-century painting of *Susanna and the Elders* in the collection of the Marquess of Exeter at Burghley House, Stamford, is also given by R. Ward Bissell to Artemisia.

out that in this case the older Elder glances out of the canvas in our direction, so that we all become joint voyeurs. Diderot was probably unaware of the existence of this painting which has been in a private collection for over two hundred years.

In other representations of this subject Susanna often looks out appealingly at the spectator. Still innocent but fearful of what might befall her she seeks our help. In the Rembrandt panel of *Susanna and the Elders* in the Gemäldegalerie in Berlin, signed 1647, the Elders are already pulling off her garment. Rembrandt's rather waif-like Susanna, unlike other examples in the seventeenth century, conveys none of the sensuousness shown by contemporary artists. I do not propose to discuss the voyeurism inherent in this painting because this has been fully and eruditely analysed in the chapter entitled 'Between Focalization and Voyeurism: The Representation of Vision' in *Reading 'Rembrandt'* by Mieke Bal.

When compared to the brave and sword-swinging Judith, the heroine of decapitation fame par excellence, who showed no fear even when left alone with the drunken and lascivious Holofernes, Susanna's courage almost fades into insignificance. Nevertheless, we must not forget that it was not her physical courage but her mental bravery in withstanding the sexual pressure from these two perfidious Elders, that place her highly in the hierarchy of biblical heroines. In terms of moral courage Susanna has more in common with Queen Vashti in the Book of Esther who boldly refused to have her beauty paraded in front of King Ahasuerus, his people and his drunken officials (Esther 1:10).

Susanna has been criticized for not being more forceful, merely groaning when the Elders first approached her, for not defending herself in court and not protesting her innocence while being led away to her execution. It is easy to accuse Susanna of cowardice, but what happened to Joachim? He is mentioned at the beginning of the story and then miraculously disappears from the narrative when events take a turn for the worse. He does not question the accusation, nor does he defend Susanna. He only resurfaces at the end of the story, together with Susanna's mother and father and all her other relatives, to praise God because she was found to be innocent of this shameful deed. It is therefore not surprising that artists have no interest in depicting

Joachim. His place in art is minimal, only occasionally appearing as part of this last scene.

What prevented Susanna from giving way to these persuasive Elders? Firstly she was the wife of a rich, high-ranking and greatly respected man of the town. It would therefore have been unseemly for her to engage in any kind of sexual escapade or adulterous relationship with these two scoundrels. She had her own and her husband's position to consider. As a devout Hebrew woman she was also well aware of the Law of Moses as regards adultery. She was totally faithful to Joachim and exclusively his property. Artists recognise this marital faithfulness and symbolically often include a small dog in their pictures. In the Altdofer painting in Munich to which we have already referred Susanna holds a small dog on her lap.

While most artists see Susanna as the innocent victim, there are others such as Peter Paul Rubens who regard her as an evildoer, temptress and second Eve. He makes this abundantly clear in his later painting of *Susanna and the Elders* (*c*.1636–40) in the Alte Pinakothek, Munich where one of the Elders stares at Susanna from a safe distance between the protective branches of an apple tree (see Leach, 120–7), instead of a 'mastic tree' (verse 54) or an 'evergreen oak' (verse 58) under which, according to the separate accounts of the two Elders, Susanna is supposed to have been intimate with the young man. The image of the apple tree is no doubt a reference to the tree in the Garden of Eden from which Eve, the first seductress, tempted Adam with the fruit from this tree. The temptress in Rubens's eyes is Susanna, who sits naked in the classical crouching Venus position[10] with her back towards the viewer in an attractive yet decent pose because we cannot see her feminine attributes. She turns her head and glances seductively and challengingly at the spectator. She is no longer the blameless and chaste Susanna of the Early Christian and Medieval period.

Let us now move away from Susanna for a moment and discuss the position of the Elders. These judges, who had been appointed by the people, were well regarded in the community and should have

10 An example of a marble Graeco-Roman *Crouching Venus* (*c*.250–240 BCE) can be seen in the Louvre.

known better. They represent Evil and their deeds are the work of the Devil. This had already been recognized as such by the early Christian Church. Bishop Hippolytus of Rome stated in the third century; 'For as of old the Devil was concealed in the serpent in the garden, so now too, the Devil, concealed in the Elders, fired them with his own lust that he might a second time corrupt Eve.'[11] Susanna, therefore, becomes a redemptive figure and also represents the Church.

We can see the cumulative effect of this Evil in the painting of *Susanna and the Elders* by Tintoretto of 1555/6 in the Kunsthistorisches Museum in Vienna where it is no coincidence that one of the Elders takes on the guise of the serpent in the Garden of Eden who after the Fall of Adam was condemned to creep for the rest of his life on his belly (Genesis 3:14). The bald Elder snakes his way along the ground to where the beautiful naked Susanna sits making an intellectual display of admiring herself in a mirror, which reflects the light onto her white translucent skin, here painted to perfection by this Venetian master.

These hot-blooded and passionate Elders, without any self-control, are not decent. They contrive, plan together, lie through their teeth to compromise her, they gloat; they plan a sexual assault on this innocent girl. As far as these Elders are concerned their attraction is indecent. Not only are they shown leering, peering through the undergrowth, smiling and grimacing, but also their activities are covert: hidden like spies in the bushes or foliage they become peeping Toms. Their lewd ugly faces and hideous expressions are the epitome of wickedness and vice. Artists, especially north European ones, purposely depict them with evil-looking expressions with eyes often bulging with desire (for instance, in the painting dated 1567 by Jan Massys entitled *Susanna and the Elders* in Musées Royaux des Beaux-Arts de Belgique in Brussels). In the seventeenth-century canvas by Domenichino (Domenico Zampiere, 1581–1641) of *Susanna and the Elders* of 1603 in the Galleria Doria Pamphilj in Rome, their wicked intentions are not left in any doubt. While one of the Elders tries to remove the cloth which lightly covers her body,

11 St John Chrysotom and Bishop St Asterius of Amasus also recognized the comparability of Susanna and Eve.

the younger Elder leaps over the balustrade 'burning with desire' (verse 20).

This action of molestation, so common in sixteenth- and seventeenth-century images, which in extreme cases can lead to Susanna being physically manhandled or fondled – as, for example, in the painting by the Dutch artist Willem van Mieris (1662–1747) of *Susanna and the Elders* dated 1691, where the Elder on the right caresses her breast, or those images where her garments are being pulled from her body, also occurs in works of the nineteenth century. However, we now notice a distinct difference in attitude in line with the modern emergence of feminist perspectives. No longer is she the righteous, timid and terrified or surprised maiden of Renaissance and Baroque paintings. In the painting by the Danish painter Laurits Tuxen (1853–1927) executed in 1882 and now in the Ny Carlsberg Glyptotek in Copenhagen[12] she stands erect on the step leading down to the bath, covering her nakedness, and looks down contemptuously on the two old men. The grey-haired Elder tugs desperately at the dark-coloured drapery clutched by Susanna. She is now very much in control, heroically defends her virtue and proudly displays her wedding ring on her left hand. The image has now become much more secularized; a trend which is continued into the twentieth century.

We do not know the ages of the Elders, but presumably because of their high standing in the community and, by their own admission, inability to restrain the young man who was embracing Susanna (verse 39), they are considered old. Artists therefore play safe and depict one Elder as being older, portrayed with a white or grey beard, while the other is either beardless or has a short brown beard. This can be clearly seen in the 1620–5 painting of *Susanna and the Elders* by Guido Reni (1575–1642) in the National Gallery, London. Often the intention is to demonstrate that they were too old for rape: in which case, Susanna was never in any real danger. In the early wall painting of *c.*1410–20 which is part of a series of three roundels of the *History*

12 I am grateful to Professor Dr Lena Johannesson of the University of Göteborg for drawing my attention to the article by Dr Solfrid Söderlind, 'Moraliska täckmantlar och ohölijda ögonkast, *Klädd och okläddʼ*, in the National Museum Katalog, Stockholm, 1996, pp. 42–3.

of Susanna situated in the westernmost crossing of the nave, together with Delilah, Judith and Esther, in the church of Santa Maria in Risinge in Östergötland in Sweden, on the other hand, the two Elders are shown young and beardless, and are therefore much more threatening. We can see this in the drawing by C. F. Lindberg after the original which is now in a rather poor state of preservation. The Latin inscription informs us SUSANA:LAVATOR ('Susanna:bather'). She sits rather quaintly and unerotically in a barrel, her head covered, but her naked breasts subtly indicated by a few deft strokes of the brush. She raises one hand feebly in protest but she knows that she is 'completely trapped' (verse 22).

In view of Susanna's coy and virtuous behaviour, almost to the point of naïveté, it was therefore just as well that the young Daniel in all his wisdom, seen in the painting by Paul Troger (1698–1762; Carolino Augusteum Museum, Salzburg) should have been sent by God to rescue Susanna, not only from the scheming, lying, lecherous and vindictive Elders but also from being stoned to death according to the Law of Moses. By separating these scurrilous Elders he is able to arrive at the truth while he examines their account of events. Like a latter-day Solomon, but depicted more like an image of Jesus Christ in the Troger painting, he confutes them and demonstrates that they were bearing false witness. In the end Susanna is exonerated, evil is vanquished; justice rules and the Elders are lead away to be put to death. The moral of this tale is that the wages of sin is death and that indecent attraction can lead to fatal exposure.

Plate 1. Drawing by C. F. Lindberg of the wall painting by the Risinge Master, *Susanna Bathing*, Church of Santa Maria, Risinge, Östergötland, Sweden, *c.*1410–20.

Plate 2. Peter Paul Rubens, *Susanna and the Elders*. Bayerische Staatsgemäldesammlungen, Alte Pinakothek, Munich.

Plate 3. Guido Reni, *Susanna and the Elders*. The National Gallery, London.

Plate 4. Laurits Tuxen, *Susanna in the Bath*. Ny Carlsberg Glyptotek, Copenhagen.

Works of art mentioned

1. Lorenzo Lotto, *Susanna and the Elders*, Galleria Uffizi, Florence, 1517.
2. Dutch oak and ebony cabinet, *Story of Susanna*, Rijksmuseum, Amsterdam, *c.*1630–50.
3. Jacopo da Empoli, *Susanna*, Kunsthistorisches Museum, Vienna, 1600.
4. George Engelhard Schröder, *Susanna Bathing*, Nationalmuseum, Stockholm, eighteenth century.
5. Peter Paul Rubens, *Susanna and the Elders*, Galleria Borghese, Rome, *c.*1607.
6. Jean-Jacques Henner, *The Chaste Susanna*, Musée d'Orsay, Paris, 1864.
7. *Susanna*, Catacomb of Praetexatus, Rome, fourth century CE.
8. Albrecht Altdorfer, *Susanna and the Elders*, Alte Pinakothek, Munich, 1526.
9. Followe of Jan Massys, *Susanna and the Elders*, Musées Royaux des Beaux-Arts de Belgique, Brussels, sixteenth century.
10. Circle of Adam Elsheimer, possibly Johann Koenig, *Susanna and the Elders*, Dulwich Picture Gallery, *c.*1607.
11. Artemisia Gentileschi, *Susanna and the Elders*, Schönborn Collection, Schloss Weissenstein, Pommersfelden, 1610.
12. Rembrandt van Rijn, *Susanna and the Elders*, Gemäldegalerie, Berlin, 1647.
13. Peter Paul Rubens, *Susanna and the Elders*, Alte Pinakothek, Munich, *c.*1636–40.
14. Tintoretto, *Susanna and the Elders*, Kunsthistorisches Museum, Vienna, 1555/6.
15. Jan Massys, *Susanna and the Elders*, Musées Royaux Beaux-Arts de Belgique, Brussels, 1567.
16. Domenichino, *Susanna and the Elders,* Galleria Doria Pamphilj, Rome, 1607.
17. Willem van Mieris, *Susanna and the Elders*, sold at Christie's 27 November 1973, lot 318.
18. Laurits Tuxen, *Susanna in the Bath*, Ny Carlsberg Glypotek, Copenhagen, 1882.
19. Guido Reni, *Susanna and the Elders*, National Gallery, London, 1620–5.
20. The Risinge Master, *Susanna and the Elders*, Church of Santa Maria, Risinge, Östergötland, Sweden, *c.*1410–20.
21. Paul Troger, *Susanna Before Daniel*, Carolino Augusteum Museum, Salzburg, eighteenth century.

Bibliography

Ambrose. *Seven Exegetical Works,* translated by Michael P. McHugh. *The Fathers of the Church*, vol. 65. Washington, DC: 1972.

Bal, Mieke. *Reading 'Rembrandt': Beyond the Word–Image Opposition.* Cambridge: CUP, 1991.

Garrard, May D. *Artemisia Gentileschi: The Image of the Female Hero in Italian Baroque Art.* Princeton and Oxford: Princeton UP, 1989.

Humfrey, Peter. *Lorenzo Lotto*. New Haven and London: Yale UP, 1997.

Leach, Mark C. 'Rubens' *Susanna and the Elders* in Munich and Some Early Copies', *Print Review*, 5 (1976).

Murray, Peter. *Dulwich Picture Gallery: A Catalogue*. London: 1980.

Murry, Peter and Linda. *The Oxford Companion to Christian Art and Architecture*. Oxford: OUP, 1996.

Rooses, Max, and Ch. Ruelens. *Correspondance de Rubens et documents épistolaires concernant sa vie et ses œuvres*, 6 vol. Antwerp, 1887 1909.

Saunders, Gill. *The Nude: A New Perspective.* London: 1989.

PETER STILES

To the Threshold: Window Scenes in Elizabeth Gaskell's *Ruth*

The value of binary oppositions as a model

The notion of binary oppositions is a useful one for any close examination of the fiction of Elizabeth Gaskell. Critical insight can be advanced by a consideration of the constantly emerging interdependent polarities or contraries in her work. The problematic nature of her fiction is best resolved by accepting the tensions that such antinomies create. Opposing notions such as moral determinism and freewill, or social conservatism and radicalism, exhibit, in the strength of their juxtaposition throughout her work, an acute appreciation of the maturity of her intuitive judgement about the nature of life.

In her subliminal acknowledgement that each extreme position is dependent for its truth and cogency on the existence of its opposite, she also maintains a position that greatly enhances the quality of her work. The reader is rarely confronted with categorical understandings, but left to balance the irreconcilable, the enigmas which make the human predicament interesting, if not at times perplexing. Her fiction, in its complex patterning of such oppositions, provides the reader with room to assess the validity of seemingly contradictory propositions. In this way her work is never tendentious or monochromatic.

Further examination of her work would undoubtedly reveal other oppositions. The examples of oppositions in Elizabeth Gaskell's work given above (such as moral determinism and freewill, conservatism and radicalism) are broadly descriptive of polarities that have their basis in some of the theological ambiguities to which she was exposed as a Unitarian. In this essay a frequently utilized motif in Elizabeth Gaskell's fiction is examined. It demonstrates the consistency with which her work renders in a variety of ways the same recurrent oppositions.

Window scenes in fiction

> What could be more mystical or magical than ordinary daylight coming in through an ordinary window? […] Why should not that wonderful white fire, breaking through the window, inspire us every day like an ever-returning miracle? […] The mere fact of existence and experience is a perpetual portent. Why should we ever ask for more? (Chesterton, *The Common Man*)

> I wrote a paper on Victorian women's imagination of space. 'Marginal Beings and Liminal Poetry'. About agoraphobia and claustrophobia and the paradoxical desire to be let out into unconfined space, the wild moorland, the open ground, and at the same time to be closed into tighter impenetrable small spaces – like Emily Dickinson's voluntary confinement, like the Sibyl's jar. (Byatt, 54)

Windows allow an observer to look out of or into a building. As it is physically impossible to be both inside and outside at the same time, a window distinguishes between an area occupied by the observer and an area observed but physically unoccupied by the observer. Thus a window situates the observer and differentiates between physical presence and mental awareness.

But there is no real detachment between the observer and the scene observed. All observation involves psychological complexity and reflexivity. It is coloured by the personal history of the observer and involves complex cognitive processes. In this sense there is a strong connection in any observation through a window between the exterior and the interior.

Scenes in fiction depicting observation through windows operate in a similar manner. While a character within a fictional text may appear to be preoccupied with looking out of a window at the scene outside (most are of this kind), the reader is frequently made aware simultaneously of the subject of observation and the observer. The transcendent reader can be both within and without at the same time, aware of the physical appearance and emotional or psychological state of the observer as much as of the nature of the scene outside the window that is being described.

The reader in such scenes, however, is often given the advantage of looking both inwards and outwards with an objectivity that the character involved lacks. This occurs because of the freedom that the reader is allowed in having several vantage points from which to observe both the exterior physical attributes of the scene observed, as well as the intricate psychological relationship between the observer and the observed. Rarely, in nineteenth-century fiction, does the character have the ability to view him- or herself in the same manner that the reader does.

A most effective exception is a scene from *The Turn of the Screw* (1898), by Henry James. One Sunday afternoon the Governess sees the spectre of Quint through the window in the dining room. Thinking that she has seen a prowler, she rushes outside to confront the offender. Obviously not achieving her objective she then looks in at the same window where she first saw Quint:

> I applied my face to the pane and looked, as he had looked into the room. As if, at this moment, to show me exactly what his range had been, Mrs. Grose, as I had done for himself just before, came in from the hall. With this I had the full image of a repetition of what had already occurred. She saw me as I had seen my own visitant; she pulled up short as I had done; I gave her something of the shock I had received. She turned white, and this made me ask myself if I had blanched as much. She stared, in short, and retreated on just my lines [...]

An interesting vehicle for interpretation is provided by window scenes. Discrete, exterior observations from a window can be seen as a projection of the character's inner turmoils and yearnings and can be read as a subtext for the overt textual explication of the relationship between the observer and the scene observed. The view from the window can effectively frame a series of cameo insights into the psychological state of the character which go well beyond any surface reading of the text.

Climatic conditions in Victorian England obviously ensured that much time was spent looking out of windows. The limitations imposed by inclement weather forced anyone seeking relief from the tedium of life indoors to observe the outside world from behind glass. The following observations about window scenes in Victorian fiction are based on the work of one author, Elizabeth Gaskell. While they share much in common with similar scenes from other authors, they also indicate some very particular concerns in her work.

Window scenes in *Ruth*

From the outset, *Ruth* by Elizabeth Gaskell highlights a textual concern with views from windows. The assize-town which provides the setting for the beginning of the work is said to be 'amusing' because of 'the infinite variety of windows […] crammed into [its] walls' (*Ruth*, 1).[1] There follows in the rest of the novel a number of scenes in which Ruth or another character views and assesses life through a window. Scenes of this type frequently signify critical moments in the text.

In *Ruth*, such scenes can be broadly characterized as alluding to the desire for escape at a time of crisis or the availability of restorative influences in the larger world outside the window. Interspersed as they are, such scenes serve to demonstrate the ebb and flow of anguish and serenity in Ruth's emotional state throughout the novel.

Window scenes depicting crisis

On several occasions Ruth seeks to escape from the oppressive nature of her problems. The victim of her own sexual innocence, she has to confront the shameful consequences of her relationship with Bellingham (later Donne) when she gives birth to an illegitimate son, Leonard. At first abandoned, later in the novel she also has to deal with the renewed advances of her former lover. Many of the crises arising from this situation are depicted in passages where Ruth is

1 The much later novel *Wives and Daughters* also opens with a window scene.

looking out of a window. All such scenes involve heightened emotion and are concerned with the complexities of morally appropriate actions in conflict with repressed desires.

There are three scenes of particular relevance in this regard. In the first Ruth seeks to escape from the near-imprisonment of her work as a seamstress by striving to gain access to the night air. Later, after rejection by her seducer, and while in Benson's care, her thwarted desire for reconciliation with Bellingham is well conveyed in another window scene. Finally, the most dramatic scene of the three occurs when Ruth is reunited with Bellingham (now the budding politician Donne). The exploitation Ruth suffers as a seamstress in the first scene is quickly exchanged for an alternative source of marginalization, this time through sexual exploitation and moral dilemma. The latter two scenes both stem from difficulty of this kind. Only Thurstan and Faith Benson, the kindly minister and his sister, make any impression upon the series of repressive influences to which she is subjected. All three window scenes referred to above convey Ruth's desire to live a more unrestricted existence, one in which, as a young, orphaned woman, she is not repeatedly victimized. Such scenes, with their heightened emotion, demonstrate the point of desperation to which Ruth is driven in an attempt to resolve her personal struggles.

Utilizing the language of entrapment the first scene effectively conveys the parlous plight of the Victorian working classes. With other young seamstresses in an airless room at two o'clock in the morning Ruth exhibits claustrophobic behaviour:

> Ruth Hilton sprang to the large old window, and pressed against it as a bird presses against the bars of its cage. She put back the blind, and gazed into the quiet moonlight night […]
>
> Ruth pressed her hot forehead against the cold glass, and strained her aching eyes in gazing out on the lovely sky of a winter's night. The impulse was strong upon her to snatch up a shawl, and wrapping it round her head, to sally forth and enjoy the glory; and time was when that impulse would have been instantly followed […] (*Ruth*, 4–5)[2]

2 There seems to be a good case for suggesting that Elizabeth Gaskell readily identified with feelings of claustrophobia. Scenes involving female protagonists

Here, a window clearly distinguishes between the immediate and real and the unattainable, the separating and joining window pane accentuating the cruel reality that the observing Ruth is restricted only to visual impressions. She is denied the benefits of feeling and inhaling the restorative night air. While for most of the episode the reader is alongside Ruth within the room, the reader's ability to be outside has clearly been demonstrated earlier, as the scene begins with the reader looking into 'a window (through which the moonlight fell on Ruth) with a glory of many colours' (*Ruth*, 3).

The second window scene, set in Wales, is rendered in such a way as to project dramatically onto the observed scene the distress suffered by Ruth at the point of her abandonment by Bellingham. Her emotional confusion and uncertainty as to whether she should pursue Bellingham is mirrored in the kaleidoscopic nature of the changing sky:

> Ruth stood in the little bow-window, looking out. Across the moon, and over the deep blue heavens, large, torn, irregular-shaped clouds went hurrying, as if summoned by some storm-spirit. The work they were commanded to do was not here; the mighty gathering-place lay eastward, immeasurable leagues, and on they went, chasing each other over the silent earth, now black, now silver-white at one transparent edge, now with the moon shining like Hope through their darkest centre, now again with a silver lining; and now, utterly black, they sailed lower in the lift, and disappeared behind the immovable mountains; they were rushing in the very direction in which Ruth had striven and struggled to go that afternoon; they, in their career, would soon pass over the very spot where he (her world's he) was lying sleeping, or perhaps not sleeping, perhaps thinking of her. The storm was in her mind, and rent and tore her purposes into forms as wild and irregular as the heavenly shapes she was looking at. If, like them, she could pass the barrier horizon in the night, she might overtake him. (*Ruth*, 99–100)[3]

anxiously seeking fresh air are frequent. A good example is to be found in *Wives and Daughters*: Roger's proposal to Cynthia throws Molly Gibson into a state of confusion. She sought refuge in her bedroom, but 'the room grew stifling, and instinctively she went to the open casement window, and leant out, gasping for breath' (*WD*, 391).

3 The concept of figuratively projected emotions is reminiscent of the third of the 'Preludes' by T. S. Eliot, where 'The thousand sordid images / Of which your soul was constituted [...] flickered against the ceiling'. With reference to this

This description lacks, after the initial sentence, any sense of an intervening windowpane, or the window mediating or obstructing the scene Ruth observes. There is, rather, an indistinguishable similarity between her emotional state and the unsettled night sky. Their mutually mimetic quality makes it difficult to determine which is the antecedent of the other. But, despite Ruth's close identification with her nocturnal observations, she is as much restrained as in the previous scene. Her moral guardian Benson observes (as the reader also does) her 'longing gaze outwards upon the free, broad world' (*Ruth*, 100) and appeals, through reference to Ruth's mother, to her sense of moral propriety. Although not physically restrained (Benson is incapable of that) she remains within, relinquishing what she believes to be her last opportunity for reconciliation with Bellingham. This is entrapment of another kind.

The most dramatic window scene occurs towards the end of the novel. Now, having lived a peaceful and productive life with the Bensons for a number of years, and with the further complicating factor of her love for their son, Leonard, any prospect of reconciliation with the morally unscrupulous but tempting Bellingham (now Donne) is even more fraught. Her behaviour becomes almost suicidal in this scene. In an attempt to gain freedom from her anxious and confused station as observer, she comes close to achieving the desired therapeutic transition from detached observer to one in close harmony with the observed.

There is, as she throws open the window, a deliberate emphasis on her ability to remove any intervening pane of glass, to achieve a sense of physical engagement with the elements to which she is exposed. But although the recipient of some restorative influences through this experience, she is, however, in this liminal state denied any ability to transcend her human limitations as observer. This

passage and others Felicia Bonaparte makes some interesting comments on projected emotions. She compares Ruth with the mythological character, Persephone. She states: 'the mood itself is externalised in nature. Nature itself does not exist. The storm is not outside the window. It is raging in Ruth's heart [...] As Persephone in the myth is the divinity of nature, in the novel Ruth is nature and the natural world is Ruth' (Bonaparte, 90–91).

episode, nevertheless, does provide her with more than the visual impressions of the first and second scenes. The very restricted visual dimension available to her in the dark night sky is more than compensated for by the rain and the invigorating air. This offers some consolation:

> She fastened her door, and threw open the window, cold and threatening as was the night. She tore off her gown; she put her hair back from her heated face […]
>
> She threw her body half out of the window into the cold night air. The rain beat down on her. It did her good. A still, calm night would not have soothed her as this did. The wild tattered clouds, hurrying past the moon, gave her a foolish kind of pleasure that almost made her smile a vacant smile. The blast-driven rain came on her again, and drenched her hair through and through. The words 'stormy wind fulfilling his word' came into her mind. (*Ruth*, 272, 274)

As if fascinated by the possibilities for sacramental significance and resolution offered in such a window scene, in the space of sixty pages Elizabeth Gaskell has Jemima Bradshaw attempting to come to terms with her jealousy of Farquhar's attentions to Ruth in a very similar manner. Opening a window to the elements and to the variety of a changing, natural vista is a recurrent motif in this work and one which deserves attention because of its sheer frequency. Again it is a young female protagonist who is depicted, someone similarly caught up in the confusion of moral loyalties and sexual desire:

> At length Jemima could stand it no longer, and left the room. She went into the schoolroom, where the shutters were not closed, as it only looked into the garden. She opened the window, to let the cool night air blow in on her hot cheeks. The clouds were hurrying over the moon's face in a tempestuous and unstable manner, making all things seem unreal; now clear out in its bright light, now trembling and quivering in shadow. The pain at her heart seemed to make Jemima's brain grow dull; she laid her head on her arms, which rested on the window-sill, and grew dizzy with the sick weary notion that the earth was wandering lawless and aimless through the heavens, where all seemed one tossed and whirling wrack of clouds. (*Ruth*, 332–3)

The preceding passages stress, in the main, the inability of the characters involved to achieve the desired transition from dissatisfied observer to a state of integration with the scene observed. The observer is described as 'pressed [...] against the cold glass', 'in the little bow-window', 'half out of the window', 'on the window-sill' (*Ruth*, 4, 99, 274). All these images suggest that the critical moment of transfer is imminent, but in each case it is not accomplished. Rather, there follows a need for the character to be resigned to the limitations and difficulties of the present situation. Consecutively through the scenes Ruth stands 'dreaming of the days that were gone', is 'calm, in the absence of all hope', or resorts to repentant prayer, while Jemima, similarly, resigns herself to overwhelming inevitabilities of cosmic origin (*Ruth*, 5, 101, 274, 333).

In addition, throughout the novel there are scenes in which Ruth, as passive observer simply accepts the sadness and limitations of her position in life. As a lonely young seamstress, on her Sundays 'she would sit at the window, looking out on the dreary prospect till her eyes were often blinded with tears' (*Ruth*, 34) and in the most agonizing moments of her abandonment in Wales, through the window she observes the dark mountains 'like giants, solemnly watching for the end of Earth and Time' (*Ruth*, 83). Later in the novel a window scene tells Ruth 'of the lapse of time and life' (*Ruth*, 392).

Window scenes depicting restorative agencies

Interspersed with these scenes, however, are numerous scenes in which characters are exposed to the restorative influences available to an observer through a window. They counterbalance and compensate for the protagonists' inability to achieve transcendence. For the text affirms that transcendence is the substance of dreams, and not a solution to personal need. In a telling scene, Ruth and her young son Leonard, apart for the first time, dream about each other. Ironically, in Leonard's dream of Ruth she achieves what has been unattainable in reality:

> He [...] dreamt of her sitting watching and smiling by his bedside, as her gentle self had been many a morning; and when she saw him awake (so it fell out in the dream), she smiled still more sweetly, and bending down she kissed him, and then spread out large, soft, white-feathered wings (which in no way

surprised her child – he seemed to have known they were there all along), and sailed away through the open window far into the blue sky of a summer's day. (*Ruth*, 258)[4]

Although Ruth is prevented in real life from achieving such freedom, the open window frequently becomes a source of restoration to the observer within. Refreshing air, rain, warmth, floral fragrances, effects of light, all demonstrate that the observation, so appreciated, yet frustratingly detached, can breach, through these agencies, the divide between observer and observed, thus connecting with and restoring an otherwise helpless character, one so restricted in the role of observer. There are numerous scenes of this type in the novel.

Fragrances are a good example. Elizabeth Gaskell's interest in floral diversity has recently been noted again (Eve),[5] and in numerous instances throughout this novel Ruth is consoled by floral beauty. An exception, however, is when, waiting at the inn for Bellingham to return and take her off to Wales, she stands in moral confusion at the window:

4 Felicia Bonaparte offers an alternative interpretation of this dream. In the context of her argument that in Ruth 'Gaskell allows the son metaphorically to become the lover' this scene then has sexual connotations (Bonaparte, 227).

5 Reference can been made to Mrs Gaskell's appreciation of and dependence on rural beauty, so much of which seems to stem from her childhood experiences in Knutsford.

It is interesting to note that in *North and South*, after Margaret and her father leave the rural idyll of Helstone and move to the industrialized and debilitating Milton-Northern, there are very few window scenes involving restorative agencies. Window scenes there suggest a much bleaker aspect. Examples sush as the following indicate this: 'Outside a thick fog crept up to the very windows, and was driven into every open door in choking white wreaths of unwholesome mist' (*NS*, 104); 'The window, placed at the side of the oblong, looked to the blank wall of a similar projection, not above ten feet distant. It loomed through the fog like a great barrier to hope' (*NS*, 105); 'The mill loomed high on the left-hand side of the windows, casting a shadow down from its many stories, which darkened the summer evening before its time' (*NS*, 213–14); 'The windows were half open because of the heat, and the Venetian blinds covered the glass, – so that a gray grim light, reflected from the pavement below, threw all the shadows wrong, and combined with the green-tinged upper light to make even Margaret's own face, as she caught it in the mirrors, look ghastly and wan' (*NS*, 228).

> The girl left the room. Ruth became as hot as she had previously been cold, and went and opened the window, and leant out into the still, sweet, evening air. The bush of sweetbrier, underneath the window, scented the place, and the delicious fragrance reminded her of her old home. I think scents affect and quicken the memory more than either sights or sounds; for Ruth had instantly before her eyes the little garden beneath the window of her mother's room [...] (*Ruth*, 60)

But this is an exception. Later in the novel, when Ruth is secure in the care of the Bensons and happier in her role as mother of Leonard, it is only the pleasant sensations of floral fragrances through windows that are mentioned: 'the peacefulness of the time, the window open into the little garden, the scents that came stealing in, and the clear summer heaven above, made the time be remembered as a happy festival for Ruth' (*Ruth*, 186).[6] In a later similar scene, floral fragrances are inferred in addition to the pleasing visual effects created through the window:

> But whatever poverty there might be in the house, there was full luxuriance in the little square wall-encircled garden, on two sides of which the parlour and the kitchen looked. The laburnum-tree, which when Ruth came was like a twig stuck into the ground, was now a golden glory in spring, and the pleasant shade

6 A close examination of *North and South* and *Wives and Daughters* also reveals a number of scenes in which characters are exposed to floral fragrances through open windows. The following examples are from *North and South*: 'The middle window in the bow was opened, and clustering roses and the scarlet honeysuckle came peeping round the corner' (*NS*, 55); 'The little casement window in Margaret's bed-chamber was almost filled up with rose and vine branches' (*NS*, 474). Some further examples are taken from *Wives and Daughters*: 'Then to the window, and after some tugging she opened the casement, and let in the sweet morning air. The dew was already off the flowers in the garden below, but still rising from the long hay-grass in the meadows directly beyond' (*WD,* 1–2); 'The muslin curtains flapped softly from time to time in the scented air that came through the open windows' (*WD,* 15); 'First of all, she went to the window to see what was to be seen. A flower-garden right below; a meadow of ripe grass just beyond, changing colour in long sweeps, as the soft wind blew over it' (*WD,* 62–3); 'Molly looked out of her chamber window – leaning on the sill, and snuffing up the night odours of the honeysuckle' (*WD,* 70).

> in summer. The wild hop, that Mr. Benson had brought home from one of his country rambles, and planted by the parlour-window, while Leonard was yet a baby in his mother's arms, was now a garland over the casement, hanging down long tendrils, that waved in the breezes, and threw pleasant shadows and traceries, like some Bacchanalian carving, on the parlour walls, at 'morn or dusky eve'. The yellow rose had clambered up to the window of Mr. Benson's bedroom, and its blossom-laden branches were supported by a jargonelle pear tree rich in autumnal fruit. (*Ruth*, 208)

The visual effects and benefits that occur in this redolent description are to be found in other window scenes as well. Earlier in the novel Ruth 'lay very still in the moonlight calm of her sick bed' (*Ruth*, 164). Later, in the period of her greatest personal contentment:

> She rose while the hedge-sparrow was yet singing his reveille to his mate; she dressed and opened her window, shading the soft-blowing air and the sunny eastern light from her baby. If she grew tired, she went and looked at him, and all her thoughts were holy prayers for him. Then she would gaze a while out of the high upper window on to the moorlands, that swelled in waves one behind the other, in the grey, cool morning light. These were her occasional relaxations, and after them she returned with strength to her work. (*Ruth*, 177)

What Ruth loses, in an inability to transcend her limitations as observer, is compensated for by the pleasures that come from looking through windows. Such pleasures have wide sensory appeal. Escape may not be possible for the moment, but the comforting alternative signals to the disappointed that despair is unwarranted, that passive acceptance is appropriate (and not without its rewards) and the hope of transcendence elusively remain.

Scenes involving windows abound in *Ruth* and not of all of them have been referred to in this analysis. Collectively they indicate an interesting, recurrent dichotomy in Elizabeth Gaskell's work. As has been demonstrated such scenes point to an unsuccessful desire on the part of the observer (usually Ruth) to escape from the inherent tensions and frustrations encountered in her sadly exploited life, or, they indicate the many restorative agencies available to the observer through no action on her own part other than merely opening the window.[7]

The theological implications of window scenes in *Ruth*

Thus these contrasting scenes starkly delineate a consistently espoused theological imperative throughout her work: efforts to achieve individual freedom are frequently overridden by divine expectations, and a need to be submissive to such expectations must ensue; but, to counterbalance this, divine favour is unexpectedly provided for those who are existentially limited and restrained by divine determinism.

Figuratively, this dichotomy is so clearly enunciated through the window scenes in *Ruth*. Try as she may Ruth is unable to pass through the window into any realm of sacramental union with that beyond. She is unable to assume the same vantage point as the omniscient reader, who is able to see in and empathize with Ruth, yet remain unscathed by the experiences she suffers. But the reader is encouraged to rejoice when Ruth receives temporary relief as a result of the restorative agencies available to her through the open window. The juxtaposition of scenes of both types is a noticeable feature of the novel.

7 Thus, some of the scenes in which Ruth is exposed to restorative influences from outside accentuate the shift from a desire to escape, to a contentment with the passive pleasures of observation. They echo the distinction Ruskin makes, in commenting on the work of Turner and Constable, between observations made through windows, and paintings which capture and frame the same scenic beauty. The difference, he suggests, is one of degree, not really of a disappointing contrast: 'For, observe, although I believe any sensible person would exchange his pictures, however good, for windows, he would not feel, and ought not to feel, that the arrangement was entirely gainful to him. He would feel it was an exchange of a less good of one kind, for a greater of another kind, but that it was definitely exchange, not pure gain, not merely getting more truth instead of less. The picture would be a serious loss; something gone which the actual landscape could never restore, though it might give something better in its place' (Ruskin, 138).

While a psychosexual interpretation of these contrasting scenes is possible, they also illustrate a recurrent theological emphasis within Elizabeth Gaskell's fiction. The author's indebtedness to the principles of mid-Victorian English Unitarianism is generally acknowledged,[8] and in these scenes the tension that exists between Ruth's desire to transcend her restricted, exploited existence, and her eventual compliance and resigned acceptance of her plight (along with whatever compensating factors that might imply) can best be understood against this background.

The sense in this novel, as elsewhere, that efforts to achieve individual freedom are frequently outweighed by divine expectations and a need to be submissive to such demands, demonstrates that Elizabeth Gaskell subscribed to conflicting doctrinal precepts. The pursuit of individual freedom, a strong vein in the dialectic of Romanticism, as well as in aspects of Unitarianism, was counterbalanced by a residual adherence to the influence of Joseph Priestley's theory of necessity (Priestley).

Elizabeth Gaskell, like other English Unitarians of her day, was conscious of the struggle that her forebears had undergone in their efforts to achieve social and political rights for themselves within England. Early to embrace more liberal attitudes to biblical interpretation, English Unitarians at the end of the eighteenth century had also been keen proponents of widespread social change. Their high view of the freedom of the individual in decisions relating to nuances of religious and social doctrine should not be underestimated. They had supported the French Revolution (Uglow, 9–10), and their egalitarian aspirations were reflected in their involvement in all aspects of social reform.[9] They were amongst the Nonconformist intellectual elite of England, sceptical of many establishment values and strong advocates of the benefits of general education. They had a strong commitment to personal freedom.

8 For the place of English Unitarianism in the life and work of Elizabeth Gaskell see Webb. Detailed biographical information concerning her Unitarian heritage is given in Uglow.

9 A good account of this influence is in Holt.

Ironically, however, because of the powerful influence of Joseph Priestley in shaping English Unitarianism, well into the nineteenth century the residual influence of a strong sense of determinism persisted as well. It was not until James Martineau became the dominant influence within English Unitarianism, and elements of Transcendentalism were introduced from its New England counterpart, particularly through Ralph Waldo Emerson, that the influence of determinism began to decline (Drummond, Waller). Determinism is a very obvious element in the fiction of Elizabeth Gaskell. Freedom is always conditional in her work, always constrained by a strong compliance with and accountability to moral categories and divine expectations.

But the desire to express a need for individual freedom is also intense. Thus the tension expressed in Elizabeth Gaskell's work between the pursuit of freedom and the need for compliance and resignation can be explained in terms of her lifelong exposure to conflicting strands within Unitarian teaching. Window scenes in *Ruth* provide an interesting vehicle for exploring this opposition.

Appendix

(A) A more recent example of a character's awareness of being simultaneously within and without, of having privileged dual insights regarding the psychological state of the protagonists is in F. Scott Fitzgerald's novel *The Great Gatsby* (1926). Nick Carraway, disillusioned by the intrigues at Tom Buchanan's drunken party in New York, comments:

> I wanted to get out and walk eastward toward the park through the soft twilight, but each time I tried to go I became entangled in some wild, strident argument which pulled me back, as if with ropes, into my chair. Yet high over the city our line of yellow windows must have contributed their share of human secrecy to the casual watcher in the darkening streets, and I saw him too, looking up and wondering. I was within and without, simultaneously enchanted and repelled by the inexhaustible variety of life. (Scott Fitzgerald, 42–43)

A sense of connectedness between the observer and the observed is evident in the following scene from *Middlemarch*, by George Eliot. Dorothea reflects on the sociological implications of this inevitable interrelationship:

> She opened her curtains, and looked out towards the bit of road that lay in view, with fields beyond, outside the entrance-gates. On the road there was a man with a bundle on his back and a woman carrying her baby; in the field she could see figures moving – perhaps the shepherd with his dog. Far off in the bending sky was the pearly light; and she felt the largeness of the world and the manifold wakings of men to labour and endurance. She was part of that involuntary, palpitating life, and could neither look out on it from her luxurious shelter as a mere spectator, nor hide her eyes in selfish complaining. (Eliot, 846)

(B) *Rear Window* (1954), Alfred Hitchcock's classic cinematic treatment of voyeurism, adds an interesting dimension to any consideration of the use of windows as a device for conveying the unstable, even threatening nature of human perception. When L. B. Jeffries (James Stewart), confined to his room by a fractured leg, observes the activities of all his neighbours in the courtyard, he looks both out of his window and in through the windows of others. Safely ensconced in his own apartment (he draws back from the window when his own privacy is threatened by recognition from outside) he is able to penetrate, unbeknown to his neighbours, deep into their private lives.

His careful observations, sometimes with binoculars or telescopic lens, lead him to witness a murder. He is able to preserve his safety and anonymity within his sanctuary as observer, until the murderer discovers his whereabouts, and comes seeking to eliminate this witness to his crime. The film ends with Jeffries being pushed, not fatally, out of his window, but not before a struggle on his part to remain within. Thus, the climax of the film occurs when the observer is forced, for the first time in the film, across the threshhold between within and without, into the realm of his observations. Like Margaret Hale in *North and South*, he has to deal with the ambivalence (alluded to in the epigraph from *Possession*) of being within or without.

(C) The psychological relationship between the observer and the observed is recognized by the persona in Coleridge's 'Dejection Ode', when it is stated that:

> I may not hope from outward forms to win
> The passion and the life, whose fountains are within. (Coleridge, 242)

(D) The restrictive or deceptive nature of observations through windows is equally well demonstrated by the virtually interchangeable notions of projection and reflection. Some window scenes become a projection of the inner turmoils and incapacity on the part of the observer to transcend reality. But because human perception involves all the complexities and subtleties of the psyche of the observer, it is also possible for such projections to be marred, distorted or manipulated in some way.

Images of restricted vision, of translucence or opacity in perception, are not uncommon in fiction. They suggest that sometimes the observer is unable to view the outside world clearly from a vantage point such as a window and that, visually, the world may be partially or fully denied to the observer.

A scene in Elizabeth Gaskell's novel *Ruth* where this restriction occurs is when Ruth, at one point, thrusts herself out of a window into the dark night air (pp. 272–4). There is no visual comfort in this instance, just a formless void confronting her. Only wind and rain are available to the observer, the opacity of the night scene preventing the creation of an alternative realm into which the observer can venture.

Window scenes depicting deception also occur in fiction. In Charlotte Brontë's *Villette* Lucy Snow believes she sees a ghost through a window. Conversely, the Governess, in *The Turn of the Screw* by Henry James, believes she observes an intruder at the window, whereas she really is witnessing a spectre, perhaps one of her own making (see main text, p. 97 above).

The observations that female protagonists make through windows in Elizabeth Gaskell's fiction are not of this latter type, however. Whereas window scenes may act as projections of the psychological struggles of the characters involved, such scenes in her work retain their integrity as faithful, often detailed descriptions of natural landscapes. They are not distorted perceptions, but, nevertheless, provide obvious typological significance.

Reflection is essentially the ultimate image of perceptual restriction. As Felicia Bonaparte indicates, mirror scenes are occasionally used very effectively in Elizabeth Gaskell's work. They provide a useful mechanism for ensuring that the observer is constantly forced to look back to the inner life rather than to the prospect of a world beyond the self. In this sense they are like window scenes in that they force the observer to seek for solutions that are to be found within and not in some transcendent experience.

Reflection can also shape the reader's attention. In *Our Mutual Friend* (1865), by Charles Dickens the scene in which the 'great looking-glass above the sideboard reflects the table and the company' at the Veneerings dinner party, reflection limits the perception of the reader in that it creates a focal point for character description. A series of portraits of the comical assortment of characters assembled at the dining table is provided. Each description begins with the word 'Reflects', limiting the attention to one character at a time, but also accentuating the illusory nature of these figures, and further satirizing their superficiality (Dickens, 10).

1 Corinthians 13:12a highlights the similarities between projection and reflection. The Authorized Version translates the verse as 'For now we see through a glass, darkly', as if the restricted observation were being made through translucent glass, or at a scene without sufficient light to distinguish features. Matthew Henry comments (using the AV) that the verse means that 'Now we can only discern things at a great distance, as through a telescope, and that involved in clouds and obscurity.' This is quite different from more modern translations, where the image is of a mirror. The Good News Bible translates the verse as 'What we see now, is like a dim image in a mirror'; the New English Bible as 'Now we see only puzzling reflections in a mirror'; and the New International Version as 'Now we see but a poor reflection', to take but a few. While projection and reflection may be seen as opposites, they have qualities that are very similar.

Bibliography

Bonaparte, Felicia. *The Gypsy-Bachelor of Manchester: The Life of Mrs. Gaskell's Demon*. Charlottesville and London: Virginia UP, 1992.

Brontë, Charlotte. *Villette*. London: Penguin, 1985.

Byatt, A. S. *Possession: A Romance*. London: Vintage, 1990.

Coleridge, S. T. *The Poems of Samuel Taylor Coleridge*. London: OUP,1963.

Dickens, Charles. *Our Mutual Friend*. London: OUP, 1963.

Drummond, James, and C. B. Upton. *The Life and Letters of James Martineau*, 2 vols. London: James Nisbet and Co., 1902.

Eliot, George. *Middlemarch*. London: Penguin English Library, 1965.

Eve, Jeanette. 'The Floral and Horticultural in Elizabeth Gaskell's Novels', *The Gaskell Society Journal*, 7 (1993).

Gaskell, Elizabeth. *North and South*. London: Penguin Classics, 1970.

—— *Ruth*. Oxford: OUP, 1985.

—— *Wives and Daughters*. Oxford: OUP, 1987.

Hitchcock, Alfred (director). *Rear Window*. 1954.

Holt, R. V. *The Unitarian Contribution to Social Progress in England*. London: Allen and Unwin, 1938.

James, Henry. *The Turn of the Screw*. London: Signet, 1962.

Priestley, Joseph. *Disquisitions Relating to Matter and Spirit, and the Doctrine of Philosophical Necessity Illustrated*. New York and London: Garland, 1976.

Ruskin, John. *Modern Painters*, vol. III. London: George Allen, 1897.

Scott Fitzgerald, F. *The Great Gatsby*. London: Penguin, 1964.

Uglow, Jenny. *Elizabeth Gaskell*. London: Faber and Faber, 1993.

Waller, Ralph. 'James Martineau: his engagement as a theologian, his Christology, and his doctrine of the Church, with some unpublished papers.' Unpublished doctoral dissertation, King's College, University of London, 1986.

Webb, R. K. 'The Gaskells as Unitarians', in Shattock, Joan (ed.), *Dickens and Other Victorians*. Basingstoke: Macmillan, 1988.

JEFFREY F. KEUSS

'Seeing' *Adam Bede* – An Iconographic Reading[1]

> So that ye may have
> *Clear images before your gladden'd eyes*
> Of nature's unambitious underwood
> And flowers that prosper in the shade. And when
> I speak of such among the flock as swerved
> Or fell, those only shall be singled out
> Upon whose lapse, or error, something more
> Than brotherly forgiveness may attend.[2]

Adam Bede (1859) is an exercise in bringing 'clear images' before the reader's 'gladden'd eyes'. George Eliot opens her story by citing this passage from Wordsworth's *The Excursion*, of which *Adam Bede* can be seen as a prose echo. In the poem by Wordsworth, a pastor mourns his dead parishioner Ellen, who is buried next to her dead baby and is described as 'a virtuous women, in pure youth', 'delivered to distress and shame' by a lover who breaks his promise of fidelity and leaves her alone when she becomes pregnant. It is interesting that of all the portions of *The Excursion*, this is the stanza which George Eliot chooses to reference, one that is an admonition *to see clearly images that are before the reader*. Given this agenda by George Eliot from the outset, I would like to propose a reading of *Adam Bede* that observes the iconographic signifiers of her narrative and *sees* them for what they are. In this regard, I will be utilizing Mieke Bal's definition of 'iconographic signifier' as that which the artist utilizes to

1 An earlier version of this essay appears as chapter seven in Keuss, *A Poetics of Jesus: The Search for Christ through Writing in the Nineteenth Century* (Aldershot: Ashgate, 2002).

2 William Wordsworth, *The Excursion* (1814), book VI, lines 651–8. Cited on the title page of the original printing of *Adam Bede* (William Blackwood and Sons, 1859).

> help the reader recognise the preceding visual tradition, which in turn refers to the verbal text; in the second case the recognition is directly related to the text and works with the text's verbal devices. [We utilize] the term 'iconographic sign' for the sign that travels the visual-verbal route. The sign based upon the solely verbal reference then falls under the more encompassing concept of intertexuality and exemplifies the subcategory of pre-textual thematic reference. (Bal, 184)

As noted by Valentine Cunningham, 'the distinction of *Adam Bede* is to tell a story, and also tell about telling a story. This is a novel about obscure lives, and also about *how* to be a novel about obscure lives' (Cunningham, viii). More than 'reading' in a traditional sense, George Eliot wants the reader to 'see' the world by 'viewing' well. In this way there is more to 'reading' *Adam Bede* than merely acknowledging the words on the page. This is an attempt at creating a bridge between the visual and the verbal accounts of reality to bring forward that which is without language and yet has meaning.

Adam Bede is a sentient novel, fully aware of the story it is portraying and equally aware that it is being 'read' by the reading subject. Akin to Samuel Johnson's statement in *Preface to Shakespeare*, Eliot takes seriously the edict that 'the end of writing is to instruct'. Additionally, this is a narrative that finds part of its genesis as a reported history, told to Eliot by her aunt. Eliot's choice not to record her aunt's tale, but to tell it herself moves this narrative to a form that is neither fiction nor fact, yet is more than both. As noted by Cunningham:

> It's *My* Aunt's Story – a narration of George Eliot's own, her own design, her particular narrative blend, the product of a real, live author, one who is neither dead nor disappeared (in those curious formulas of Roland Barthes and Michel Foucault), the written sum of all her intentions, beliefs, philosophies, her various discourses (as they say), her assumptions about how lives and stories should go. It's also My *Aunt's* Story – a historically rooted narration, a story steeped in the real, datable, historical world of real lives, actual locales, living persons and tractable bits of religious history and social circumstance. Again, it's also My Aunt's *Story* – a story, emphatically a story; a poeticization, a rhetoricization, a fictionalising of a history and a philosophy. This is a text obedient and susceptible to the constraints and conventions of numerous available narrative forms past and present. (Cunningham, xxxvi)

Eliot strives in her poetics to show that there are certain laws that apply in both the fictive and historical realities, utilizing the alignment of the two worlds as a reciprocal testimonial to the truth of each – each 'world' backs up the claims of the other. For example, life has cause and effect in both the world of *Adam Bede* and the world of the reader and actions do have their consequences, albeit the difference between choice and determinism is often blurred. In Chapter XVI, 'Links', the Rector, Mr Irwine, speaks to Arthur Donnithorne of the 'Nemesis' that is the 'unpitying' nature of consequences due to one's 'deeds':

> A man can never do anything at variance with his own nature. He carries within him the germ of his most exceptional action: and if we wise people make eminent fools of ourselves on any particular occasion, we must endure the legitimate conclusion that we carry a few grains of folly to our one ounce of wisdom […] Our deeds carry their terrible consequences […] consequences that are hardly ever confined to ourselves. And it is best to fix our minds on that certainty, instead of considering what may be the elements of excuse for us. (*AB*, 172–3)

Eliot shifts from the fictive realm of her created characters to address the reading subject directly in Chapter XXIX, 'The Next Morning'. These actions or 'deeds' reflected upon in the fictive dimension in Chapter XVI, 'Links', that determine one's subjectivity and are 'hammered home in narrative reflections' (Cunningham, xxx) by the narrator to the reader amidst the narrative:

> Our deeds determine us, as much as we determine our deeds; and until we know what has been or will be the particular combination of outward with inward facts, which constitutes a man's critical actions, it will be better not to think ourselves wise about his character. (*AB*, 313)

The nature of determinism and causality is questioned in both the fictive and historical reality and this synchronicity gives a testimony to the truth of each realm's claim: the fictive supports the historical and the historical supports the fictive.

The claims of subjectivity are also supported in such a manner. In the case of Dinah Morris, her identity is self-creating and self-sustaining as evidenced in her resolute assertion: 'I am Dinah Morris.' As Cunningham notes,

> this is clearly an 'I' worth attending to, whatever we might have thought before of mill-girls, rural eloquence, provincial intelligence, and Nonconformist religious sincerity. The banished, muted, disregarded selfhood of the Victorian margin crowds thus on to the centre-stage, in an arranged renovation of sympathy and imagination that has the male, scathing, educated and uneducated Anglican audience awed into silence. (Cunningham, xix)

The query in the opening sentence of *The Impressions of Theophrastus Such* (1879), 'it is my habit to give an account to myself of the characters I meet with: can I give any true account of my own?' (*TS*, 3), is responded to in Dinah Morris's declaration of identity: we can make an account of ourselves, and in many respects are the only ones who can. The first person singular of Dinah Morris stands against any other characterization of her – she is who she is because she says so. (This has particular resonance in Dinah Morris as the incarnate 'I am' who is the new Adam, as will be discussed in further depth.) In this way, George Eliot through the narrative of *Adam Bede*

> exactly mirrors, and thus mightily animates and energises, the struggle by whole segments of English society and geography to be heard and seen in Victorian England, to be taken seriously, to be known for themselves, and to have their selfhood, their identity, their name recognised, in the pages of the English Novel [...] For George Eliot, being realistic and true to life will result in a fiction whose plot exemplifies, inexorably, some such laws of the material and human world. (Cunningham viii, xxx)

Identity and the 'selfing' of the subject are central to Eliot's textuality. In Chapter XVII of *Adam Bede*, Eliot repeatedly refers to the 'reader' directly – acknowledging that the one who reads the story is to be identified *and* to be identifying oneself. Eliot calls out specifically through direct discourse to the reader, binding one to the fictive encounter as a member in the cast of characters and expanding the identity of the reading subject to a mythic level. As noted by Cunningham:

> it is also the case that George Eliot had, and just as foundationally, been influenced by the argument that for a narrative to have any force of a religious

> or sacred nature – for it to be great in the way she wanted – it would have to amalgamate the historical and the philosophical with the poetic so as to comprise the mythic. This was the line of argument adopted by David Friedrich Strauss about the Bible. (xxxv)

Yet while it was an argument adopted by Strauss, it was not truly actualized. In this way Eliot picks up where the 'Concluding Dissertation' of Strauss failed – to realize a 'true fiction' of the life of Jesus that serves as *a poetic frame* through which to view life. Addressing the reader, Eliot makes this note:

> But you must have perceived long ago that I have no lofty vocation, and that I aspire to give no more than a faithful account of men and things as they have mirrored themselves in my mind. The mirror is doubtless defective; the outlines will sometimes be disturbed; the reflection faint or confused; but I feel as much bound to tell you, as precisely as I can, what that reflection is, as if I were in the witness-box narrating my experience on oath. (*AB*, 175)

M. H. Abrams states that 'as late as the middle of the eighteenth century important critics continued to illustrate the concept of imitation by the nature of a looking glass' (Abrams, 32). In Goethe's *Die Leiden des jungen Werthers*, this 'mirror' is located within the artist reflecting the Ideal onto the blank page:

> I feel the presence of the Almighty Who created us in His own image, and the breath of that universal love which sustains us, as we float in an eternity of bliss [...] I often think with longing, Oh, If only I could express it, could breathe onto paper all that lives so warm and full within me, that it might become the mirror of my soul, as my soul is the mirror of the infinite God! (Goethe, 6)

In this dimension of Goethe's rendering, the reading subject is invited into a house of mirrors – the writer's soul mirroring the Ideal mirrored from God which is mirrored onto the page to be mirrored onto the reader. Yet Eliot's poetic mirror 'is doubtless defective; the outlines will sometimes be disturbed; the reflection faint or confused'. She is aware that what is being offered before the reader is not a mimesis, but a *disturbed outline* which frames and focuses the reader's attention for viewing reality. Given the scope of her project as suggested by the choice of title *Adam Bede*,[3] George Eliot utilizes her narrative project to suggest a 'viewing' of humanity and history via this narrative frame. With regard to 'framing', I refer to Jonathan Culler's assertion that

> since the phenomena criticism deals with are signs, forms with socially-constituted meanings, one might try to think not of context but of *the framing of signs*: how are signs constituted *(framed)* by various discursive practices, institutional arrangements, systems of value, semiotic mechanisms [...] The expression *framing the sign* has several advantages over context: it reminds us that framing is something we do; it hints of the framing up ('falsifying evidence beforehand in order to make someone appear guilty') [...] and it eludes the incipient positivism of 'context' by alluding to the semiotic function of framing in art, where the frame is determining, setting off the object or event as art, and yet the frame itself may be nothing tangible, pure articulation. (Culler, ix)

By the creation of visual-verbal signs, George Eliot recovers that which can be lost and submerged and *frames* it for the reader, both undoing institutional arrangements that hinder a proper 'reading' and, at the same time, offering a re-imagined poetics through which to view life. In Chapter XVII, 'In Which the Story Pauses A Little', George Eliot states that her thesis is 'to tell my simple story, without trying to make things seem better than they were; dread nothing, indeed, but falsity, which, in spite of one's best efforts, there is reason to dread. Falsehood is so easy, truth so difficult' (*AB*, 177). To illustrate this thesis, George Eliot goes on to use an illustration *of* illustration:

> The pencil is conscious of a delightful facility in drawing a griffin – the longer the claws, and the larger the wings, the better; but the marvellous facility which we mistook for genius, is apt to forsake us when we want to draw a real unexaggerated lion. (177)

In this way George Eliot 'draws' an iconographic sign that travels the visual-verbal route. 'Falsehood' is not explained by Eliot as much as it

3 'Adam Bede' brings together the references to 'Adam', who in the biblical account of Genesis is the first created human, and Venerable 'Bede' whose *Ecclesiastical History of the Church* is an ancient accounting of the 'history' of the Church.

is *portrayed* through the act of visual poetics which subvert written language and thereby frees text through this act of intertexuality in grafting the *verbal* to the *visual* – in order to understand 'falsehood', one must *see* as well as understand it. Visual poetics force the reader to ask what the visual counterpart of a word is. 'Falsehood' in this instance is tethered with an *image* – a mythical griffin – which creates a sense of 'density' through the verbal-visual tethering. 'Density' in this instance refers to that which is defined by Nelson Goodman as conveying a bridged intertexuality of visual and verbal:

> [*Density* is] the fundamental inseparability of individual signs, as opposed to discreteness. This view eliminates at once difference between discourse and image [...] the same density that characterises visual texts obstructs the propositional clarity of verbal texts [...] This recognition means that the difference between verbal and visual texts is no longer one of the status and delimitation of the signs that constitute them. And the visual model, apparently predominant, overwhelms the concrete particularity of the signifier, giving rise to the 'cloudiness' in each medium [...] language is as dense as pictures. (Bal, 13–14)[4]

The use of visual poetics allows for an expansion of meaning and ultimately a density that makes visible that which can (and often does) get overlooked. What is possible is the framing of that which language cannot display. The sign based upon the solely verbal reference then falls under the more encompassing concept of intertexuality and exemplifies the subcategory of pretextual thematic reference.

As a reference to this act of intertexuality between the verbal and visual, George Eliot proceeds to refer the reader in Chapter XVII to the works of the sixteenth-century Dutch Realists:

> It is for this rare, precious quality of truthfulness that I delight in many Dutch paintings, which lofty-minded people despise. I find a source of delicious sympathy in these faithful pictures of a monotonous homely existence, which has been the fate of so many more among my fellow-mortals than a life of pomp or of absolute indigence, of tragic suffering or of world-stirring actions [...] 'Foh!' says my idealistic friend, 'what vulgar details!' (*AB*, 177)

4 Bal is citing the notion of 'density' in reference to Nelson Goodman's *Languages of Art: An Approach to a Theory of Symbols* (Indianapolis: Hackett, 1976).

Dutch Realism created a remarkable shift in sixteenth-century art through its seeming lack of discrimination regarding the detail considered germane to a given work.[5] No detail could be considered irrelevant – a stray dog, a fallen tree branch, an overturned water bucket. Each item must be considered if the whole is to be truly framed. No sign is therefore neutral but is valued to the sense of wholeness for the composition. Furthermore, as the verbal calls to the visual, a desire for illustration is provoked into a tension between verbal and visual. This provoked moment, where sign is now the event of the visual and verbal exchange, creates 'framing'. Moving this notion to reading and writing text, one can engage in what Bal terms 'iconographic reading':

> [Iconographic reading] is a discursive mode of reading because it subordinates the visually represented element to something else, thus privileging the symbol at the expense of the icon, while displacing the indexicality that allowed this semiosis in the first place. *Iconography means, literally, writing by means of images*. It is this challenge to the unwarranted assumption that visual art is iconic and verbal art symbolic that turns the iconographic mode of reading into a powerful critical tool, a tool that can be used to undermine the opposition between word and image. (Bal, 178)

Bal is referring to a 'reading' of paintings in this instance, yet the principle remains the same for the 'reading' of text. Iconographic reading allows for a powerful release from both language and image and approaches a reclaiming of what is lost when each (language and image) is isolated in distinction from the other.

In the case of *Adam Bede*, the reader is prompted to view/read the narrative and recognize the 'density' of the underlying story that can so easily be overlooked – the role of women, the question of class, the forgotten rural life, the face of God. In this way, George Eliot

5 Hugh Whitemeyer makes an extensive study of George Eliot's knowledge of the visual composition in *George Eliot and the Visual Arts* (New Haven: Yale University Press, 1979). In speaking of her use of portraiture in relation to her character development, Whitemeyer holds that Eliot in *Scenes of Clerical Life* and *Adam Bede* was 'primarily concerned to show that looks do mirror personality', that there are, as G. H. Lewes put it, 'subtle connections between physical and mental organisation' (p. 45).

juxtaposes the evoked against the narrated story (for example, the image of humanity's Fall from Grace against the image of Hetty Sorrel's fall in the garden of Hayslope, the image of Jesus against the image of Dinah Morris) in order to let them interact and to let the tensions between the stories produce new meanings. As Bal notes, 'Iconographic reading tends to obliterate the other story because stories are sometimes so generally known that reader/viewers have difficulty realising to what extent the visual work responding to the story signifies its own story' (207). This is similar to John Ruskin's use of *ut pictura poiesis* throughout *Modern Painters* (1843–60) where painting and writing are used together as hermeneutic lens for the interpretation of true 'poetry'. According to Ruskin, 'Painting is properly to be opposed to *speaking* and *writing*, but not to *poetry*. Both painting and speaking are methods of expression. Poetry is the employment of either for the noblest purposes' (Ruskin, vol. 5, 31). For Ruskin, it is in bringing works of art together – the visual and the textual – that allows for 'Great art [...] produced by men who feel acutely and nobly [...] some sort of expression' (32). As George Landow notes, 'It is thus particularly appropriate that a work [*Modern Painters*] which had been undertaken to defend the value of painting should have referred to the principle of *ut pictura poiesis*, for throughout the Renaissance and eighteenth century, poetry and painting had been juxtaposed as a means of defending the prestige of the visual art' (Landow, 43).

(Wo)men in the Garden

George Eliot offers an interesting (re)reading of the Genesis account of humanity's Fall in the Garden of Eden. As opposed to offering a dualism between the sexes that results in a view of women as a gender of weaker flesh that bends to Satan's lure and in humanity's expulsion from the Garden of Eden, Eliot disturbs this rendering by showing *two* women in the Garden of Hayslope – Hetty Sorrel and Dinah Morris. They are portrayed as humanity in the first and second Adam, respectively, yet embodied in the female. Gender guilt is further overturned in this action through the secondary 'Eves' of Arthur Donnithorne and Adam Bede who also show the extremes of damnation and grace. In this way fallen and obedient characters represent *humanity* rather than *gender* so that neither male nor female holds exclusive claim to sin or salvation. But it is a story told primarily through Hetty and Dinah – for it is their story which is most 'visible' in this accounting. While the novel is entitled *Adam Bede*, it is that which is veiled beneath this title, namely the female characters, who are ultimately the centre of the reader's concern. In this new accounting of the narrative of the Fall, we are asked to 'see' a side that had no language to be told – namely the choice, and lack of choice, of women.

Dinah and Hetty are mirrors of each other and humanity itself throughout the unfolding narrative of *Adam Bede*. Hetty wants to cast her past life behind her; but her 'narrow bit of an imagination' only leads her to make 'ill-defined pictures' of the future (*AB*, 154). Dinah's sympathetic intuition, on the other hand, is based on her awareness of biblical history, and yet Hetty 'for any practical result of strength in life, or trust in death, (had) never appropriated a single Christian idea or Christian feeling' (384). She is guided only by her current sensual responses. As noted by U. C. Knoepflmacher, parallels can be drawn between Milton's Eve in *Paradise Lost* and the portrait we are offered of Hetty Sorrel in *Adam Bede*. In *Paradise Lost*, Eve's appetite is aroused 'by the smell / So savoury of that Fruit' as she approaches the Tree of Knowledge (Milton, Book IX, lines 740–1). Similarly, Hetty is stimulated by the 'sweet languid odours of the garden at the Chase' where she will lose her innocence (*AB*, 136). Milton's Eve wants to be immortal, to rise in station. She fancies herself heightened 'through expectation high / Of knowledge, nor was God-head from her thought' (Milton, Boox IX, lines 789–90). Hetty, later, 'without knowing what she should do with her life […] craved the means of living as long as possible; and when we desire eagerly to find something, we are apt to search for it in hopeless places' (*AB*, 380), flutters between 'memory and dubious expectation' as she passes the gates of the forbidden Fir-Tree Grove:

> That was the foreground of Hetty's picture; behind it lay a bright hazy something – days that were not to be as the other days of her life had been. It was as if she had been wooed by a river-god, who might at any time take her to his wondrous halls below a watery heaven. (136)

Milton's Eve indulges in a pagan worship of the tree from which she has eaten. Arthur mythologizes the wood in which he seduces Hetty as a 'sacred grove' immune to time:

> His arm is stealing round the waist again, it is tightening its clasp; he is bending his face nearer and nearer to the round cheek, his lips are meeting those pouting child-lips, and for a long moment time has vanished. He may be a shepherd in Arcadia for aught he knows, he may be the first youth kissing the first maiden, he may be Eros himself, sipping the lips of Psyche – it is all one. (137)

Yet this 'garden' is not fashioned by Keats. George Eliot is quick to show the reader that this sublime moment is but a figment of Arthur's imagination. The novelist's mythological references are every bit as ironic as those Milton uses to describe Adam and Eve's lovemaking after the Fall. If Adam and Eve soon feel ashamed in their nakedness, Arthur, too, becomes uncomfortable, suddenly conscious that 'something bitter had begun to mingle itself with the fountain of sweets' (138). Adam and Eve are reminded of God's rule; Arthur is reminded of time. As Knoepflmacher notes, Arthur 'pulls out his watch and wonders "how late it is". He hopes that his watch is too fast. It is later than he thinks' (Knoepflmacher, 274–5).

Hetty and Arthur stand and fall together in symbiosis through the choices they make. With the evoking of visual poetics, George Eliot calls to mind in the fir grove of Hayslope a mythical place *outside* the normal order of things – a fantasy akin to that of Keats, filled with wondrous halls found in Arcadia and rivers teeming with river-gods. These images are clear and vivid, so much so that the reader who passes out of the world of Hayslope and into the mythical land of Hetty and Arthur's creation clearly notes that this is *not* Eden, but an imagined fantasy that evaporates under the density of the more compelling reality of Hayslope, the 'true fiction' of time and place. This is where Eden is to be – amidst the dairy maids, real shepherds, and common people of the land. This is not an Eden populated by idealised Greek shepherds who are known only through poetry, but is a realist composition in the midst of real life. In this way, fiction gives way to a 'truer' fiction.

Arthur notes in the realization of time ('how late it is'), in his attempt to create sublimity, that this Arcadian grove is a fiction that will not last; and 'something bitter' has indeed entered into his fantasy. But there are no serpents in this garden, nor is evil mediated by a third party – the bitterness that arises is found between the two momentary lovers and they alone. Humanity is to own its destiny and its choices. But the traditional narrative of theFall is further overturned. The tempter of the garden, Arthur Donnithorne, freely escapes and lives seemingly above moral law. Where the Adam of Milton's *Paradise Lost* leaves the garden to head toward the hope of salvation, Hetty Sorrel as the fallen 'Eve' of Hayslope leaves her encounter in the garden as a character under erasure. Hetty is left to her 'objectless wandering, apart from all love […] clinging to life only as the hunted wounded brute clings to it' (*AB*, 389). She wishes to disappear, to vanish, to 'wander out of sight, and drown herself where her body would never be found, and no one should know what became of her' (383), which stirs an image that compels one to 'see' Goethe's *Elective Affinities* played out anew. Throughout the narrative of *Adam Bede*, the reader is aware that Hetty is not truly alone in her Fall and that Arthur is living beyond the moral code by denying his relationship with her. In this way George Eliot puts before the reader the claim that guilt is never black and white, and that one person's fall from grace is surely tied to a larger circle. Arthur is exposed in the end, but remains to live another life. Hetty's fate does not contain this option. It is shown that Hetty is not fully to blame for the events that lead to her demise, yet neither is she fully absolved from them. In the end justice is rendered more to some than to others, and with differing consequences. In the garden of good and evil there are no pure victims nor are there pure villains. For Eliot, choices that are made are always part of a community, never in isolation. The plight or salvation of humanity is not to be found in finding one at fault, be it a gender or a class, but in acknowledging the interwoven nature of all people who ultimately share triumphs and defeats together in seen and unseen ways. It is the unseen that concerns Eliot, and it is that which she not only describes but displays through the frame of *Adam Bede*.

A poetics of Jesus in *Adam Bede*

Another compelling overturning of narrative in *Adam Bede* is with regard to the image of Jesus, the 'new Adam'. As noted in George Eliot scholarship, Eliot felt distraught during her translation of Strauss's rewriting of the life of Christ in *Das Leben Jesu*. She felt that Strauss had lost 'the beautiful story' in his attempt to reimagine the life of Jesus through his treatise that was bound to the restrictions of German Higher Criticism. Ultimately, it would be the space of fiction where 'the beautiful story' was fully reimagined outside of nineteenth century Higher Criticism. Multiple attempts had been made to rewrite a 'life of Jesus' within the Victorian Zeitgeist. The Victorian poetics arising in novels such as Mrs Ward's *Robert Elsmere* (1888), Froude's *The Nemesis of Faith* (1849), Pater's *Marius the Epicurean* (1885) and others strove to place this 'story of stories' in a context germane to the day. For George Eliot, the issue was not to rewrite the old Gospel tale as repetition as much as it was a returning of the narrative to its humanity in the refiguring act of 'true fiction' that is Gospel as writing. The humility, grace, and mercy of Jesus that Strauss blithely dismantled in his Hegelian project was to be returned by George Eliot with a fusing of image and word that gave a greater density to this 'beautiful story' than Strauss was capable of. Also, by creating a tension between the orthodox understanding of Jesus within Victorian England and the 'true fiction' that was 'the beautiful story' that was lost to Higher Criticism, George Eliot not only challenged the traditional images, but framed the tradition itself in a viewing within the framing of her poetics. To exemplify this in the case of visual poetics, we must look at the iconographic images that Eliot figures in *Adam Bede* employed from Dutch Realism, and specifically, the rendering of Jesus by Rembrandt.

In 1635 Rembrandt completed a sketch entitled *Last Supper, after Leonardo da Vinci.* The copy looks like a simple sketch, most likely to help the copyist memorize the work and reflect on the possibilities its composition offered. This sketch serves as a representative work of the painter's renderings of Jesus. As noted by Mieke Bal:

> What the sketch has in common with the composition of da Vinci's fresco is in the first place the isolation of the Christ figure, surrounded by the disciples who are ostensibly busy doing other things. In this respect, the 'Rembrandt' sketch is closer to the fresco than to the Birago copy through which presumably 'Rembrandt' read it. The static character of Christ is opposed to the down-to-earth commerce of the others. If the disciples of the left can be interpreted as listening and responding to the master with the exception of the figure next to Christ, those at the far right are definitely not attending to him. They are arguing among themselves, maybe plotting, maybe responding in their own way; Christ, in contrast, is not engaged with any of them. Christ is thus suspended from the narrative of talk, of worldly futility. He is absorbed [...] He is also emphatically alone. His hands, from a narrative standpoint, are engaged in the gestures of teaching; but his absorption undermines the teaching. It separates him from the others (who are clearly not listening anyway), as does the halo around his head. (Bal, 201)

It is interesting to note that Rembrandt never went to Italy and therefore never saw the original da Vinci fresco which his sketch emulates. What is evident here is that imitation or *mimesis* was not the most important goal for Rembrandt. Instead, sharing the *framework* of da Vinci's fresco rather than work itself provided Rembrandt with a language of signs that the 'reader' will acknowledge even if not overtly. Rembrandt's sketch, although 'written' in da Vinci's language, is not identical to the work from which language was borrowed, nor was it trying to be. This exemplifies 'the difference between language and utterance, between system and actual signs' (431–2) which underscore the framing project of the iconographic.

Referring back to the Rembrandt sketch of *Last Supper, after Leonardo da Vinci*, one can observe that behind Christ's head is *another* head – that of a woman, leaning toward Christ with attentiveness. This is a clear shift from the 'narrative' of da Vinci although the *composition* is strangely coherent in Rembrandt's sketch, as if this 'person' has been there all along. Bal makes the following remarks:

> Since this is merely a sketch, nothing would be easier than to ignore it. For example, it can be easily dispensed with as an earlier but rejected attempt at drawing Christ's head. The pointed finger of the bald man next to Jesus can be directed toward Jesus or toward one of the figures on the other side, and the strangely unreal second head does not need to be a woman's head, although it alone has long, curly hair. Moreover, that second head can be taken as a proleptic allusion to Judas, who will later come up to kiss Jesus, thus identifying himself as the traitor. So one would think we need not worry about this second head, although the depiction of this Judas as a woman is remarkable. (201)

It is noted by Bal that women-in-excess are, as she states, 'quite "Rembrandtesque". They are readable, never mind how enigmatic they may otherwise be.' Here, this shadow woman seems to be uninvited as one only able to listen and not partake. To the 'reader', this figure is compelling in that she is the only one who seems to be attending to what Christ is saying. In this way, the 'reader' is led to wonder what she hears as one who is so close, what she feels as one who listens but only from outside the circle. Moreover, the 'reader' is taken to *her* place at the table, which is what Bal terms *'excurse'* – that figuring within compositional form which leads the reader/viewer out of the story entirely. In this case, the 'reader' is drawn away from the distracted table, and into the space where the absorptive Christ figure has gone. As Bal surmises, Rembrandt's sketch *Last Supper, after da Vinci* 'tells us no more; it just suggests the sheer possibility of an "elsewhere"' (201).

Rembrandt utilizes da Vinci's compositional template of *The Last Supper* fresco in a 1638 painting entitled *Samson posing the Riddle to the Wedding Guests*. Painted three years after the sketch *Last Supper, after da Vinci*, here is a work of strikingly similar composition with a completely different subject: the episode of Samson's wedding in which Samson proposed the riddle to the wedding guests taken from Judges 14:12–20. Bal notes that:

> Since the subject [of *Samson posing the Riddle to the Wedding Guests*] is so different from the sketch, it is not sufficient to use the iconographic mode of

> reading to identify the subject matter itself. Yet, in spite of the tradition of wedding painting, it is compelling to relate the *Samson* to the Leonardo rather than to works, say, like Brueghel's *Peasants' Wedding* (ca. 1560), which is closer in subject but different in composition. (202)

This is an important difference between *compositional* and *figural* iconography: we cannot use the iconographic mode of reading to identify theme, but we can use it to identify a very relevant meaning, to make the two subjects speak to each other, and to see how, for example, Rembrandt through the *Samson* painting appropriates unseen pre-texts – both Leonardo and the Gospel narrative – for its own ends. This approach for Bal 'requires a semiotic attitude that abhors meaninglessness. Not all viewers will share this attitude, but those who do cannot leave the similarity of composition to accident' (202). Putting the sketch *Last Supper, after Leonardo da Vinci* into play with *Samson posing the Riddle to the Wedding Guests* shows a heritage that is truly striking and provocative. The compositional structure of the Leonardo fresco *frames* both works. Yet the shift that has taken place in the three years between the sketch *Last Supper* to the painting of the *Samson* is even more striking. Where the women in the Last Supper sketch is in *excurse,* she is now portrayed as filling the space of Christ in the *Samson*. Bal makes the following comparisons:

> The woman is as isolated as Christ. She is not, as he was, engaged in a stillness outside of time and of the world, for she is not the son of God. But she, too, is lonely and about to die. Christ's inward gaze was directed to no one in particular; the bride's gaze is also directed outside of the story that the others are busy acting out; but whereas Christ's gaze is inward, the bride's is outward, toward the viewer. Thus she steps out of a diegetic situation that is as frightening and as threatening as Susanna's situation when she is trapped by the Elders. (203)

Other textual similarities are also evident between these works of Rembrandt as we put them into play. The woman's head in the *Samson* is adorned with the curls of the head behind Christ in the *Last Supper* sketch, as if the woman, still hidden there, has stepped forward to tell her story of sacrificial death. Of course, no halo surrounds her head, but the figure in the background tapestry is just a little bit lighter around her head than elsewhere. This shows a truly ironic turn in Rembrandt's compositional choice:

> The irony here is one of shifting, of displacement, of turning the highest subject into a low one – the genre scene. But the displacement does not effect the woman at the centre. She remains separated from the promiscuous scene, isolated in this way just as she is diegetically and pictorially isolated. In addition, there is no confusion, no extension of the reference to 'the Biblical' in general. The sign is compositional, but no less precise and delimited [...] In *Samson's Wedding*, a specific moment of the one pre-text – of the Leonardo and, through it, of the Gospel – is seen to be used to compose the framework of the painting in which other pre-text – the Judges episode – is then made to fit. The context, the contemporary habit of typological interpretation, is used in a way that makes a highly sympathetic representation plausible. (205–6)

This compositional shape that is iconographically implied between the works brings about a tension between narratives. This provokes what Bal terms as a 'double, differential reading, which juxtaposes the evoked against the narrated story, in order to let them interact and to let the tensions between the stories produce new meanings' (207). This reading radically challenges assumed foundational narratives by allowing differing subjects to occupy identical compositional reality. This goes to the heart of the reading event, where signs and signifiers are replaced by the item that is absent and only alluded to by language.

In *Adam Bede*, George Eliot evokes a similar compositional form through a visual poetics of Dinah Morris. In Chapter II entitled 'The Preaching' (note the definite article), Eliot calls to mind the biblical account of Jesus' Sermon on the Mount. Yet it is not Adam to which the title refers but Dinah Morris, who is central to the compositional structure of the scene and the Adam upon whom George Eliot bestows the 'title' of new Adam. Like Jesus, she too is marginalized despite her prophetic gifts due to her common heritage as merely the 'niece to Poyer's wife', one who is a 'Methodis' – those who are prone to go 'stark starin' mad wi' their religion' (*AB*, 16). She is a compelling figure, at odds with tradition as a woman in 'quaker-like costume' and draws a crowd of 'stronger curiosity' to the village green. As noted by a stranger in the crowd, she is merely a 'sweet woman [...] but surely nature never meant her for a preacher' (23). She is described as one of 'no particular beauty, beyond that of expression' whose eyes 'looked so simple, so candid, so gravely loving'. Her hand is stretched out 'towards the descending sun' and her head is covered with a 'net'. She is placed in the centre of the crowd by the composition of the narrative, who gather around, listening but distracted throughout her sermon. In the sermon itself, Eliot gives visual cues that are to 'see' a portrait of Christ as one reads the sermon voiced through the compositional centre of Dinah Morris:

> *'See!'* she exclaimed, turning to the left, with her eyes fixed on a point above the heads of the people – '*see* where our blessed Lord stands and weeps, and stretches out his arms towards you.' [...] In a pleading reproach, turning her eyes on the people again. '*See* the print of the nails on his dear hands and feet. It is your sins that made them! Ah, how pale and worn he looks! He has gone through all that great agony in the garden [...] And he is upon this earth too; he is among us; he is there close to you now; I *see* his wounded body and his look of love.' (307; emphases added)

With these visual cues George Eliot evokes the following image: a crowd that is gathered around a central figure whose gaze is turned outward. The central figure is set apart even though placed compositionally in the centre. This central figure has its arms extended to show the palms of hands where one is to 'see' 'the print of nails' that can be imagined and a covering about the head. The crowd is present yet not attentive to the one they gather around. Through her evoking of visual images tethered to verbal description, George Eliot has given density to this scene that is compositionally compatible with Rembrandt's works that utilize the compositional language of various pre-texts – namely da Vinci and ultimately the Gospel accounts. As noted with Rembrandt, who stands central to the tradition of Dutch realism which George Eliot addresses in Chapter XVII, this compositional iconography allows for a double, differential reading that juxtaposes the evoked image of Jesus figured by da Vinci's compositional template against the narrated story of *Adam Bede*, in order to let them interact and to let the tensions between the stories produce new meanings. With this compositional iconography framing the text, both *imago* and *verbum* are challenged. This tension challenges assumed foundational narratives and allows for differing subjects to occupy identical compositional reality. As mentioned before, this goes to the heart of the reading event, where signs and signifiers are replaced by the item that is absent and only alluded to by language. So compelling is this image presented in chapter II that upon reading *Adam Bede*, Queen Victoria had this scene commissioned in 1861 as a painting by Edward Henry Corbould entitled *Dinah Morris Preaching on Hayslope Green*. In looking at the painting, the compositional form of the scene transcends the visual poetics into an image true to da Vinci and Rembrandt's compositional heritage and calls back to both the narrative of *Adam Bede* and ultimately, the deeper narrative of Jesus. The words indeed become flesh in this vivid rendering of image which gives further density to the verbal. The compositional iconography in *Adam Bede* allows for an image made word that enables images to speak beyond the limits of language. It is this possibility that is central to Eliot's poetics and key to a poetics of Jesus. As demonstrated in *Adam Bede*, Eliot evokes a 'new Adam' that is neither 'new' nor 'Adam', yet a visual-verbal paradox arises that overturns assumptions through an intertexuality of the visual and the verbal. In a poetics of Jesus, narrative overturns narrative and allows for possibilities of new subjects, formerly unseen, to inhabit traditional compositional forms.

Bibliography

Abrams, M. H. *The Mirror and the Lamp: Romantic Theory and the Critical Tradition*. Oxford: OUP, 1953.

Bal, Mieke. *Reading 'Rembrandt': Beyond the Word–Image Opposition*. Cambridge: CUP, 1991.

Culler, Jonathan. *Framing the Sign: Criticism and its Institutions*. Oxford: Blackwell, 1988.

Cunningham, Valentine. *Introduction to* Adam Bede. Oxford: OUP, 1996.

Eliot, George. *Adam Bede*. Oxford: OUP, 1996. (AB).

—— *The Impressions of Theophrastus Such*. London: J. M. Dent and Sons, 1995. (TS)

Goethe, Johann Wolfgang von. *The Sorrows of Young Werther*. In the *Collected Works*, vol. 11, ed. David E. Wellbury. Princeton: Princeton UP, 1988.

Knoepflmacher, UC. 'On *Adam Bede*', in Ian Watt (ed.), *The Victorian Novel: Modern Essays in Criticism*. London: OUP, 1971.

Landow, George P. *The Aesthetic and Critical Theories of John Ruskin*. Princeton: Princeton UP, 1971.

Milton, John. *Paradise Lost*. 1667.

Ruskin, John. *The Works of John Ruskin*, 39 vols, ed. E. T. Cook and Alexander Wedderburn. London: George Allen, 1903–12.

CATHERINE RAINE

Sin and Theodicy – Victorian and Modern Style

I want to understand what conviction of sin and theodicy mean in the context of spiritual autobiography and American Civil Rights history. Can the journal of a Victorian governess, Emily Bowes, share anything with *Freedom Summer*, Sally Belfrage's book about her experiences in Mississippi? Both women write autobiographical accounts which articulate a sense of sin. For Miss Bowes, it is 'the sin of storytelling' which condemns her to wickedness, while for Sally Belfrage it is her fellow white volunteers' acknowledgment of 'the world's evil in themselves' (Belfrage, 5) which paradoxically makes them heroes compared to the complacent.

Can evil confessed in silent prayer in 1835 and evil in 1964 Mississippi share a common source? Can a theodicy be conceived in which social good flowers from inner convictions of sin? I would like to support a theodicy which bears witness to the experience of Belfrage. The alternative position on human depravity represented in Bowes's *Recollections* echoes Paul in Romans 7:25: 'I am a slave to the law of sin.' In other words, white Mississippians hated because they personified a law of wickedness; in a mob they were a 'beast on the march' (Roosevelt, xix). Yet the theological comfort suggested in *Freedom Summer* is that of an honesty which allows movement from self-condemnation to dynamic engagement with voter registration and freedom schools. In the words of Belfrage:

> Maybe these clothes, this guilt and hate, don't fit me at all […] [but] the hate is there. If it's not mine, then whose? To act at all, perhaps one has to assume the sins which led to the need to act, whether or not they fit, make them one's own. To take on the deep hates with the deep loves, exist inside them, and somehow find a way out (Belfrage, 83).

For Emily, to flee from inner doom was to write the story of her pilgrimage from sinful childhood to conversion. For Sally, escape from the suffocating burdens of history is possible only after they are internalized, however inappropriately. For me, if there *must* be sin and sinners, the preferred sin is one which offers a chance to participate in social change. I'm curious about the territories to which conviction of sin opens the gate – whether the sinners who enter experience them as sloughs of despond or transcendent mass meetings that absorb and absolve the self.

Emily Bowes characterized her soul as wicked from a child. Born in 1806, she came of age during a great Evangelical revival. Like the Civil Rights era in the States, early nineteenth-century Britain was a time of political upheaval, including the slave trade's end in 1807 and emancipation in British colonies in 1838. Parliament passed the 1832 Reform Act, which shared the 1964 Civil Rights Act's concern with voting rights, three years before Emily wrote her *Recollections*. Roughly five years later, she joined the Plymouth Brethren, a community which embraced radical simplicity, stripping preachers and ritual from their worship and leaving bare a Bible-centered core. Although she was not a member of the Brethren at the time of writing the *Recollections*, she, like them, 'always had a love for the Bible' (Bowes, 24).

She also had a weakness for preachers and 'would have sacrificed any enjoyment' to hear a Mr Marsh, of Hampstead (22). In fact, it is a preacher's sermon on Deuteronomy which inspires the writing of her Recollections. She begins with a scriptural verse:

> Thou shall remember all the way which the Lord thy God led thee these forty years in the wilderness to humble thee and to prove to thee *to know what was in thine heart*, whether thou wouldest keep his commandments or no. (Deut. 8:2; 11).

John Bunyan's *Grace Abounding to the Chief of Sinners* (1666) quotes exactly the same biblical passage in its preface (Bunyan, 2). Here, the Exodus story can be read as an allegory of the soul, the wilderness internal, with inward movement to self-knowledge imperative before the idea of freedom can even be considered. (Yet in the summer of 1964, the physical turn is a journey from the freer North to slave-like conditions in Mississippi, simultaneous with a movement of inner freedom for the volunteers).

In Emily's heart lies what she considers deep sinfulness. Like Bunyan, she was convicted with a sense of wickedness and turned to spiritual introspection to provide openings to the possibility of grace and freedom from fear. The wilderness in Deuteronomy represents Emily's twenty-nine year sojourn in the world. Her *Recollections* propose to 'examine her past life' according to a pattern borrowed from a preacher, meditating on: her religious development, afflictions, mercies, sins, and God's providence. She follows the Deuteronomy quotation with an explanation: 'A sermon on these words having enforced the necessity of a frequent and minute enquiry into our past lives […] I propose considering and noting down some of my recollections' (Bowes, 11).

Emily's enquiry reveals a profound worthlessness. Moreover, it is insufficient recognition of her depravity which troubles her: 'The great and worst defect in my religious education was that I was never fully impressed with the utter depravity and helplessness of my nature, with the efficacy of the Atonement, of the new birth, and the work of the Spirit' (12). Of the five meditation topics suggested by the preacher, the one which engages her most is *sins*. It is by far the longest section. Thus, at the heart of her story, Emily settles down to the serious business of confessing her sins. She's not even sure how to begin, sounding like a penitent St Augustine who wonders if there are any evil deeds that he has *not* done, spoken, or willed (Augustine, 204). Yet Emily's sins have limited shock value. They include: storytelling, unbelief, selfishness, sneaking food from the kitchen, dissembling because of surprise or pride, and concealing her opinions while pretending to agree with friends and family (Bowes, 16–14). She scrambles about for sins, as if she wishes to provoke grace by exaggeration, grace the more abounding to the stars among sinners. Alas, she must resort to books: 'I have also taken a wicked pleasure in reading of wickedness' (19).

Emily's sense of wickedness makes a doubly reflective turn and focuses on the process of writing itself:

> When a very little child I used to amuse myself and my brother with inventing stories, such as I read. Having as I suppose naturally a restless mind, and busy imagination, this soon became the chief pleasure of my life [...] Miss Shore [a Calvinist governess] finding it out lectured me severely, and told me it was wicked. From that time I considered it a sin, and often repented and confessed it, but it was too deeply rooted in my affections to be resisted in my own strength, and unfortunately I knew neither my corruption nor my weakness, nor did I know where to gain strength. (16–19)

She describes the sin of storytelling as if it were a private manifestation of original sin. Her mind is 'naturally' restless, the sin is 'deeply rooted', and she is weak and corrupt, fatally bereft of free will. Corruption is a strong word to describe the spirituality of a nine-year-old girl, calling to mind James's *The Turn of the Screw*. Emily's conviction of fiction's sin strengthened as she grew older:

> and the folly, vanity, and wickedness which have disgraced and polluted my heart are more than I am able to express. Even now, tho' watched, prayed, and striven against this is still the sin that most easily besets me [...] It has made me to know more of the depths of sin than I could ever otherwise have believed [...] (17)

Storytelling has made her sympathize with other sinners, for even though they may have been more 'openly wicked', she may nevertheless be 'worse in the eyes of God'. But there are compensations, for sin 'teaches me the desperate wickedness of my heart, and makes me thereby understand the scriptures and the need of a Saviour' (18). The sin of storytelling precipitated Emily's fortunate fall; she didn't know she was wicked and needed saving until the depth of her corruption became clear. So also, the *Freedom Summer* volunteers were optimistic about America until they confronted the poverty and racism lurking beneath its democratic rhetoric; corruption, both internal and external, was forced to the surface and connected to the state of the union.

Did Emily truly believe she was as wicked as she said? Was it a defect or a strength that she was 'never fully impressed' with her depravity as a child? I wonder how much is pulpit rhetoric and how much heart-felt sorrow. Sins are very much like fashions, and nineteenth-century sins can seem hopelessly quaint. For never once did Emily mention the sin of racism or xenophobia. The notion of calling them sins at all would have been as surprising to the majority of Victorians as it would to Citizen Council Members in the American South, shrouded as racist thinking was with Christian jingoism. Yet Emily was aware of the abolitionist cause. Her husband wrote a tract entitled *The Negro Slave* which appeared in a book of Emily's collected tracts. It declares: 'the devil is a worse slave-holder than the most severe planter in the southern states; and to a certainty you are in his chains' (Grosse, 3).

The movement described in the *Recollections* is an inward one which does not seem to allow escape into active atonement. It's all about the forbidden, about repression, about sins that beset and beset again despite prayers and resolutions. Setting out with Moses as he escapes from slavery, Emily's story goes inward and circles round and round the crucible of sin. In contrast, *Freedom Summer* started from an idea of sin for many, but a sin which encouraged movement from introspection to social action, from inner turns of self-doubt to immersion in the larger Civil Rights movement.

Yet the white volunteers' right to participate in this Movement was passionately debated by the members which made up the Council of Federated Organizations. COFO organized the 1964 Mississippi Summer Project and its component parts included SNCC (The Student Non-Violent Coordinating Committee), the Congress of Racial Equality, the Southern Christian Leadership Conference, and the Mississippi branches of the NAACP (Belfrage, 4). SNCC was the dominant group, and many of its leaders argued that the student volunteers would undermine the confidence of local black leaders who had recently sprung up and whose Mississippi summer was a lifetime, not a choice. African-American civil rights workers like Fannie Lou Hamer, Bob Moses and Anne Moody had suffered imprisonment, death threats, and day-to-day harassment. Importing the volunteers might show disrespect to the martyrs who had battled alone against the Klan in its multiple guises as night terrorist, policeman, and judge. The danger was that the media would ignore the grass roots and forget that: 'The movement, despite any white illusions [...] is an indigenous one, before, during, and after the summer' (80).

The decision to invite over seven hundred and fifty, mostly white, out-of-state volunteers to conduct voter registration drives, freedom schools, and to organize community centres was to a large degree driven by the realities of the American media. In an interview, Dave Dennis, second in command after Bob Moses, framed the project in terms of 'speaking the language' of 1960s America: 'We knew that if we had brought in a thousand blacks, the country would have watched them slaughtered without doing anything about it […] They would respond to a thousand young white college students, and white college females who were down there. All right?' (Raines, 274).

Sally Belfrage was one of those females. *Freedom Summer* doesn't catalogue Sally's sins as exhaustively as Emily did but the influences mentioned seem more firmly rooted in a sense of history: 'During the war I remember asking an adult to explain why Jews were being killed […] "What are Aryans?" I asked, and the answer was: "People who look like you"' (Belfrage, 82). Here the guilt is mystifying to a child, seeming to fly from an alien place but coming to rest on a face, a hair colour, a random appearance assigned. The leaders of the Summer Project stressed the idea that the white volunteers were 'the victims of the very prejudice we fought' (81), and did not encourage self-congratulation for taking up a fight which after all was a shared one. Why expect thanks for simply being a decent person?

Belfrage wonders if her motivation to participate did not ultimately come down to guilt: 'Try it. Yes, I feel guilty. I am guilty of the sins of the world, the sins of the past, the sins of the foreign.' The tone is slightly edgy, sarcastic, a sharpness that is missing in the *Recollections*. Yet are Sally's sins different from Emily's? Like original sin, Sally's guilt includes the past, the ancestors, but the link is also horizontal, not just the linear chain of heritage, but absorbing the wider world's history of racial violence. For Sally, Mississippi is an easier place to making atonement than New York City, her home. Mississippi is 'a pilgrimage to a foreign country; traveling there, I can leave my guilt behind and atone for someone else's' (Belfrage, 82).

Mississippi eroded belief in personal innocence. Belfrage lost her belief in it and turned instead to the question of justice: 'Maybe it is just a cool question of feeling, impersonally, that some things are right and others wrong, and that I must do what I can for the right' (82–3). For a fellow volunteer, it is 'recognition of the disease' which ought to make 'action necessary' (Sutterland, 10). Accepting the sin, claiming it, is the catalyst for action, a peculiar freedom, a fortunate fall, in that this nugget of hatred so seemingly foreign, is the volcanic core from which more honest love can erupt. It is a force which can bathe you in the light of a mass meeting like this one: 'there's a direct tie between every person in that church and God and every person with me and I with them' (51). Two volunteer teachers describe freedom schools in a similar way: 'Every class is beautiful. The girls respond, respond, respond.' 'I can see the change. The 16-year old's discovery of poetry, of Whitman and Cummings [...] After two weeks a child finally looks me in the eye, unafraid' (96–7).

It is the looking outward, the witness of possible trust, which appealed to many of the volunteers, the imperative 'to peel off the layers of do-nothing spiritualists, apathetic worshippers, navel-gazers, and to institute people who will make a sacrifice, a radical [...] witness' (16). Yet who bears the responsibility when radical witnesses get beaten or killed? The shadow of James Chaney, Andrew Goodman, and Michael Schwerner's murders touched the Summer Project from the beginning; news of their disappearance broke during the second orientation session on a college campus in Ohio (Belfrage, 11–12).

The sense of sin which Emily Bowes experienced differed from that of Sally Belfrage. But both are abstractions compared to that of civil rights leaders who suffered from the agonizing knowledge that their actions could lead to Mississippians getting killed. Dave Dennis explained: '[The white violence] caused problems – I mean, psychologically – for me [...] you felt responsible for what happened to people [...] But it was something that had to be done' (Raines, 274). Anne Moody was on a Klan hit list and could not return to Wilkinson County, Mississippi for fear of reprisals against her family. She understood Bob Moses's guilt feelings over the deaths of Herbert Lee, a civil rights worker, and Louis Allen who witnessed Lee's 1961 murder. Moody wrote: 'I could detect in him [Moses] a feeling of guilt, disgust, and helplessness. I also knew he could tell that I, too, felt guilty about my uncle's death' (Moody, 332).

The torment that Dennis, Moses, and Moody felt was more grounded in the actual world of events than that of the volunteers who just came for the summer. Yet this guilt does not seem justified in the sense that true guilt lay where it was least being admitted, that is, the perpetrators of Klan violence who used that very guilt to scare local black people into submission. The guilt which freed the Sallys into recognition and action is now the guilt which paralysed many potential Anne Moodys into inaction for fear of endangering their families. In this light, white guilt seems a kind of luxury guilt, guilt light that turns out so right. The prominent Northern families of the volunteers were not likely to be firebombed because of civil rights activity.

For a movement to be beautiful, either religious or political, there must be a turn, a momentum from self-hate to love, from injustice to justice. If theodicy is to be encouraged, perhaps it can be found in a powerful turn from the soul's portrait of Dorian Gray to the cameras, however cynical, which told the story of the three murder victims (among countless others) and finally acknowledged evil on a scale far removed from the sensitive musings of a Victorian governess. The sin of this story is its monstrous truth. Guilt revealed made the innocence of the United States impossible to uphold and helped to galvanize a change, still incomplete, which partly grew out of convictions of sin. For the Summer started to unravel a Mississippi contradiction which imprisoned the innocent and rewarded the guilty.

Bibliography

Augustine, St. *The Confessions*. London: Hodder and Stoughton, 1997.

Belfrage, Sally. *Freedom Summer*. Charlottesville and London: Virginia UP, 1965.

Bowes, Emily. 'The Recollections of the Earlier Life of Emily Bowes to the Year 1835'. Unpublished Manuscript in Cambridge University Library, Manuscript Room (Add. 7035).

Bunyan, John. *Grace Abounding to the Chief of Sinners*, 1666; ed. Roger Sharrock. Oxford: Clarendon Press, 1962.

Gosse, E. and P. *Gosse's Narrative Tracts*. London: Moran and Chase, 1857.

Moody, A. *Coming of Age in Mississippi: An Autobiography*. London: Peter Owen, 1968.

Roosevelt, Eleanor. Foreword to D. Bates, *The Long Shadow of Little Rock*. New York: David McKay, 1962.

Raines, H. (ed.). *My Soul is Rested: Movement Days in the Deep South Remembered*. New York: Penguin Books, 1977.

Sutterland, E. (ed.). *Letters From Mississippi*. New York: McGraw Hill, 1965.

DAVID E. KLEMM

Re-entering the Magic Theatre: The Trace of the Other in Hermann Hesse's *Steppenwolf* (1927)

In the American counterculture of the late 1960s and early 1970s, the hippies were in ecstasy over the fiction of Hermann Hesse. They carried Hesse's novels in their knapsacks along with their prayer beads, tarot cards, and other talismans. *Demian*, *Siddhartha*, *Steppenwolf*, *Narcissus and Goldmund*, *The Journey to the East* and *The Glass Bead Game* became sacred scripture. The world of the text was more real to them than the supposedly real worlds of politics and economics, for these young pilgrims understood and interpreted their own inner changes in light of the holy texts. Even more strongly, Hesse's novels opened new symbolic worlds, which shaped their dreams, imagination, and emotional life. Hesse was really 'far out, man'. All one could say was 'Wow!'

This Hessomania did not go unchallenged, however. Anxious parents paid good money for psychologists and psychiatrists to explain the dementia of their supposedly uncommitted sons and daughters who followed this Pied Piper into alien spiritual communities. Literary critics jumped into the fray as well. Through the public media, they exposed what many of them took to be the pernicious influence of Hesse on young minds (Ziolkowski, 1973, 1–15). It became commonplace to read that Hesse was a second-rate thinker whose novels cheaply combine German Romanticism's sense of longing for the absolute with a Nietzschean existentialism. The purported result of Hesse's concoction was the illusion of a spiritual freedom to be found somewhere beyond good and evil.

I know both sides of this debate firsthand. In 1967, a mere lad of twenty and enchanted by Hesse's spell, I considered myself a member of an important League on an eternal journey to the East. Fifteen years later (1982), with a doctorate earned in theology, I joined the literary and philosophical critics of Hesse. Today, as a Professor of Theology, I understand the power of literature in the undergraduate classroom, and I wonder which side was right in the debate about Hesse. My inquiry has led me to re-enter the Magic Theatre of Hesse's fiction, this time with my eyes open, for my own sake and possibly for the sake of my students. This paper arises from a recent encounter with Harry Haller – the tormented middle-aged intellectual and figure of otherness whose tracks are left like pawprints in the snow across the pages of *Steppenwolf*.

What kind of novel, exactly, is *Steppenwolf*? The received interpretation, best articulated by Theodore Ziolkowski, is that *Steppenwolf* is similar in kind to the Romantic Märchen as crafted by E. T. A. Hoffmann (Ziolkowski, 1965, 178–228).[1] Ziolkowski further claims that the novel's thematic development within this form tightly resembles that of the three-movement sonata. *Steppenwolf*, he concludes, is a Romantic fairy-tale written as a sonata in prose.[2] In this paper I propose an alternative interpretation. I argue that *Steppenwolf* is a serious study of human nature, which takes the form of a spiritual handbook for the healing of the diseased soul. My interpretation of the genre of *Steppenwolf* is corroborated by the revealing prefatory note that Hesse wrote to the new edition of the novel in 1961. Hesse allows that poetic writing can be understood and misunderstood in many different ways, and he admits that the author is not the right authority to decide whether the reader's interpretation

1 Chapter 9, on *Steppenwolf* was published originally in *Modern Language Quarterly* 19 (1958) and was revised for the book. It also appears in German in *Materialien zu Hermann Hesses 'Der Steppenwolf'*, edited by Volker Michels (Frankfurt am Main: Suhrkamp, 1975), as 'Hermann Hesses *Steppenwolf*. Eine Sonate in Prosa', 353–76.

2 '*Steppenwolf* is a long realistic narrative of contemporary life in which a dualistic view of reality is rendered through a contrast between everyday reality and the inner vision of the hero. The fairy-tale atmosphere is created technically by the fact that the inner vision is projected as though it were real in the ordinary sense of the word; the author identifies himself at crucial points with the hero's point of view, describing the world as fantastically as the hero sees it in his vision. The implications of the whole are broadened by reference to an interpolated myth which is fulfilled symbolically by the characters of the realistic framework story' (Ziolkowski, 1965, 205–6).

in fact understands or misunderstands the text. Nonetheless Hesse ventures to say that 'of all my books *Steppenwolf* is the one that was more often and more violently misunderstood than any other, and frequently it is actually the affirmative and enthusiastic readers, rather than those who rejected the book, who have reacted to it oddly.' Hesse goes on to remark that part of the reason for the misunderstandings is that the book was written when he was fifty years old to deal with the problems of that age, and it often fell into the hands of very young readers who were ill-prepared to receive it. But even among readers of his own age, he continues, many of them perceived only the sufferings and grief of Harry Haller. They overlook the fact that 'this book knows of and speaks about other things besides Harry Haller and his difficulties, about a second, higher, indestructible world beyond the Steppenwolf and his problematic life,' namely, 'a positive, serene, superpersonal and timeless world of faith.' *Steppenwolf*, Hesse insists, 'pictures a disease and crisis – but not one leading to death and destruction, on the contrary: to healing.'

In other words, the book has both a theoretical and a practical dimension. It both conveys an understanding of who or what the Steppenwolf is within a range of possibilities for being human, and even more importantly it instructs the reader concerning what to do about it if she or he is in the position of the Steppenwolf. The basis for my interpretation is grounded in a structural analysis, which reveals most strikingly that this novel is not divided by a single narrator into chapters according to the principle of plot development, but is rather divided into discrete parts according to four different narrative voices. The structure of the novel makes possible its remarkable unity of theoretical and practical interests. Clearly, the reader's task is to follow the trace of the other through each of the different voices to the standpoint at which all the voices can be appropriated as a unity expressing itself in diversity. Let me explain.

The author's theoretical interest is expressed in the novel's articulation of a human cosmology – a set of five possible modes of human being in the world, each one of which is explainable with reference to two basic principles that Hesse calls 'nature' and 'spirit'. In the economy of the self, 'nature' denotes the organic function of desire, governed by the passive principle of receptivity to, rootedness in, and longing for meanings that arise in and are satisfied by sensible and affective life. 'Spirit' denotes the intellectual function of thought, governed by the active principle of reason as it determines reality by subsuming intuitions under concepts and inclinations under projects. The centre of the self, and the finite origin point of conscious activities, is the concretely embodied subject – the 'I am' – as it combines spirit and nature. The final aim or goal of conscious life is the absolute horizon of the fully differentiated unity of spirit and nature – the unifying unity of the Godhead. Any concrete individual or self is always a living combining and combination of these two principles of spirit and nature. Hesse's spiritual cosmology presents five possibilities for combining these two principles in human life, and each one is posited in ascending hierarchical order. The five possibilities are: (1) the libertine, (2) the bourgeois individual, (3) the tormented Steppenwolf, (4) the transformed Steppenwolf, and (5) the Immortal.

The author's practical interest is expressed in the novel's clear instruction with regard to how one can move from one mode of being to the next and thus make the ascent from innocence through despair to redemption or wholeness. The theoretical and practical interests are unified in this text through the division of the whole into different narrative voices. Each voice is ascribable to a place within the human cosmology, and each voice instructs the reader how to live. Each voice (and therefore each instruction) is valid at its own level. The book, with its sequence of voices, enjoins the reader to master the instruction at each level and then to proceed sequentially to the next instruction. The use of these different voices allows the author both to communicate a vision of the human plight grandly conceived, but also to lead the reader to a condition beyond the plight. In other words, rather than finding a musical idiom as subtext of *Steppenwolf*, I link this work to the subgenre of spiritual guidebook. This subgenre includes such well-known texts as Saint Bonaventura's The Mind's Road to God, Erasmus's *Handbook of the Christian Soldier*, and even more directly, Kierkegaard's pseudonymously written *Stages on Life's Way*, which shows the humorous and ironical possibilities of this subgenre for the modern literary and theological mind. Like all of the aforementioned works, *Steppenwolf* lays out both a principled system and a progressive method of spiritual realization. Like both Erasmus's and Kierkegaard's works, *Steppenwolf* aims to transform the diseased soul rather than the natural one. And like Kierkegaard's literary inventions in particular, the author of *Steppenwolf* speaks through multiple voices of instruction, each representing a possible mode of being human that must be appropriated successively in order to reach the goal. Let us now walk through the novel in order to listen to the voice of the other in each of the different parts.

I

The first part of *Steppenwolf* is called the 'editor's preface' ('Vorwort des Herausgebers'). The editor is a bourgeois observer of the Steppenwolf, who explains that he discovered Harry Haller's written records quite by accident and has decided to edit and publish them. The editor's voice is thus the first narrative voice, and the compiler of the materials to follow. The voice of this bourgeois individual provides the primary instruction in this part of the book, but he alludes to three of the four other possibilities for being human that are represented in Hesse's cosmology, namely the libertine, the bourgeois individual and the tormented Steppenwolf.

The voice of the libertine appears here only indirectly, through the suspicion of the editor who observes Haller intently when he inquires about a flat to rent from the editor's aunt. Haller's obvious otherness, exhibited in the disturbing first impression of a man who 'comes out of an alien world', causes the bourgeois narrator to worry that Haller may have filthy habits and an uncouth nature. That is, the narrator suspects that Harry Haller may be a libertine whose structural type is defined by a maximal domination of the principle of bodily desires (nature) over the principle of thinking (spirit), so that appetite negates reason. The bourgeois narrator spends days and nights intently observing, nay, spying on the Steppenwolf with rapt attention, and he quickly concludes that Harry Haller is no libertine. Thus the libertine's mode of being appears in the book only as an unrealized possibility for Harry Haller.

Through his observations, the bourgeois editor reveals his own mode of being in the world. It is determined by love of order, predictability, cleanliness, meticulousness, and, above all, duty. The bourgeois mode of being in the world is defined precisely by its intention to bind nature and spirit together in such a way that neither body nor soul can recognize, much less actualize, its own potentiality for bodily passion or for genuine intellectuality. Its maxim is to avoid extremes at all costs. The dominant force is that of the self's commitment and activity to contain the organic and intellectual principles of nature and spirit in a weakened state of moderation.

Harry Haller, the wolf of the Steppes, appears to the editor as coming from a higher order than the bourgeois mode of being. The reason for the editor's view of Haller is that he has broken the bourgeois social contract that binds and debilitates the principles of nature and spirit. In the being of Harry Haller, the two principles are in open conflict, and he himself evokes extreme and opposing responses from others. The editor is at once fascinated by 'this significant, uncommon, and unusually gifted man', a man who 'had thought more than other people'; yet at the same time, the editor is repulsed by the depth of emotion in Haller's frightful loneliness, his unsociability, and his estrangement from others. The editor observes that Haller is diseased in spirit, that he is in fact a genius of suffering with a boundless capacity for pain; the editor recoils from Haller with the instinct of the healthy shunning the ill.

From the voice of the bourgeois editor, we glean the following instruction: *Control your impulses, moderate your desires, and observe carefully and cautiously the world around you! Something quite unusual may appear.* That is the first practical instruction arising in *Steppenwolf*, and it identifies the primary audience among the bourgeoisie.

II

In the second part of the book, the observed tormented Steppenwolf assumes the narrator's voice. Here we have Harry Haller's own written records entitled 'For Madmen Only'. These writings comprise an autobiographical account that Haller left behind him after his departure from the rooms he once occupied. These writings express the malaise and despair of a conflicted man. Haller's texts are striking in giving direct voice to what Paul Ricoeur calls the *pathétique* of misery, namely, the painful self-awareness of a soul that in its ontological constitution is marked by a rupture or fault, a disproportion between natural desires and spiritual desires.[3] How so?

On one hand, the Steppenwolf howls about how unbearable the ostensibly good, normal, and tolerable days have become, for they lack all intensity of extreme pleasure or pain; they contain no inbreaking of power and meaning. 'A wild longing for strong emotions and sensations seethes in me, a rage against this toneless, flat, normal and sterile life.' On the other hand, the Steppenwolf moans when he recalls moments in the past, perhaps while listening to music, or reading a poet or philosopher, when a trace of the divine did in fact break in, and of a sudden a door was opened to the other world. 'I sped through heaven and saw God at work. I suffered holy pains. I dropped all my defenses and was afraid of nothing in the world.' Yet such moments of transcendence pass, leaving one adrift in 'this besotted humdrum age of spiritual blindness, with its architecture, its business, its politics, its men!' The Steppenwolf's misery becomes a sickness unto death, as Haller discovers that the spiritual drive to transcend the world of natural desires itself produces an unreconcilable conflict. The spirit strives to surpass its own natural desires and thereby ironically refuses to accept its own otherness; it desires to negate itself. Death appears to be the only cure for this sickness of the soul.

3 Paul Ricoeur, *Fallible Man*, revised translation by Charles A. Kelbley, introduction by Walter J. Lowe (New York: Fordham University Press, 1986), pp. 6–15.

The practical instruction rendered through the voice of the Tormented Steppenwolf is the following. *When, for whatever reason, you become an alien in your own world, a living contradiction between nature and spirit: Express yourself! Howl at the moon, if you must, but somehow write or otherwise record the true story of your anguish.* The reader gleans this message just from the fact that Haller has expressed his spiritual sickness in the form of autobiographical writing. Haller's work of active imagination opens him to what is to come.

III

The third part of the novel is narrated in the voice of an Immortal, a visitor from the dead to the living – or perhaps more accurately, a visitor from the undead to the spiritually dying. Haller, in despair, pursues a mysterious man in the marketplace bearing a sign that says *'Magic Theatre. Entrance not for everybody. For madmen only!'* At an auspicious moment, this man presents a text called 'Treatise on the Steppenwolf' to Harry Haller. The treatise is a theoretical study of the nature of the Steppenwolf written by an Immortal.[4]

The treatise begins with a reflective diagnosis of Haller's illness. According to the Immortal, this Steppenwolf believes himself to have two natures – a wolfish one and a human one – and neither will accept the other. In craving freedom, independence for himself, Haller has condemned himself to a suffocating solitude. He is suicidal in that he is both overwhelmed by his own sense of guilt and finds his only solace and support in the thought of taking his own life, even as he struggles against the act. The Immortal also analyses the Steppenwolf's ambiguous relationship to the bourgeois world. In his own

4 In many German editions of *Der Steppenwolf*, to emphasize that the treatise has an altogether different origin than the records of Harry Haller, the treatise is presented as a book within a book, with separate covers, a different kind of paper, and printed in Fraktur rather than in Roman type.

view, Haller stands altogether outside the world of family, duty, and social ambition, but in fact he is deeply attached to the world of order and comfort. So he lives as a lone wolf among sheep, as dependent on them as they are dependent on the Steppenwolves in their midst. The bourgeoisie lack any vital force of their own, and so out of envy they torment the living Steppenwolves; just as out of need for their spiritual vitality, they pay homage to the dead and crucified Steppenwolves.

The Immortal finally prescribes a cure for Haller's disease. According to the immortal narrator, there are two paths beyond the sickness unto death. The first is the path of *humour*, and it is appropriate to artists and intellectuals who despise the bourgeois world and yet lack the courage or strength to sever their attachment to it. Humour makes it possible both to recognize and to accept the difference between nature and spirit; to make the opposites meet by embracing their difference.[5] But humour is recommended only for those who are cut short of the second path beyond the sickness unto death – the highest goal of *tragic wisdom*, for which many are called but only a few are chosen. To achieve the tragic, one must agree to break free of all attachments to the bourgeois world, to wear the crown of thorns that is the reward of those happy few, and to attain the unconditioned goal by accepting one's defeat by the conditions of finitude.

Seeing that the Steppenwolf shows some indications of possessing a higher nature, though not one likely to attain the tragic wisdom born of suffering (for Harry Haller presently even lacks humour), and understanding his profound need of self-knowledge, the immortal narrator proposes an experiment with Harry Haller. Haller will have to discover a few things for himself, we learn, including that his attachment to the image of his twofold being – both wolf and man – nature and spirit, is a crude simplification. In truth, as a unifying unity

5 Humour makes it possible 'to live in the world as though it were not the world, to respect the law and yet to stand above it, to have possessions as though "one possessed nothing", to renounce as though it were no renunciation' (*Steppenwolf*, p. 55).

between nature and spirit, his being is a manifold unity, a mirror of the infinite whole, a magic theatre of eternal possibility.

The voice of the Immortal narrator speaks from the pinnacle of Hesse's cosmology, for his comprehension of the Steppenwolf's plight presupposes the attainment of both cosmic humour and tragic wisdom. The Immortal's mode of being combines and transcends the opposing principles of nature and spirit into the manifold unity of which he or she speaks. The voice of the Immortal speaks this lesson to the Steppenwolves of the world: *After you express your anguish, reflect in a principled way on that primary language of testimony. Strive to attain the standpoint from which to grasp all reality in a vision of its systematic unity in difference. Through reflection you will prepare yourself to enter the magic theatre of your own immortal soul.*

IV

The narrative voice of the fourth and final part of *Steppenwolf* is once again Harry Haller, but a Harry Haller who is changed by the experiment of the Immortals and is led into the Magic Theatre. Consequently, I call this voice the Transformed Steppenwolf. The sequence of events runs like this: Haller is led by the Immortals into the Black Eagle pub where he meets Hermine, the voluptuous agent of his transformation.

Who is Hermine? Literally speaking, she is a high-class prostitute, and therefore a fitting counterpart to the compromised Steppenwolf. But on a more miraculous level, she is his *anima*, the otherness of his own soul, a mirror sent to him by the Immortals. Through Hermine, Haller learns that his purported difference from the bourgeoisie is mostly a pretence, and he begins to overcome his mostly bourgeois inhibitions. Hermine teaches him not to retract but to expand his soul so as to appropriate his own sensible and emotional nature. She initiates him into the world of dancing, jazz, sensual love, and drugs. Most importantly, she teaches him not to take himself so seriously.

At the masked ball, Haller dances in ecstasy with Hermine in a mystical union of the two poles of his being. She leads him into the Magic Theatre, which literally speaking is an opium den, but magically speaking is the site of his initiation into the truth of his soul. In this dream world, Haller enters a series of four booths where he appropriates previously repressed and dismissed parts of the manifold unity that is his own soul. In the final booth, 'How One Kills for Love', Harry is put to a great test. Standing before a mirror in which the image of a beautiful wolf leers back at him, he solemnly states, 'I am only waiting. I am waiting for death.' But Haller's serious mood is interrupted by a surprise appearance of the Immortal Mozart who laughs at Haller's affectation, while the music from the last scene of *Don Giovanni* sounds from a radio or record player in the background. Haller falls into despondence and sleeps. He has failed the first round of the test. On regaining consciousness, he recalls that Hermine awaits him, and he longs for the final consummation of his symbolic wedding with her. Final union with her would represent the total acceptance of his own otherness, the unifying of the disparate elements of his Steppenwolf nature. But on opening the door to her room in feverish anticipation, Haller finds her locked in embrace with Pablo, the libertine, and in a fit of jealousy he seems to take a knife and kill her. Mozart's music once again is heard through a tinny radio. Mozart now summons Haller before the jury of the Immortals, where he is accused of confusing the apparitions of the Magic Theatre with so-called reality. The jury convicts Haller of taking himself too seriously by 'stabbing an imagined girl with an imagined knife'. His punishment is to endure laughter from the Immortals. His further penalty is to remain in the world and to learn how to laugh properly at the world and his place in it. Haller must learn to venerate the eternal spirit behind the illusory appearances of external reality, to appreciate what is essential and immortal in life without quarrelling with what is accidental and trivial in life. Haller has failed to pass the test, but in a crucial moment of tragic insight he accepts his failure and thereby gains the insight into the potential unity behind his divided being that the tormented Steppenwolf so sorely lacked. His final words are 'One day I would be a better hand at the game. One day I would learn how to laugh. Pablo was waiting for me, and Mozart too.'

The voice of the Transformed Steppenwolf represents a mode of being in which spirit no longer contends with nature but seeks a unity with it, and nature is no longer impervious to spirit but yields to it. Haller as the transformed Steppenwolf now understands and accepts the finitude of his being. He knows that Hermine is not other than himself, and that the obscene jazz musician Pablo is not other than the divine Mozart. This realization signals his appropriation of the truth that spirit and nature are ultimately not other than each other.

What is the lesson of the final voice? *Open yourself to experience the other, and in this opening experience the other as yourself and yourself as the other! Learn to laugh at yourself, and strive for the tragic wisdom that that is the prize of spiritual suffering.*

In conclusion, I want to reiterate my hypothesis. *Steppenwolf* is structurally composed in four different narrative voices to present both a theoretical reflection on five fundamental possibilities of being human and a practical instruction with each of four voices contributing a rule. Taken together the instruction reads:

- Observe yourself disinterestedly as you live and move in the world around you.
- Express the conflicts both within you and between yourself and the world.
- Reflect on the expressions of your tormented soul from the standpoint of received immortal wisdom.
- Open yourself to the other; experience the otherness of the other in yourself and yourself in the otherness of the other.

Finally, I want to return to the question of evaluating Hesse's contribution in this book. Who was right – the youthful admirers of Hesse or his cultured despisers? Is Hesse himself among the Immortals or is his novel a matter of second-rate thinking? My answer is that insofar as his own possibly adolescent prose enables words of immortal wisdom from the undead to be heard and understood by the spiritually dying, it still works for me as a tinny radio through which the most divine sounds may be heard.

Bibliography

Ziolkowski, Theodore. *The Novels of Hermann Hesse: A Study in Theme and Structure*. Princeton, NJ: Princeton UP, 1965.

—— (ed.). *Hesse: A Collection of Critical Essays*. Englewood Cliffs, NJ: Prentice-Hall, 1973.

Darren J. N. Middleton

Scratching the Barthian Itch: A Theological Reading of John Updike's *Roger's Version*

Karl Barth [...] who helped me believe. (Updike, 1989, 230)

The Gospel proclaims a God utterly distinct from humanity. (Barth, 1933, 28)

1. Introductory comments

In John Updike's 1997 'Remarks upon Receiving the Campion Medal', recently made availiable as part of the first book-length analysis of his religious vision, the Pulitzer Prize-winning author describes his novels as 'illustrations for texts' from the Danish Lutheran Søren Kierkegaard (1813–55) and the Swiss Calvinist Karl Barth (1886–1968) (Updike, 1999, 5). This remark is certainly true of Updike's *early* work. In *Rabbit, Run,* Updike's second novel, published in 1960, Harry 'Rabbit' Angstrom, whose surname recalls the German word for 'flow of anxiety', displays an unsatiated yearning for transcendence, an agitated yet heroic response to the mysterious motions of grace, and so appears to signify Updike's most imaginative construal of 'the Kierkegaardian Man'. Using Kierkegaard's model of the three basic stages on life's way, Updike portrays Rabbit Angstrom as a man who embodies the aesthetic form of existence. He lives on an existential frontier, trapped between his weaknesses and his conscience, and yet, as the novel unfolds, we find him loving and fighting his way into an unseen world, the divine vision getting nearer and nearer. Properly viewed, Updike, as a writer, is interested in how men and women become lonely and afraid without God, and this fascination stems from his reading of both Kierkegaard and Barth.

The Centaur, Updike's third novel, which won the 1964 National Book Award, carries an epigraph from Barth's *Dogmatics in Outline* (Barth, 1959, 59). Here Barth speaks of women and men caught in the strange territory between heaven and earth, powerless to escape from this 'betwixt and between' unless they are rescued by the redeeming love found in the Father–Son relationship revealed in Jesus Christ. Caldwell and Peter, the main characters in *The Centaur*, become anxious when, from different perspectives, they become increasingly aware of the *existential aporia* between heaven and earth. And yet, through numerous Christological allusions, Updike suggests that Caldwell, because of his own peculiar gestures of goodness, gladness, relinquishment, and praise, *hints* at the hope and promise represented by Jesus Christ, the supreme model of the relationship between Creator (heaven) and creature (earth).

Since the publication of *Rabbit, Run* and *The Centaur*, literary critics have worked long and hard to research and document a 'history of the question' of Kierkegaardian and Barthian influences on Updike's *early* work.[1] While their passion for reading and interpreting Updike has never diminished, these scholars have avoided theological

1 For example: Harold Bloom (ed.), *Modern Critical Views: John Updike* (New York: Chelsea House, 1987); Robert Detweiler, *John Updike*, revised edition (Boston: Twayne Publishers, 1984); David Galloway, *The Absurd Hero in American Fiction: Updike, Styron, Bellow, Sallinger*, second revised edition (Austin, Texas: University of Texas Press, 1981); Donald J. Greiner, *John Updike's Novels* (Athens, Ohio: Ohio UP, 1984); Alice and Kenneth Hamilton, *The Elements of John Updike* (Grand Rapids, MI: Eerdmans, 1970); Howard M. Harper, *Desperate Faith: A Study of Bellow, Salinger, Mailer, Baldwin, and Updike* (Chapel Hill, NC: University of North Carolina Press, 1967); George W. Hunt, *John Updike and Three Great Secret Things: Sex, Religion, and Art* (Grand Rapids, MI: Eerdmans, 1980); William R. Macnaughton, (ed.), *Critical Essays on John Updike* (Boston: G. K. Hall, 1982); Judie Newman, *John Updike* (New York: St Martin's Press, 1988); David Thornburn and Howard Eiland, (eds.), *John Updike: A Collection of Critical Essays* (Englewood Cliffs, NJ: Prentice Hall, 1979); and Suzanne Henning Uphaus, *John Updike* (New York: Frederick Ungar, 1980).

accounts of his *later* work, even though Updike's more recent writing is suffused with theological influences, choosing instead to explore his treatment of politics, of sexuality, of midlife progress, of patriarchy, and his images of contemporary America. Therefore, I propose to use this essay to investigate and analyse how *Barthian theology* appears in *Roger's Version*, one of Updike's *later* novels published in 1986, concentrating on how Updike appears to use the character of Dr Roger Lambert, a New England seminary professor, pointedly to pronounce the demerits of natural theology, represented in this novel by Dale Kohler, the obsessed computer scientist who attempts to prove God's existence with the aid of physics, mathematics, and his desktop monitor. Before I investigate how Barth's ideas enliven *Roger's Version*, though, it seems appropriate to examine Updike's appreciation of Barth more closely.

2. John Updike on Karl Barth: some brief remarks

John Updike's 'great period' of reading Karl Barth was in 1960 and 1961, when he was in his late twenties, and at this time he encountered Barth through *The Word of God and the Word of Man*, a collection of Barth's sermons and speeches (Plath, 102–3). As a young man gripped by a sense of his own finitude, a feeling he called his 'existential terror', Updike found much to admire in Barth, especially his belief that *the Word of God is the dynamic and transformative event of God, speaking to us in Jesus Christ,* and this in spite of the fact that Barth was considered theologically unfashionable in an age marked (as it was then) by the so-called 'death of God' (Campbell, 301–2). In effect, reading Barth changed, perhaps even redeemed, Updike's life. A writer in the 26 April 1968 edition of *Time* magazine remarks:

> Though he was raised a Unitarian amid the Lutherans and Amish of southeastern Pennsylvania, Updike joined the more middle-road Congregationalist Church in 1959. Then, a year later, as he was writing *Rabbit,*

> *Run*, the awareness of time passing pressed so closely on him that he felt a constant 'sense of horror that beneath this skin of bright and exquisitely sculpted phenomena, death waits'. It was a full-dress religious crisis lasting several months, and Updike says now that he got through it only by clinging to the stern, neo-orthodox theology of Switzerland's Karl Barth. In Barth's uncompromising view, reason can prove only that the nonexistence of God is absurd; the positive assertion, that God does exist, can come only by means of revelation. (74)

In his 1969 autobiographical poem *Midpoint*, Updike celebrates Barth's life-changing wisdom: 'Praise *Barth*, who told how saving Faith can flow / From Terror's oscillating Yes and No' (Updike, 1969, 58). Addressing the literary critic Jeff H. Campbell in 1976, and looking back on his reading of Barth in the 1960s, Updike states:

> I think it was the frank supernaturalism and the particularity of his [Barth's] position, so unlike that of [Paul] Tillich and the entire group of liberal theologians – and you scratch most ministers, at least in the east, and you find a liberal – whose view of these events is not so different from that of an agnostic. But Barth was with resounding definiteness and learning saying what I needed to hear, which was that it really *was* so, that there was something within us that would not die, and that we live by faith alone – more or less; he doesn't just say that, but what he does say joined with my Lutheran heritage and enabled me to go on. (Campbell, 301–2)

Today, numerous years after his initial exposure to Barth, Updike continues to find the Swiss thinker 'bracing and interesting', a theologian he feels he can 'trust', and whose construal of 'God as the enormous Other […] the totally inscrutable Other' seems 'congenial' (Plath, 188, 249, 251). In Barth, Updike detects a powerful theological response to the emotional maladies that affect every thoughtful human being, including Updike himself, and which works at cross-purposes with what Updike, following Barth, takes to be the glib and facile nature of much modern theological thought. Furthermore, 'what lingers of Barth, still ringing in the air of churches and seminaries', is Barth's unmistakable 'tone of fearlessness, his bold, encyclopedic, and hearty exposition of the word of God as over against the word of Man' (Updike, 1983, 836). Writing in *More Matter*, his most recent collection of essays and criticism, Updike notes that Barth (and

Kierkegaard, whom Barth admired) 'gave me a philosophy to live and labor by, and in that way changed my life' (Updike, 1999, 843).

While I want to be careful enough to say that Updike is not a simple versifier of Barth's theology, it is fairly accurate to claim that Barthian ideas are scattered throughout Updike's fifty-three books.[2] And 'like meandering through the muddle of Mme Blavatsky to appreciate Yeats or confronting the opacity of Swedenborg to appreciate Blake', writes the critic George W. Hunt, 'a plunge into the cold water of Barth's theology freshens and deepen's one's understanding of Updike' (Hunt, 35). It is to Barth's theology that I now turn.

Two key points in Barth's theology are his belief that God is Wholly Other, sovereign over humankind and nature, and that liberal theology, which posits a natural point-of-contact between God and God's creation, is a humanly-constructed religious endeavour, and therefore a form of unbelief, and in the next section I pay special attention to both ideas. After noting these two concepts, placing them in the context of Barth's own life, I move to discuss *Roger's Version*, and here *my inclination is to understand Updike's 1986 novel as a literary meditation on Barth's God-centred view of reality*, which claims that to comprehend God, we must begin with God, not humankind, and with God's self-disclosure in Jesus Christ as made manifest in Holy Scripture and attested to by the power of the Holy Spirit. Having facilitated a specific 'conversation' between Barth and Updike, I close my essay with a short reflection on the seemingly complementary yet antagonistic relationship between theology and literature in general.

2 For Updike's most succinct appreciation of Barth's theology of the Word of God, the novels notwithstanding, see his essays 'Faith in Search of Understanding', *Assorted Prose* (New York: A. Knopf, 1965), 273–82; and 'To the Tram Halt Together', *New Yorker*, 12 March 1979, 135–44.

3. Karl Barth's theology in outline

The son of a professor of New Testament and Patristics, Karl Barth was born on 10 May 1886 at Basel in Switzerland. After early schooling in Berne, he studied in a number of German universities, reading theology with popular liberal theologians Adolf von Harnack and Wilhelm Hermann, and under their tutelage he expressed some initial enthusiasm for Friedrich Schleiermacher's attempt to use experience as a foundation for constructing a theological world view. Upon graduation, Barth spent several years serving the Church as a minister. After an early stint as a junior pastor in Geneva, he was appointed pastor of the village of Safonwil. In a way, his ministerial experience shaped the theological outlook which was to come.

In August 1914, on the eve of the First World War, many of Barth's former professors attached their names to a controversial document supporting Kaiser Wilhelm II's pre-war policies. Reacting with utter disbelief, Barth chastized his former theological professors for their *Kulturprotestantismus* ('cultural Protestantism') – their apparently glib and dangerous identification of the Gospel with secular culture, particularly German nationalism. From this 'black day' onwards, Barth cultivated a deep distrust of late-nineteenth- and early-twentieth-century theology. Profoundly suspicious of cultural Protestantism's presumptuous attempt to establish the Kingdom of God on earth, in the form of an ethical commonwealth of citizens, Barth pressed on to assert God's sovereignty, human fallibility, and Jesus Christ's saving function as Electing God and Elected Man.

While these three theological ideas first appeared in Barth's famous 1922 commentary on the Apostle Paul's epistle to the Romans *Der Römerbrief*, Barth initially shared his convictions with his students at Göttingen in 1921, and then later, in 1925 and 1930, with his students at Münster and Bonn respectively.[3] Confident of his

3 The first edition of Barth's commentary on Paul's epistle was dated 1919, although it originally appeared at Christmas 1918. This first edition was never translated into English, because Barth rewrote his commentary in 1920–1, and

beliefs in God's transcendence, in human sinfulness and in Christ's uniqueness, Barth embarked upon the task of writing the multivolume *Church Dogmatics*, an activity he initiated in 1932 and which he continued, off and on, until his death on Monday, 9 December 1968 at the age of eighty-two.[4]

Following the Apostle Paul's emphasis on the universality of sin in Romans 1–3, Barth taught that all men and women are personally unworthy to approach a holy and transcendent God. In Barth's eyes, we are beset by selfishness; as a result, there is no avenue from humanity to God. Furthermore, in keeping with the letter and spirit of the Reformers, Barth believed we are not able not to sin; thus, we are unable to earn our salvation. Even religion, though it comes disguised as a friend, is nonetheless an adversary, because religion – broadly conceived – seeks to ignore the devastating truth that there is no route from humankind to God. Resolute in his belief that 'the Gospel is not a religious message to inform humanity of their divinity, or to tell them how they may become divine', Barth opined that 'the Gospel proclaims a God utterly distinct from humanity'. Consequently, God issues a profound and unambiguous *No* to the idea that we are able to justify ourselves through religion, through human effort (Romans 3–4). And yet, the divine *No* exists for one simple reason – it paves the way for the risen Christ, God's emphatic *Yes* (Barth, 1933, 28–9).[5]

it is this second edition that caused the bombshell among *English-speaking* theologians.

4 Barth's *Church Dogmatics* is in four volumes, each addressing a specific topic within Christian theology: the doctrine of the Word of God (I); the doctrine of God (II); the doctrine of creation (III); and, finally, the doctrine of reconciliation (IV), the longest of all four volumes. Barth did not live to write the fifth and final volume on eschatology.

5 Karl Barth, *Epistle to the Romans*, 28–9, *passim*. Barth's emphasis on God's 'Yes' and 'No' to humanity displays traces of Kierkegaardian influences, because Kierkegaard himself spoke of the 'infinite qualitative difference' between divine holiness and human sinfulness, a distinction dissolved by the Absolute Paradox (the Incarnation) only. See Søren Kierkegaard, *Philosophical Fragments / Johannes Climacus*, two books in one volume, edited and translated by Howard V. Hong and Edna H. Long, with an Introduction and Notes (Princeton, New Jersey: Princeton UP, 1985), 37–48.

Armed with this scripturally-based 'dialectical theology', Barth believed that all our attempts to comprehend God – philosophical argumentation, moral virtue, spiritual discipline, and scientific proof – are tainted by our natural propensity towards selfishness and ego. As a way for humans to approach God, then, and from God's own perspective, religion is a form of idolatry and unbelief. To quote Barth:

> From the standpoint of revelation religion is clearly seen to be a human attempt to anticipate what God in His revelation wills to do and does do. It is the attempted replacement of the divine work by a human manufacture. The divine reality offered and manifested to us in revelation is replaced by a concept of God arbitrarily and wilfully evolved by man [...] 'Arbitrarily and wilfully' means here by his own means, by his own human insight and constructiveness and energy. (Barth, *Dogmatics*, I/2, 302)

There is no avenue from ourselves to God; however, there is a route, the only route, from God to us, and this is God's objective and personal self-disclosure in the person and work of Jesus Christ. In short, God's *No* to human religiosity is God's *Yes* to divine revelation:

> two worlds meet and go apart, two planes intersect, the one known and the other unknown. The known plane is God's creation, fallen out of its union with him, and therefore the world of the 'flesh' needing redemption, the world of human beings, and of time, and of things – our world. This known plane is intersected by another plane that is unknown – the world of the Father, of the Primal Creation, and of the final Redemption. The relation between us and God, between this world and his world, presses for recognition, but the line of intersection is not self-evident. The point on the line of intersection at which the relation becomes observable and observed is Jesus, Jesus of Nazareth, the historical Jesus. (Barth, 1933, 29)

Like a tangent touching a circle, Jesus Christ is the point at which God's world connects with our world, and the Bible bears testimony to this single moment when eternity converged with time: Jesus Christ as the Electing God and the Elected man (Barth, *Dogmatics,* II/2, 103, 161–7).

According to Barth, one cannot speak of God by speaking of humanity in a loud voice. Rather, God makes Godself known through the person and work of Jesus Christ, witnessed to in Scripture, attested to by the Holy Spirit, and proclaimed through the agencies of the Church. In a way, then, the mistake of nineteenth- and early twentieth-century liberal theology of the type promulgated by Schleiermacher, von Harnack, and Herrmann, is that it successfully – but disastrously – locates theology in the human condition, in religious experience, and not in God as Wholly Other.[6] Putting a God-centred view of reality in place of a human-centred view, Barth proclaimed the sovereignty of God, and while theologians such as Dietrich Bonhoeffer and Reinhold Niebuhr expressed serious reservations about Barth's work, Barth nonetheless held a strong belief in the authoritative Word of God. And he championed its 'event-like' qualities – its ability to challenge us, to overtake us, and to address us in our wretchedness.[7]

A sense of the Word of God as 'event' permeates Updike's vast and impressive literary output, and nowhere is this made more clear than in *Roger's Version*, which uses the narrative form to deliver a stern rebuttal to any theologians seeking to orient themselves on anything other than the Gospel. As Dr Roger Lambert, the protagonist in Updike's novel, would say, one must subject oneself to the Word of God as it is witnessed to in Scripture and proclaimed by the Church and then, only then, begin one's theologizing, one's human and therefore fallible reflection on the gift that is God's self-disclosure in

6 Barth's disavowal of liberal theology's 'turn to the subject' is scattered throughout his work. Schleiermacher is the father of modern liberal theology, and a sustained criticism of Schleiermacher forms the basis of Barth's 1968 essay 'Concluding Unscientific Postscript on Schleiermacher', which is available in Green, (ed.), *Karl Barth: Theologian of Freedom*, 66–90.

7 Dietrich Bonhoeffer objected to what he called Barth's *offenbarungs-positivismus*, the so-called 'positivism of revelation'. Allegedly Barth's crime was to assume the *givenness* of divine self-disclosure; according to Bonhoeffer, Barth's 'like it or lump it' understanding of Christian doctrine appears to be an offensive attempt to avoid the demands of rigorous theological investigation. See Dietrich Bonhoeffer, *Letters and Papers from Prison* (London: Collins, 1953), 95. For a recent and careful study of the relationship between Bonhoeffer and Barth, see Andreas Pangritz's *Karl Barth in the Theology of Dietrich Bonhoeffer* (Grand Rapids, MI: Eerdmans, 2000). For Reinhold Niebuhr's critique see 'We Are Men and Not God (On the Theology of Karl Barth)', in E. J. Tinsley, (ed.), *Modern Theology: Selections from Twentieth-Century Theologians* (London: Epworth Press, 1979), 263–70.

Jesus Christ. It is to Roger's version of Barth's neo-orthodox theology that I now turn.

4. Protesting theologies of false reasonableness

A professor of Christian theology in a 'liberal seminary dominated by gracefully lapsed Unitarians and Quakers', Dr Roger Lambert becomes frustrated when he encounters Dale Kohler, a young computer specialist who believes he possesses scientific proof of God's existence (Updike, 1986, 27). The intellectual and emotional contest between these two characters consitutes the best part of Updike's novel, and it serves as an introit into Updike's own understanding of the frequently uneasy alliance between faith and reason.

Charmed by the advances of contemporary science, and equipped with the software necessary to track developments in relativity physics as well as evolutionary biology, Dale Kohler advocates his own form of the famous argument from design. 'Everywhere you look,' he instructs Lambert, 'there are these terrifically finely adjusted constants that have to be just what they are, or there wouldn't be a world we could recognize, and there's no intrinsic reason for those constants to be what they are except to say *God made them that way*' (14). The basic structure of the universe is the handiwork of a benevolent God, or so Kohler maintains, and a consideration of the mathematics of cosmic, planetary and biological developments supports, or is about to support, as Kohler avers, that everything is as it is because God willed that it should be precisely so. Against Kohler, Roger Lambert asserts that all knowledge of God is grounded in God's self-disclosure, Jesus of Nazareth, and he holds that because we are, as sinful human beings, incapable of comprehending God, we have no right to think we can *demonstrate* divine existence. Upholding theological mystery, then, Lambert objects to what he calls 'the sheer, sickening extravagance' of all attempts to show the 'intelligibility' of Christian theism; in his view, God cannot be adequately grasped or expounded on the basis of reason (17). Even Thomas Aquinas, the most famous exponent of the design or cosmological argument, did not, Lambert claims, 'postulate a God who could be hauled kicking and screaming out from some laboratory closet, over behind the blackboard' (21). Undeterred by Lambert's disquiet, which is cloaked in Lambert's own special brand of fideism, Kohler asks the seminary administration to fund his plan to prove God's existence.[8] Not surprisingly, Lambert mounts a vigorous protest against Kohler's grant application:

> I said to him, 'The church preaches, I believe, and the Old Testament describes, a God Who acts, Who *comes to us*, in Revelation and Redemption, and not one Who set the universe going and then hid. The God we care about in this divinity school is the living God, Who moves toward us out of His will and love, and Who laughs at all the towers of Babel we build to him.' I heard myself echoing Barth and the exact quotation flickered at the edge of my mind. (22)

As part of his polemic against Dale Kohler, Roger Lambert draws on the work of Karl Barth, who reacted against liberal theology, with its confidence in our ability to comprehend God, after the horrors of the First World War. As I noted earlier, Barth introduced 'dialectical theology', a way of thinking that emphasizes the *infinite qualitative difference* between God and the world. One of the most trenchant critics of any desire to domesticate transcendence, to trivialize God by thinking of the divine with the aid of human categories, Barth believed we are unable to grasp God unaided:

> God's Word is no longer grace, and grace itself is no longer grace, if we ascribe to man a predisposition towards this Word, a possibility of knowledge regarding it that is intrinsically and independently native to him [...] The fact of God's Word does not receive its dignity and validity in any respect or even to the slightest degree from a presupposition that we bring to it. Its truth for us, like its truth in itself, is grounded absolutely in itself [...] Men can know the Word of God because and insofar as God wills that they know it, because and insofar as there is a revelation of God's will in his Word in which the impotence of disobedience is set aside. (Barth, *Dogmatics*, I/1, 194, 196)

8 Fideism is a way of thinking theologically that refuses to accept the need for, or possibility of, analysis or evaluation from sources outside the circle of faith (*fiducia*: a Latin term, literally meaning 'faith' or 'trust').

Roger Lambert strongly criticizes Dale Kohler's project. 'For myself,' he confesses, 'I find your whole idea aesthetically and ethically repulsive. Aesthetically because it describes a God Who lets Himself be intellectually trapped, and ethically because it eliminates faith from religion, it takes away our freedom to believe or doubt' (Updike, 1986, 24). To understand God, we must start with God, not with humankind's so-called 'proofs' and 'demonstrations', and with that disclosure in Jesus Christ as revealed in the Bible, the witness to the Word of God. A key point in Lambert's Barthian theology comes when he takes his nightly walk home from the Divinity School:

> Really, what a preposterous glib hope, his [Dale's] of extracting God from the statistics of high-energy physics and Big Bang cosmology. Whenever theology touches science, it gets burned [...] Barth had been right: *totaliter aliter*. Only by placing God totally on the other side of the humanly understandable can any final safety for Him be secured. The positivism of revelation, as Bonhoeffer described it. (31–2)

Following Barth, Lambert maintains that God's emphatic *No* to all so-called proofs of God – including proof by an intricate decoding of numbers that appear on a computer screen – leads to God's insistent *Yes* to God's self-disclosure to humankind in Jesus Christ. The *No* and *Yes* form the main thrust of Lambert's dialectical theology.

While some might say that Dale Kohler's collection of statistical information is humanly interesting, especially when seemingly disparate data merge together to create a brief and flickering image, tantalizingly suggestive of Christ himself, Roger Lambert nonetheless rejects Kohler's belief that 'God is showing through' his PC (10, 248–9). For Roger, Dale's project displays classic signs of *hubris*, intellectual pride. And in the words of the critic Stephen H. Webb, 'Roger is disdainful of Dale's theological Pelagianism, the idea that we can win salvation by relying on what we know about God' (Webb, 155). Finally, when Kohler meets with the seminary grant committee and tries to state his case, Lambert listens and turns to his colleagues, invoking Barth's name (and theological project) for the last time:

> 'You know me, Jesse [a scholar, a colleague of Lambert's],' I said, with a false jocosity that barked in my own ears. 'A Barthian all the way. Barth, I fear,

> would have regarded Dale's project as the most futile and insolent sort of natural theology. I also agree with Jere [a second scholar]: apologetics mustn't leave ground where it's somewhat safe for ground where religion has been made to look ridiculous time and time again. Like Rebecca [another colleague], I don't think God should be reduced purely to human subjectivity; but His objectivity must be of a totally other sort than that of these physical equations [...] A God Who is a mere fact will just sit there on the table with all the other facts: we can take Him or leave Him. The way it is, we are always in motion *toward* the God Who flees, the *Deus absconditus*; He by his apparent absence is always with us. What is being proposed here for us to finance, I'm sorry, just strikes me as a kind of obscene cosmological prying that has little to do with religion as I understand it. As Barth himself says somewhere – I can't give you the exact reference offhand – "What manner of God is He Who has to be proved?"' (Updike, 1986, 218–19)

It appears that Dale Kohler secures the last laugh in Updike's novel because Roger Lambert's pointed use of Barth, 'the scornful enemy of religious humanists and accomodators', finds little favour with the committee, whose members swing towards Dale, granting him the money he needs to pursue his project (219). Roger's version of Barth's theology is left to stand alone, then, a somewhat strange and solitary witness to what the critic Jeff H. Campbell calls 'the futility and failure of all attempts to reduce God to the level of phenomena analyzable by the human mind' (Campbell, 260).

I want to say that *Roger's Version* is an ingenious narrativization of Barthian dialectical theology or neo-orthodoxy. It is so much more than this, of course, for Updike's polymorphic novel opens out to multiple readings, not one, but, if the American-Jewish writer Cynthia Ozick is correct when she says that Updike's work displays the irresistible 'itch of theology', it must surely be a theology of the Barthian variety (Ozick, 122).[9] By consolidating the references to

9 Another 'reading' might focus on the theme of sexuality in *Roger's Version*, for example. While I have not addressed the issue of sexual licentiousness that runs throughout the novel, I am persuaded that Updike uses Roger and Esther's [Roger's embattled wife] adultery to underscore the fallen nature of our world, and this strategy enables Updike to further accentuate the infinite qualitative difference between divine holiness and human sinfulness, a classic theme in Kierkegaard's and Barth's way of looking at the world.

Barth in *Roger's Version*, I think we are able to appreciate Updike's feel for the Swiss Reformer's God-centred view of reality.

While there is but one small reference that Barth makes to Updike in his own writing, confined as it is to a letter in which he asks for a copy of Updike's review of Barth's *Anselm: Fides Quaerens Intellectum*, the purpose of the next and final section is to facilitate a conversation between Barth and Updike by asking what happens when one compares these two thinkers in the form of their writing (Barth, 1981, 139). More specifically, having noted some similarities between Updike and Barth, I conclude by wondering whether there are any differences that exist between them, and whether these specific differences serve to reveal some of the important, general contrasts between literature and theology?

5. Reading Barth, reading Updike: what's the difference?

Writing in his *Self-Consciousness: Memoirs*, John Updike describes God as 'a dark sphere enclosing the pinpoint of our selves, an adamant bubble enclosing us, protecting us, enabling us to let go, to ride the waves of what is' (Updike, 1989, 229). Such a description is as avowedly Barthian as it is richly metaphoric. Following Karl Barth, Updike believes God's superabundant grace grants us the free gift of faith – a gift which enables us to overcome the sin that isolates us from God. And such faith, furthermore, is an antidote to the poison of anxiety, the precondition of all sin. Now, any reader who examines Updike through Barthian spectacles is at some point forced to raise a particular question: How does Barth, a theologian committed to notions of orthodoxy, logical exactitude, conceptual clarity, and systematic thought, 'converse' with Updike, a creative writer resolved to exploring ideas through literary forms? Part of the answer to this question, or so it seems to me, is that each writer reminds the other, metaphorically speaking, of the *kind* of text that they are writing. Committed to Christian theology's propositionally-oriented tradition, Barth is tied to constructing arguments that proceed step by step in an elaborate network of mutual and logical implication. By contrast, Updike, eager to align himself with the narrative quality of existence, is committed to thinking theologically in prose or poetic form.

In my view, the above observation prompts the hypercritical question of whether literature and theology have anything to say to one another. In the past the relationship between these disciplines has been open to considerable misunderstanding. This is largely due to the attitude, prevalent in both fields, that the two disciplines are mutually exclusive. Theologians readily acknowledge the theological content of much creative writing, but where clashes have occurred with literary critics, then the former frequently retreat into an arcane defensiveness which accuses their critics of misreading the Christian tradition. Similarly, literary theorists happily acknowledge the importance of theological discourse in fictional narrative, but have been eager to 'deconstruct' theological language by challenging the theologian's tendency to systematize his thought. To my mind, this apparent hostility need not be present. It may prove far more fruitful to speak of the fundamental difference between the novelist and the theologian as existing in a difference of emphases. The modes of discourse and reception are different in both cases. For both the novelist and the theologian 'tell a story', to express my point in a very general way, and yet seem tuned into 'experience' differently, and so invariably write different kinds of narrative though these are never far apart from one another.

Commenting on the fundamentally sensual nature of much creative writing, Robert Olen Butler, the Pulitzer Prize-winning author of *A Good Scent from a Strange Mountain*, supports my basic thesis:

> Fiction is unlike other forms of discourse because it does not deal in the matters of the intellect: analysis, abstraction, summary, and generalization, the modes of discourse for nonfiction writing. The focus of the reader is not on an intellectual grasp of the abstractions of what the character is saying, but rather the moment-to-moment revelation of the personality of the speaker. And that is a sensual matter. There is a certain response to the ideas or the analysis, but there is a deeper response to the revelation of personality. That's the only legitimate way in which abstraction finds a place in fiction. The primary experience is moment-to-moment through the senses. (Butler, 59)

Convinced that theologians, with their hard penchant for logical coherence and conceptual plausibility, often struggle to 'thrum' to a novel or a piece of short fiction, Butler outlines one of the basic contrasts between literature and theology, a contrariety that I think may profitably be applied to the work of Updike and Barth, a difference, that is, in modes of discourse and reception:

> Those theologians [...] are comfortable expressing their vision in abstract terms. They work in terms that can be communicated as laws or principles to be grasped by the intellect and applied to life. The artist is terribly uncomfortable with that kind of expression. The artist goes back to the chaos and the ways in which it is experienced, moment to moment through our senses, and pulls out bits and pieces of that sensual experience. The artist gives it back to the reader reshaped. In selecting and shaping and structuring the sensual experience, the artist creates a vision of order for the reader, not as an idea, not as a set of principles, but as a kind of harmonic that's set up in the reader, a resonance. You thrum to a work of art; you don't understand it intellectually. (60)

In conclusion, even though I started this essay with Updike's own observation that his work is an attempt to 'illustrate' ideas first mentioned by Barth (and others), I am persuaded that important differences between these two thinkers, as between the two disciplines that they represent, exist, and so I would maintain that it is unwise to view the novelist as *merely* an illustrator of orthodox belief, even neo-orthodox belief. Neither Dante, Milton nor Updike can be read as providing, say, a poetic overcoat for the structured activities of, say, Anselm, Calvin or Barth. The relationship between literature and theology does not seem to me to be of this order. So, how may we view the alliance between these two disciplines? Very generally, I think that despite the fact that practitioners associated with both disciplines sometimes appear to write narratives which are mutually offensive to each other, some novelists and some theologians are engaging in essentially the same conversational task – contradicting one another, correcting one another, and reminding one another of the kind of narrative they are both writing.

Bibliography

Barth, Karl. *Church Dogmatics* I/1, translated by G. W. Bromiley, 1936; I/2, translated by G. T. Thomson and Harold Knight, 1933; II/2, translated by G. W. Bromiley et al., 1967. Edinburgh: T&T Clark.

—— *Dogmatics in Outline*. New York: Harper & Row, 1959.

—— *The Epistle to the Romans*, translated by W. Montgomery. Oxford: OUP, 1933.

—— *Letters, 1961–1968*, edited by Jürgen Frangmeier and Hinriech Stoevesandt, translated by Geoffery W. Bromiley. Grand Rapids, MI: Eerdmans, 1981.

—— *The Word of God and The Word of Man*, translated by Douglas Hartman. New York: Harper & Row, 1957.

Butler, Robert Olen. 'On Madness and Longing', in W. Dale Brown (ed.), *Of Faith and Fetia: Twelve American Writers Talk About Their Vision and Work*. Grand Rapids, MI: Eerdmans, 1997.

Campbell, Jeff H. *Updike's Novels: Thorns Spell a Word*. Wichita Falls, TX: Midwestern State UP, 1987.

Hunt, George W. *John Updike and Three Great Secret Things: Sex, Religion and Art*. Grand Rapids, MI: Eerdmans, 1980.

Ozick, Cynthia. *Art and Ardor*. New York: Knopf, 1983.

Plath, James, (ed.). *Conversations With John Updike*. Jackson, MS: Mississippi UP, 1994.

Updike, John. *Hugging the Shore: Essays and Criticism*. New York: Knopf, 1983.

—— *Midpoint and Other Poems*. New York: Knopf, 1969.

—— *More Matter: Essays and Criticism*. New York: Knopf, 1999.

—— 'Remarks upon Receiving the Campian Medal', in James Yerkes, (ed.), *John Updike and Religion: The Sense of the Sacred and the Motions of Grace*. Grand Rapids, MI: Eerdmans, 1999.

—— *Roger's Version*. New York: Knopf, 1986.

Webb, Stephen H. 'Writing as a Reader of Karl Barth: What Kind of Religious Writer is John Updike Not?', in James Yerkes, (ed.), *John Updike and Religion: The Sense of the Sacred and the Motions of Grace*. Grand Rapids, MI: Eerdmans, 1999.

George Newlands

Theology, Culture and the Arts

Part One

This paper is concerned with interactions of faith and culture in a number of specific instances. It deals in fragments, and does not intend to demonstrate a grand pattern of fractal similarity beneath the fragments. Most of the fragments are multifaceted, and will be seen differently when examined from different angles. If this study has an ultimate coherence, as it is intended to have, it will be solely the coherence of the shape of the Christian Gospel, and this is experienced in worship and service through the centuries. In many of the instances, it will be the darker facets of the fragments which will point to the light.

When we look at the relation between Christianity and the arts, and especially literature, we see an interesting ambiguity in the role of such central images as incarnation, for example in inspiring great poetry and at the same time perhaps in reinforcing authoritarianism in the work of T. S. Eliot. Religion and power often go hand in hand, for better and sometimes for worse. Questions of ethics and of truth in corporate and individual life are constantly thrown up by these interdisciplinary explorations, and they require answers, however provisional they may inevitably be.

There are endless different sorts of connections between Christianity, theology and the humanities. Poets and novelists may often be influenced by religious practice and by doctrine, without ever reading formal theology. There are some who did read theology and were consciously influenced by it – Eliot again by Niebuhr and Barth, Auden by Niebuhr and Kierkegaard.

We must note that very different sorts of interactions occur in different cultures. 'Intercultural theology' very often suggests to us inter-religious comparisons across the major world religions and in different continents. But there are also numerous overlapping sub-cultures in European and American societies, and in predominantly Christian contexts. And there is continuous change. It is often said rightly that the Bible has an enormous influence on literature and the humanities. It may be, however, that this influence will be nothing like as great in the next century as it was in the past. It is true that the 'secular Christianity' which many expected in the 1960s to appear did not happen, and the last decades of the twentieth century brought a renewed interest in religion and spirituality in many parts of the world. Yet in Europe at least, church attendance continues to plummet. This distancing from the churches is bound to have an effect on the role of the Bible in society. The novels of the 1980s and 1990s in Europe and even in the United States rarely make Christian or biblical themes central.

Part Two

Religion is embedded in and is part of a complex and fragmented culture. It may be much more than this, a human response to a divine initiative. It is affected by the impact of contemporary cultural trends, at this time globalization on the one hand and fragmentation on the other. The development of modern mass media assists globalization. 'Cultural studies' in many university courses has in recent years involved the analysis of 'popular' culture, sometimes in conscious contrast to the 'elite' culture of the European academic tradition. Religion has its place in this revolution, alternately pursued and marginalized by television, and now by the Internet. There is not, and perhaps never has been, a single stream of universal culture even in Europe. Knowledge of the older academic tradition cannot be taken for granted in society, though here too there is the phenomenon of particularization, in which traditional academic guilds are sometimes able to carry on in comparatively insulated circumstances.

Christianity has had much influence on human civilization, and Christians have been involved in numerous professions. Theologians have of course available a distinctive relationship between personal belief and professional output. In the world of literature, and in the visual arts, there has often been a direct reflection of faith in relation to art. In the ancient world there were direct correlations between religion and such areas as law, medicine, science and politics. In some instances these direct relationships remain. The law of marriage in Britain is still much influenced by theological considerations. Discussion of medical ethics often includes a religious input. Politics is affected by Christian traditions, with good and bad effects.

We have stressed the need for theology and the churches to build effective bridges to culture, against the anti-modern trends of much contemporary theology and practice. But of course not all accommodation to culture is good. For Christians there can be a bridge only to link up with the basic human values at the centre of the Gospel – love, peace, justice, forgiveness and reconciliation. In-culturation which encourages and intensifies coercion, oppression, racial discrimination and the like is always wrong. As is often noted, churches which have practised apartheid have been perfect examples of inculturation of Christianity with evil. Studies of the social policies of the churches often show an alliance with reaction and uncharitable prejudice. It will be important to identify ambiguities in all such correlations. But the abuse does not take away the proper use.

There will always be the need for Christian communities to gather around centres of worship. Beyond this, they may seek to act as catalysts, as the salt of the earth. Within such a framework the interaction of religion and culture, both at the margins and at the centres of cultures, becomes highly significant. It is impossible to bring support to the margins without adequate support from the centres. It is within this sort of vision that the present essay is developed. It is this transformative function, not necessarily turning everyone into traditional Christians, but offering a deeply Christian envelope for thought and praxis, which seems to offer a vital role for Christian theology and community in the future.

When we consider the influence of religion and Christianity in particular on culture and the arts we think of the influence of religion on science and medicine in the ancient world, of Christianity on painting and prose up to the early twentieth century. Yet it would be hard to think of a decisive influence of Christianity on the humanities after (say) 1950. By this time the lawyers, historians and the like are doing what the natural scientists did earlier – producing their research without any reference to religion, though they may have private religious beliefs. Scientists may be Christian but they will not attempt to produce a Christian Science, nor lawyers a Christian Law. (Exceptions may be found in some traditional Catholic lawyers – for example, John Finnis.) Even within the theological disciplines themselves there is a huge stress on academic study within a professional guild, without any reference to personal conviction or community engagement. After Auden and Eliot it is hard to think of major poets who struggle with religion in their work . As for novelists, Walker Percy is sometimes seen as the last major Catholic novelist. Writers like Susan Howatch or P. D. James can scarcely qualify as major literary figures. At least in the European and North American traditions, there appears to be a decline in that kind of professional engagement with religion. There are sociologists and philosophers of religion, but they are themselves part of the academic religious guild. Where writers do engage with religion, it is often in a highly critical style – John Updike, Tom Wolfe, Umberto Eco. In Europe decline in engagement with religion seems to follow the sharp decline in church attendance. Habermas is here more typical than Gadamer. Only perhaps in music is there still a notable existential interest in religion. In black culture there is perhaps still more engagement than in white culture – one thinks of Alice Walker and James Baldwin. But even here the secularizing influence in the liberal arts is strong.

Yet there is this paradox, that there is still a strong interest in religion in society. In North America churchgoing remains buoyant. Private religious feeling remains. Theologians still write theology, often engaging with culture. Where then is the cultural outlet for other Christians and people of religious conviction?

If religion is to be a force for good in society – and the major religions are all committed to such a vision – then it is important that not only theologians should be involved in trying to build bridges between religion and culture. What is needed is a reciprocity of dialogue and of effort to promote common human values. Part of the task of a Centre for Theology, Literature and the Arts is to examine such attempts at communicative action from all sides of the dialogue, and to encourage them to develop further in a diversity of fruitful directions. Different dimensions of culture will be involved in different ways, and it is not for any one of the dialogue partners to prescribe a methodology. At the same time, it may be possible to learn from analysis of praxis which kinds of dialogue are most likely to be fruitful, and which pitfalls are to be avoided.

There has been much concern in the liberation and emancipatory theologies for a close correlation of theology to praxis, in the name of love and justice. It will be interesting to see what response these movements produce in the wider culture beyond theological discussion. They come out of and encourage Christian communities engaged in struggle, and they invite to political and social action. Yet it will be strange if there is no corresponding engagement from other disciplines, for example from the arts. This may take the form of postmodern pluriformity, such as feminist theology in dialogue with Women's studies and Black theology with Black studies. It has to be noted here that poetry and drama are themselves not as central to contemporary culture as they were in previous centuries. The impact of the mass media has created its own culture, and though this has not neglected traditional art forms, it has led to a kind of marginalization of them. Football, television chat shows and soaps, pop music and even the national lottery arguably have a much greater role in the shaping of culture. But it would be important in all areas of the humanities to provoke constructive engagement with theological themes on a much wider front, as Kierkegaard had an impact on Auden or Anglican incarnational theology on Eliot. In Charles Taylor and Cornel West we see, largely implicitly, the beginnings of dialogue with late twentieth-century theology.

Seeking to balance an audit on the relation of Christianity to culture at the end of the twentieth century, we may say that the fairly homogenous pervasion of culture in Christendom is definitely over. We need not look back with nostalgia, for this culture raised as many questions as it solved for Christian faith – there was always the danger of unconscious and uncritical assimiliation to inappropriate types of inculturation. Christian response over centuries to many central social issues, in such areas as crime and punishment, has on the whole been anything but exemplary. And in any case, Christendom was perhaps never as absolute as we occasionally imagine. It is a very long time since daily life (say) in Britain was run along the lines of a theocracy. Even in the time of Shakespeare, where poetry and drama are often saturated in religious imagery, Elizabethan business and diplomacy ran with religion de facto as often in the background as in the foreground of events. Religion, then and now, had much to do with how people spent their leisure moments, the quality time in which they might take stock and plan new strategies.

On the positive side of the account, the radical pluriformity of contemporary culture may provide new opportunities for imaginative initiatives at different levels in specific sectors of particular cultures, in fragments which may have an impact beyond their immediate location, as cultures overlap and interact in often unpredictable ways. These fragments may involve concentrated areas of Christian transformative symbolism, as often envisaged in Christian evangelical postmodernism.

But this is not the only possible alternative. They may also involve concrete and local instances of intercultural dialogue between faith and society of a more liberal sort. Such dialogue may involve the setting out of unapologetic Christian perspectives. To describe such engagement I am inclined to prefer the word 'liberality', to indicate a critical development beyond classical liberalism. Liberality involves generosity, centred on the generosity of God in Jesus Christ, but unconditionally open to mutuality and reciprocity. To identify and pursue such avenues will involve both reference to areas of significant interaction in the present, and comparison with modes of interaction in the past. In this way we may hope to arrive at guidelines for more effective intercultural dialogue between Christianity and society in the future. In seeking to examine response to the presence of God within the fragments of multicultural pluralism we shall be pursuing further the discipline of theological intercultural hermeneutics.

Striking the appropriate balance between faith and culture is rarely easy. In the twentieth century we see this clearly in the world of Eliot and Auden. Both were highly critical of an easy accommodation with a tired liberalism. Faith provided a challenge and a place to stand *contra mundum*. Such an anti-modern stance can easily fall over into a defensive self-justification. But an effective interaction of faith and culture remains central to human flourishing.

Part Three

Characteristic of ninetieth-century, of the Modern age in Theology, not least in the work of its founding father F. D. E. Schleiermacher, was interdisciplinary study of theology and the humanities. The great theologians of the twentieth century were usually resolutely anti-modern, and their legacy in various editions of neo-orthodoxy has been an isolation of theology within its own bounds, accompanied by a marginalization of the study of theology and the arts. The greatest of the anti-moderns, Barth and von Balthasar, were not unmindful of the humanities – Barth and Mozart, von Balthasar and aesthetics. Yet the trend has been to isolationism, or at best to an ideological makeover of the realm of culture, as for example in some of the writings of Leslie Newbigin. On the credit side, there have been some modern systematic theologians who have not followed this trend – I think of David Tracy. But on the whole, the field has been relegated to marginality. This has had profound consequences, both for the important task of dialogue between the disciplines, but also for the understanding of the nature of theological inquiry itself. Beyond this, it is highly instructive to reflect on the kinds of theological and ecclesiastical perspectives which have influenced the works of poets and playwrights, musicians, lawyers and scientists. Eliot and Auden, Mozart, Blackstone and Einstein – all were much affected by particular religious doctrines – and not always, we may think, for the better.

The ways in which Christian theology has interacted with different layers of culture and different disciplines are endless. Encounters which seem particularly fruitful to one Christian perspective will seem unfruitful to others. Most of the examples of interaction which I shall examine have had, in my view, both advantages and disadvantages for the development of engagement.

This is inevitably the case. I shall attempt to suggest ways in which the advantages may be maximized and the disadvantages minimized. In this dialogue, as I see it, none of the partners has a privileged point of view. The theologian, the poet, the historian, the political scientist – all have contributions to make, and none has *the* master narrative which can encompass all else in an authoritative way. This is something which the theologians, at least, have been slow to learn. But the phenomenon also occurs in other forms of academic positivism, for example in the natural sciences.

Martha Nussbaum's *Cultivating Humanity* (1997) is a magnificent example of a series of studies which point to values at the heart of what is is to be humane, through comparison and contrast, in particular cultural contexts. It seems to me that Christian theology has an important contribution to that continuing task, and it is a contribution which is in serious need of articulation in the present. Nussbaum has been heavily criticized for her construal of human rights. It is arguable that she could have learned more from her critics and thereby strengthened her case. But what she has achieved has been deeply impressive.

Part Four

Christianity and literature, as is often pointed out, were closely intertwined until comparatively recently. Christianity has had an enormous influence on human thought over the last two thousand years, and this impact will continue to reverberate, in different forms, some more, some less muted, through the next centuries. I shall look at their interaction in two particular writers, coming from similar background and writing at the same time, Auden and Eliot. In doing so I shall try not to lose sight of the theme of Christianity and human rights, which may provide a kind of litmus test of the nature of some of this interaction.

Among the diverse group of theologians who constituted the Christian realists in the late 1930s and the 1940s were two notable literary figures, Eliot and Auden. Eliot was a friend of the Scots theologian John Baillie; he met him in Britain and America, and attended the Moot, that significant gathering of intellectual figures in England throughout the war years. Along with Barth, Temple and others, Eliot contributed an essay to the collection on *Revelation*, edited by John Baillie and Hugh Martin in 1936. Though the quality of the piece was not universally appreciated – Baillie's close friend J. Y. Campbell, who read the proofs, thought it pretentious nonsense – nevertheless it was a serious attempt by a leading poet at a piece of theologian's theology. Baillie had left New York before Auden arrived in 1939. Yet Auden was soon to become a close friend of Reinhold Niebuhr – a friendship eloquently testified to in their correspondence, published by Ursula Niebuhr in 1991. It would be hard to see any direct influence of Baillie on Eliot, though they were to keep in touch right up to Baillie's death in 1960. But Auden was to be deeply influenced by Niebuhr. In this essay I want to look at least two dimensions of the relationship of Christianity and literature through the study of Eliot and Auden. I want first of all to see how much it matters for a literary figure what sort of theology, and what sort of churchmanship, he or she embraces. Then I want to examine the possible influence of the poet on the relationship between faith and culture.

I shall begin, however, from Eliot's essay on revelation, the first in the collection. Eliot begins with the observation that 'it is because I am not a theologian that I have been asked to contribute.' He goes on to say that

> I am concerned with the general differences between those who maintain a doctrine of revelation and those who reject all revelation [...] I take for granted that Christian revelation is the only full revelation; and that the fullness of Christian revelation consists in the essential fact of the incarnation, in relation to which all Christian revelation is to be understood. The division between those who accept, and those who deny, Christian revelation I take to be the most profound division between human beings.

He then considers the nature of secularism, attacking some contemporary writers – Gerald Heard, Herbert Read, Bertrand Russell,

André Gide, Middleton Murry, at some length Irving Babbitt, and Aldous Huxley. The tone is fairly dismissive:

> M. Gide's conversion to Communism has been presented as something involving an heroic sacrifice of his creative gifts. It might, of course, be retorted that possibly the exhaustion of M. Gide's creative gifts had something to do with his conversion to Communism. There is a psychological mysticism which is not Christian.

He is more positive in his assessment of D. H. Lawrence: 'He was aware that religion is not, and can never survive as, simply a code of morals.'

Today we suffer from 'a strong and positive misdirection of the will'. He turns to 'the principal characteristics of philosophies without revelation': instability, recurrence of ancient philosophies, the tendency to evoke an opposite, and the production of immediate results. 'The whole tendency of education (in the widest sense – the forces playing on the common mind in the forms of "enlightenment") has been for a very long time to form minds more adapted to secularism, less and less equipped to apprehend the doctrine of revelation and its consequences.' He concludes that

> any apologetic which presents the Christian faith as a preferable alternative to secular philosophy, which fights secularism on its own ground, is making a concession which is a preparation for defeat [...] Should we not first try to apprehend the meaning of Christianity as a whole, leading the mind to contemplate first the great gulf between the Christian mind and the secular habits of thought and feeling into which, so far as we fail to watch and pray, we all tend to fall?

He concludes:

> What a discursive reading of secularism over a number of years, leads me to believe, however, is that the religious sentiment – which can only be completely satisfied by the complete message of revelation – is simply suffering from a condition of repression painful for those in whom it is repressed, who yearn for the fulfilment of belief, though too ashamed of that yearning to allow it to come to consciousness.

Here we see Eliot in his conservative theological mode, sharing that disillusionment with liberal enlightenment, partly as a reaction to the apparent sterility of humanist philosophy, partly in response to the clouds of communism and fascism which were all too visible on the European horizon. In this reaction he was in good company, as the following essay in the book, by Karl Barth, demonstrates. Eliot's stress on the incarnation was to lead to some of his most profound poetry. He understands the difficulty of the 'psychological mysticism' which will neither let the world be the world nor God be God. This was by no means Eliot at his best. It was too dismissive of issues which need to be tackled, too undialectical to explore the constructive tensions in the culture. It was not perhaps uncharacteristic of Eliot, who could be callous, supercilious, devout and humble by turns, and could often be extraordinarily insensitive to the human condition.

Both Eliot and Auden were, of course, immensely complex people, and the complexities led to tensions which in their poetry and prose were often immensely creative. As with all of us, there were other occasions when the tensions were more destructive, or even when the tension was lost and they were, (and we are) reduced to unreconstructed prejudice. Both Eliot and Auden had a firmly realist sense of the difference between the sacred and the profane. Neither was partial to 'psychological mysticism', though both were aware of the mystery of divine transcendence. Both were at one level prisoners of the theological and ecclesial perspectives which they inherited, largely by serendipitous means, as we all acquire knowledge which we have not studied in professional courses. Both turned these accidents to their craft with profound effect, and could produce work, at least on occasion, of the very highest order.

In his *Christianity and Modern European Literature* (1997) Daniel Murphy has an interesting chapter on Eliot entitled 'Darkness of God: T. S. Eliot's Quest for Faith'. Eliot moved from Humanism to Religion, as he explained in an essay 'Religion without Humanism', in 1931. Eliot was especially fascinated by the *via negativa*, notably in the mysticism of St John of the Cross, but also in Buddhism. These come together particularly, Murphy notes, in 'The Fire Sermon' in *The Waste Land*. While much of Eliot's early poetry had been critical of religion, *The Waste Land* explores the tension between belief and unbelief. Murphy quotes a letter of Eliot to Charles Williams: 'We are, I know not how, double in ourselves, so that what we believe we disbelieve, and we cannot rid ourselves of what we condemn.' The way of darkness is ultimately the way of light, as in 'East Coker'. These religious themes are brought to a final resolution in 'Little Gidding'. In faith, and in life beyond death, the symbol of suffering and the symbol of God's love are one:

> And all shall be well and
> All manner of thing shall be well
> When the tongues of flame are in-folded
> Into the crowned knot of fire
> And the fire and the rose are one.

Perhaps in some ways mirroring the mood of foreboding of the 1930s in Europe, there is more of the cross than of the incarnation or even the resurrection in much of Eliot's work. This gives it its power, but also a certain limitation. With Barth and Niebuhr, and also with Auden, Eliot drinks deep from the Augustinian tradition. To affirm the Gospel as good news, as transformative within the created order, without either trivializing suffering or romanticizing the world, remains a difficult task. Bonhoeffer was to struggle towards this in his *Letters and Papers From Prison*. Auden was aware of the dilemma, but perhaps too steeped in Kierkegaard to be able to address it effectively.

The debate about the extent if any to which Auden's powers declined in his later years has probably much to be said on both sides. He did somehow lose focus on the larger canvas in concentrating on occasional pieces. His theological reflection never issued in the kind of archetypal religious poetry which his middle period promised. But he did consciously seek to develop an appreciation of private and individual space, as a kind of protest against against the collectivization which he saw everywhere at work in modern society.

Eliot, despite an exceedingly turbulent private life with his two mistresses, always succeeded in remaining a respectable icon of religious establishment, high-minded and high-church. In Auden there is an almost Kierkegaardian paradox between appearance and reality. He almost appeared to cultivate a reputation for dissolute character, alcoholism, promiscuity, lack of discipline. Yet for most of his life he worked immensely hard for regular hours.

Norman Cary has noted that Auden, like Eliot, draws a clear line between the sacred and the secular, at least in theory. Auden asserts that 'To a Christian, unfortunately, both art and science are secular activities, that is to say, small beer.' The artistic imagination is purely natural, and is liable to be moved by 'certain objects, beings, and events, to a feeling of sacred awe'. This smacks of pantheism. To the Christian, on the other hand, the truly sacred is not that which naturally arouses awe in the human imagination.

The Incarnation, the coming of Christ in the form of a Servant who cannot be recognized by the eye of flesh and blood, but only by the eye of faith, puts an end to all claims of the imagination to be the faculty which decides what is truly sacred and what is profane. A pagan God can appear on earth in disguise but, so long as he wears his disguise, no man is expected to recognize him, nor can. But Christ appears looking just like any other man, yet claims that he is the Way, the Truth and the Life, and that no man can come to the Father except through him. 'The contradiction between the profane appearance and the sacred assertion is impassible to the imagination' (Auden, 456–7).

Murphy comments that 'The writings of Niebuhr, together with those of Williams and Kierkegaard, were largely responsible for shaping the Christian vision that dominated Auden's poetry from 1940 till his death in 1977' (Murphy, 323). Murphy mentions especially Niebuhr's *An Interpretation of Christian Ethics* (1935), *Christianity and Power Politics* (1940), and *The Nature and Destiny of Man* (1943). From Kierkegaard Auden derived a conception of the ethical as a fulfilment of the radical freedom of individual consciousness, and the act of moral decision as a leap from the aesthetic to the ethical.

He sees truth as the product of a dialectical tension: 'The one infallible symptom of greatness is the gift of double-focus […] We, being divided, remembering, evolving beings, composed of a number of selves, each with its false conception of self-interest, sin in most that we do' (Murphy, 344).

Following Kierkegaard, Auden stresses the inevitability of suffering, but this produces a resolution:

> It is where we are wounded that is when He speaks
> Our creaturely cry, concluding his children
> In their mad unbelief to have mercy on them all
> As they wait unawares for His world to come. (*The Enchafèd Flood*)

Faith alone is what is required. 'Our redemption is no longer a question of pursuit but of surrender to Him who is always and everywhere present. Therefore at every moment we pray that, following him, we may depart from our anxiety unto his peace.' He adds: 'The course of history is predictable in the degree to which all men love themselves, and spontaneous in the degree to which each man loves God and through him his neighbour.' Hope is founded on the cross and resurrection.

Part Five

When theologians, or even people in other disciplines, talk about culture, their conversation is often distressingly general or even banal. When they produce grand schemes for an integrated understanding of culture, they are prone to excesses of romanticism or even, say it not too loudly, of fascism. If we have learned one thing about culture in recent decades, it may be awareness of the infinite variety, subdivision and overlap of cultures. Yet there have been individuals who have had interesting things to say about culture in general, and about culture in relation to theology and to faith. One of these was Ludwig Wittgenstein. I turn here in the first instance to his collection of papers entitled *Culture and Value* (1980).

Wittgenstein fits rather conveniently into my study here because he belongs to the same period as the Baillies, Eliot and Auden, a time when the spectre of fascism was growing over Europe, when Romanticism became suspect and liberal thought appeared to call for correctives. Wittgenstein, too, was looking for a realist perspective, in this case in philosophy. Like Auden he read Augustine and Kierkegaard, and was conscious of the power of suffering and evil. Like

Auden he developed an Augustinian introspective conscience which could be a burden, increased by the influence of the psychology of Otto Weininger. We may sometimes be tempted to think that theology matters only to theologians and perhaps the clergy, and has little influence beyond these circles. In Eliot, Auden and Wittgenstein we can see how the appropriation of a particular theological perspective can have deep implications for their work, positive and negative.

Culture and Value is really in large measure a collection of aphorisms, some of which most of us will probably agree with, and some of which we may well disagree with. When he says that 'My ideal is a certain coolness. A temple providing a setting for the passions without meddling with them', most of us may find this at least interesting (Wittgenstein, 2e, 1929). When he says the following, we may think him strangely prejudiced: 'If it is true that Mahler's music is worthless, as I believe to be the case, then the question is what I think he ought to have done with his talent. For quite obviously it took a very rare set of talents to produce this bad music' (67e, 1948).

I want to list here a number of his aphorisms on culture and on theology in this volume.

> I once said, perhaps rightly: The earlier culture will become a heap of rubble and finally a heap of ashes, but spirits will hover over the ashes. (3e, 1930)

> What would it feel not to have heard of Christ?
> Should we feel left alone in the dark?
> Do we escape such a feeling simply in the way a child escapes it when he knows there is someone in the room with him? (13e, 1931)

Wittgenstein was always aware of the value of tradition, not as a blanket which stifles fresh thought, but as a legacy which spurs to renewed effort. This tradition for him included Christ. It was on the one hand the Kierkegaardian Christ, present in living life and not in dogmatic formulas, Christ in the dialectic between faith and doubt as lived. On the other hand, it was the cantus firmus of the Catholic tradition as an underlying reality:

Within Christianity it's as though God says to men: Don't act a tragedy, that's to say, don't enact heaven and hell on earth. Heaven and hell are my affair.

Christianity is not a doctrine, not, I mean, a theory about what has happened and will happen to the human soul, but a description of something that actually takes place in human life. For consciousness of sin' is a real event. And so are despair and salvation through faith. (28e, 1937)

The spring which flows gently and limpidly in the Gospels seems to have froth on it in St Paul's Epistles. Or that is how it seems to me. (30e, 1937)

Christianity is not based on a historical truth; rather, it offers us a [historical] narrative and says: now believe! (32e, 1937)

Perhaps we can say: only love can believe the resurrection. Or, it is love that believes the resurrection. We might say: redeeming love believes even in the resurrection: holds fast even to the resurrection. What combats doubt is, as it were, redemption [...] Holding fast to this must be holding fast to that belief. Then everything will be quite different, and it will be 'no wonder' that you can do things that you cannot do now. (33e, 1937)

The Christian religion is only for the man who needs infinite help, solely, that is, for the man who experiences infinite torment. (46e, 1944)

Religion is, as it were, the calm bottom of the sea at its deepest point, which remains calm however high the waves on the surface may be. (53e, 1946)

An honest religious thinker is like a tightrope walker. He almost looks as if he were walking on nothing but air. His support is the slenderest imaginable. And yet it really is possible to walk on it. (73e, 1948)

If Christianity is the truth then all the philosophy which is written about it is false. (83e, 1949)

The words you utter or what you think as you utter them are not what matters, so much as the difference they make at various points in your life [...] A theology which insists on the use of certain particular words and phrases, and outlaws others, does not make anything clearer (Karl Barth). It gesticulates with words, one may say, because it wants to say something and does not know how to express it. Practice gives the words their sense. (85e, 1950)

Life can educate one to a belief in God. And experiences too are what bring this about: but I don't mean visions and other forms of sense experience which

> show us the 'existence of this being', but for example sufferings of various sorts. (86e, 1950)

What are we to make of these examples of reflection on theology and faith within a particular cultural setting? Wittgenstein is a fascinating example. He combined what are often the most acute observations with a life of very damaged, often tragic intensity, immensely vulnerable and immensely dominating by turns. It should be noted that we cannot always be sure that in these aphorisms Wittgenstein is speaking of his own positions. When he speaks about an honest practitioner of religion being like a tightrope walker he may see himself sometimes as inside this position, sometimes outside it, sometimes torn between the two. His *obiter dicta* on religion were so varied as to provide evidence for opposing views of his attitudes to religion. This may well reflect his tortured attitude to many things. Much of what he has to say is immensely acute, and some of it is nonsense. We must take him as we find him and be grateful for what is illuminating. Given the problems with which he struggled, not least the eccentric but lasting influence of Otto Weininger, it is remarkable that he was able to produce as much as he did.

In his article in the *Wittgenstein Centenary Essays* (1991) Renford Bambrough starts out from a sentence in *On Certainty*: 'Where two principles really do meet which cannot be reconciled with each other, then each man declares the other a fool and a heretic.' He quotes Auden: 'W. H. Auden's understanding of heresy, besides associating it with public conflict, also hints that part of the purpose of orthodoxy is to bolster the individual's shaky faith: "Dogmatic theology is designed to exclude heresy rather than to define orthodoxy".' Bambrough argues, citing Wittgenstein on forms of life, that there are some continuities in the human which mean that opposing views have at least some common links:

> My conclusion is that there are *no* conflicts of principle so profound that there is nothing left for the parties to do except to cry out against folly and heresy. I am not saying that folly and heresy do not occur. I am not even saying that it is never suitable to cry out against them, only that there are always other and better ways of dealing even with the most intractable of conflicts.

This would seem to me to fit well with Wittgenstein's view of faith as a tightrope walk, a constructive tension between opposing but related values, and with the emphasis which he shares with Auden on the need for a dialectical vision, a double focus.

Wittgenstein, like Eliot and Auden, was interested in a realist understanding of faith which stressed the practical and the incarnational. Like Niebuhr and his circle of Christian realists, they were suspicious of making the wrong connections between the sacred and the secular. They looked to Augustine and to Kierkegaard, to a dialectic between faith and doubt, sin and salvation. But there the resemblance ended. For Wittgenstein and his friends, O'Drury, Rhees and the others, religion is essentially a private realm, though it may issue in public acts of devotion. This reflected the somewhat fragile private circle of acquaintance in which Wittgenstein moved. The connections between religion and philosophy are indirect. For Eliot and Auden there is a dialectical relationship between faith and literary activity. It is connected with the understanding of the self. Poets are not preachers, and to confuse the two would be disaster. For Niebuhr and his circle there is a more direct, though still dialectical relationship between religion and the public square. Theology has a clear responsibility to be active in the realm of civic society.

The Augustinian, Kierkegaardian tradition has disadvantages – in its pessimism, its dualism between the soul and the body, its introspection – and these are all mirrored in the writers we have just been considering. There were also advantages, in a profound questioning of romantic optimism and any kind of superficiality in culture, coupled with a rigorous search for self-awareness. In each of the writers we see a struggle for balance. In Wittgenstein this is the tightrope between Catholic piety and Scandinavian angst. It was after all in Norway that he was to spend months of agonizing on his own. In Eliot and Auden there is an affirmation of this world, though not without scathing critique of its failures, along with affirmation of traditional faith in the Gospel. Both Eliot and Auden are concerned to question the public square, though Auden is also determined to protest for the importance of private space in the face of increasing globalization.

Conclusion: human praxis and theological partnership

The relation between society, theology and the arts is a relationship of partnership. Christian theology is based on the divine love of God in Jesus Christ. Often its face has been of singularly loveless religion, but the abuse does not take away the proper use. Generosity even as an eschatological concept may have a considerable impact on the present. Theology as partnership should benefit from as well as contribute to the dialogue which is essential to human flourishing, and to the new creation which is God's purpose for all his creatures. Liberation theology, it has sometimes been noted, has tended in recent years to lose some of its impetus. This is partly because it has often been ignored or subverted by conservative forces in the churches. But it may also be because the narrow base of oppression which is its great and enduring strength is also limited. Emancipatory theology needs to gain the confidence to participate in the widest human dialogue, reminding the human of the humane, in the name of God. In doing so it should be able to gain new imagination and impetus, at a conceptual and also at a practical level. The crucified Christ at the centre of faith is also the risen Christ, the source of transformation, renewal and new horizons. This is not always possible in a situation of oppression. But the Christian hope is of the overcoming of evil by good.

A theology of humane praxis may seek to reimagine the basic contours of Christian doctrine, seeking to reflect a trace of the divine love in a contemporary way through its reshaping. To set this out in detail is always a major task, but to imagine some pointers should not be impossible.

Human language is inadequate to give us anything like a technical description of God. Yet there is the phenomenon of faith, which considers that in building up a cumulative case for belief in God it is responding to a source of meaning and loving purpose in the universe. Out of fragments of data, experience and interpretation, faith has developed as a community tradition, a tradition with many gaps and disjunctions, in Christianity and in the major world religions.

God is neither the patriarchal figure of the Hebrew Bible, nor the kyriarchal figure of Christian tradition, nor the mirror-image opposite of these. God includes relationship in Godself. The imagery of Incarnation and Trinity, through the Spirit of the crucified and risen Christ, reflects the concretion of this relationship. God cares about his creatures, and is the source of all generosity. God cares as humans care, as mothers, father, relatives and friends care. None of these images is privileged or excluded. But his care is perfect.

As a caring God, God thinks of his creatures' welfare and acts on their behalf. God is constantly active in creation, though not always able to act directly. God rejoices when they rejoice and suffers when they suffer. God is unable to prevent premature or tragic human death, but he brings eschatological salvation to all creation. God is concerned for the welfare of human society, as well as for non-human creatures and the cosmic environment. Divine love instantiates mutuality, reciprocity and inclusiveness. It creates forgiveness and reconciliation and the mending of brokenness. It includes justice and peace. Each of these spheres calls for infinite effort and infinite patience.

Divine love restores the damaged and injured to new creation by solidarity and unconditional identification. That is the spontaneity of grace, which is at once the great asset and the great judgement upon the community of those who believe. God's action leads towards a goal of new creation, of participation in the perfect relationship of the divine society. Because this is a society of love, peace and justice, it is the signal of direction to which all our social life is invited to move.

Bibliography

Auden, W. H. *The Dyer's Hand and Other Essays*. London: Faber & Faber, 1963.

—— *The Enchafèd Flood or the Romantic Iconography of the Sea*. London: Faber & Faber, 1985.

Baillie, J. and H. Martin (eds.). *Revelation*. New York: Macmillan, 1936.

Banbrough, J. R. and A. P. Griffiths (eds.). *Wittgenstein Centenary Essays*. Cambridge: CUP, 1991.

Murphy, Daniel. *Christianity and Modern European Literature*. Dublin: Four Courts Press, 1997.

Nussbaum, Martha. *Cultivating Humanity*. Cambridge, MA: Harvard UP, 1997.

Wittgenstein, Ludwig. *Culture and Value*. Chicago: University of Chicago Press, 1980.

CHRISTOPHER BURDON

Christian Worship in The Third Millennium: Homage or Celebration?

Bearing in mind the usual fate of those who are tempted to pontificate about the future, it would be wise at the start to say what this essay is not about. When I write of Christian worship, that does not include personal prayer, nor does it entail examination of existing liturgical texts or sketches for new ones; and when I speak of the third millennium, that may in practice not lead much beyond the year 2020. I shall not be so foolhardy as to predict what will happen in the corporate liturgy of the Churches, and I shall try to avoid dictating what I think should happen. Rather, I shall be speculating as to what might happen in the light of cultural and theological developments at the end of the second Christian millennium. Given the pace of technological change, given the collapse of political coherence and the world's exploding pluralism, it will be hard to avoid the question whether anything that could still be called 'Christian worship' will survive to the year 2020, let alone 2999. I shall, however, be giving a fairly upbeat answer to that rather absurd question – indeed, people who have discussed with me some of the ideas that follow have accused me of being over-optimistic (as well as over-traditional and over-radical).[1] I shall be restricting the range further by focusing on Europe rather than on the entire Church or world, since for all its diversity the cultural and ecclesial factors at work in Europe do seem to be substantially different from those in, say, Africa or America.

1 I am very grateful for insights from audiences who have responded to talks treating some of these themes at the University of Essex, Liverpool Hope University College, The College of the Resurrection, Mirfield, The Partnership for Theological Education, Manchester, Chelmsford Cathedral Theological Society and The Endeavour pub, Springfield.

The end of homage?

I propose to analyse the slippery concept and diverse activities called 'worship' under the two polarized heads of homage and celebration. Although the second of these terms has often been applied to Christian liturgy, it is the first that has generally had the symbolic prominence. Homage, the political act of obeisance towards a greater and more powerful being, is deeply rooted in the ritual and rhetoric of earthly synagogues, churches and temples. For Christians, it is also the reflection of the heavenly court casting their crowns before the throne. The Apocalypse of John depicts the homage of angels, 'living creatures', elders and martyrs as the fulfilment of creaturely existence. Thus John's four living creatures have innumerable eyes but fix them solely on the throne, not on the neighbour or the world; the angels and the 24 elders fall on their faces; the Christian martyrs (who alone are worthy) wait passively for the unleashing of action from the throne; and when this action occurs it is one which destroys heaven and earth so that there remains only the new city, centred on the throne and filled with perpetual worship. The former world is divided and judged on the basis of political worship – of God or of the beast – and true worship involves not only submission to absolute power but also delight in vengeance.[2] 'Mainstream' Christian theology has been wary of investing too much in the narrative and visions emanating from Patmos. Nevertheless, in liturgical performance and in popular religion, little such reticence has been shown. As D. H. Lawrence

2 Cf. Rev. 4; 7:11–12; 11:15–18; 16:5–7; 21:1–2; 22:3. For an analysis of the Apocalypse's presentation of worship, see Christopher Burdon, 'The Pathology of Worship: John's Heavenly Court and *The Four Zoas*', in Brent Plate (ed.), *The Apocalyptic Imagination: Aesthetics and Ethics at the End of the World* (Glasgow: Trinity St Mungo Press, 1999), pp. 10–25. See further Stephen Moore, 'The Beatific Vision as a Posing Exhibition: Revelation's Hypermasculine Deity', *JSNT* 60, pp. 27–55; Tina Pippin, *Death and Desire: the Rhetoric of Gender in the Apocalypse of John* (Louisville: Westminster / John Knox Press, 1992). For more benign readings, see Richard Bauckham, *The Theology of the Book of Revelation* (Cambridge: CUP, 1993); C. Rowland and M. Corner, *Liberating Exegesis* (London: SPCK, 1990), pp. 131–55.

noted a hundred years ago in the grimy chapels of the Midlands and seventy years ago in his polemical commentary Apocalypse, John's brilliant 'book of thwarted power-worship' is the one that has called the tune in Christian history (Lawrence, 86). And the stark unveiling of heavenly praise and action that the Apocalypse constitutes may do the unintended service of unveiling a pathology of worship that operates wherever men and women bow down before a greater being.

I am not saying that all the elements that normally constitute Jewish or Christian 'worship' – principally celebration, repentance, listening and desire – are pathological or illusory. But what is often presented as the sine qua non of worship is what Rudolf Otto's classic study called 'the emotion of a creature, abased and overwhelmed by its own nothingness in contrast to that which is supreme above all creatures'. To be genuinely holy, according to such a criterion, the *numen* must be not only *fascinans* but also *tremendum*, that is, awe-inspiring and terrifying. Evelyn Underhill's definition of Christian worship is only a little less absolute: it is 'the total adoring response of man to the one Eternal God self-revealed in time' (Underhill, 61). Researches more recent than Otto's and Underhill's are less sanguine about the place of power and homage in religion. René Girard, for instance, who posits a primitive crisis of 'mimetic rivalry' leading to the religious development of the 'scapegoat mechanism' as a way of restoring peace, suggests that 'the sacred' remains inseparable from human violence. However, according to Girard, the Christian gospels unmask this pathological relationship and reveal the way to its redemption. For him, the overcoming of violence and the way to peace are found by Jesus' praxis of forgiveness rather than by the Church's worship of the Transcendent Other. So his rhetorical and passionate conclusion to a lengthy consideration of the gospels in *The Scapegoat* reads:

> In future, all violence will reveal what Christ's Passion revealed, the foolish genesis of bloodstained idols and the false gods of religion, politics and ideologies. The murderers remain convinced of the worthiness of their sacrifices. They, too, know not what they do and we must forgive them. The time has come for us to forgive one another. If we wait any longer there will not be time enough. (Girard, 212)

Peter Berger meanwhile approaches the origin and persistence of religion as a sociologist rather than an anthropologist. He is less confident than Girard about some originating crisis and more sanguine about the benefits of traditional religion, having conducted an eloquent argument for taking seriously the categories of 'transcendence' and 'the supernatural'. But Berger argued over thirty years ago that religious protection and legitimation by worshipful submission frequently originate in masochism and form a powerful agency of alienation and false consciousness. 'The objectivated expressions of the human become dark symbols of the divine. And this alienation is powerful over men precisely because it shelters them from the terror of anomy' (Berger, cf. 55–8, 73–6, 90).

Now both Girard and Berger are Christians, though with considerable scepticism about the way in which the Christian Church has developed. Their approaches through the human sciences to what have traditionally been the preserve of theologians and liturgists have uncovered a shakiness in two elements on which Christian worship has almost always relied. The first of these elements is the political notion of *homage*, or service to a greater Being. As early as the Revelation of John, and certainly from the time of Constantine, we can see the presentation of God as the magnification of or replacement of the Roman Emperor: it is well known how customs of the imperial court like incense, vestments, sun-symbolism and gestures of obeisance were transferred to the worship of the Christian God, and while the Reformers of the 16th and 17th centuries, trimmed much of this only the most radical of them questioned or abolished the verbal homage paid to the Almighty God. The second element is the metaphysical notion of the *real presence* of that Being, whether apprehended through sacramental or mystical or pentecostal experience.

Now both those elements are largely bypassed by what is called postmodern culture, with its avoidance of absolutes and ultimate Reality, its sifting through many screens rather than one Book, its horizontal rather than vertical correspondences. Despite the rhetoric of politicians, Europe has moved from monarchy through republic towards the pluralist dissolution of the State, and power structures are open to inspection and criticism: where does this leave the liturgical language of almost all Christian traditions addressing their 'Almighty God' and 'Heavenly King'?

To some extent (a remarkably small extent so far, in my judgement) liturgical reformers have responded to this by being more restrained over the use of monarchical and political symbolism. But this is a difficult exercise, since it relativizes the undoubtedly monarchical and often military language of the Bible (not least, as we have seen, in the depiction of heavenly worship in the Apocalypse, and again in the Psalms, which have been as central in Christian as in Jewish liturgy). A more common response at present seems to be to affirm the traditional absolutes more shrilly – this revelation, this text, this experience, this command is the direct address from the higher realm, here is the Presence. It is hard to deny the vigour of such affirmations, whether they emerge in pentecostal, in catholic or in evangelical guises. What I would question is how far the affirmations can be more than the language of a tribe seeking certainty and identity; how far they can be liberating beyond the confines of that sub-culture; and how far the object of their homage can avoid being stranded in the third millennium as a new Ozymandias, King of Kings.

One could say, of course, that if horizontal postmodern culture bypasses the dimension of worship, so much the worse for that culture: the Church's job is to be counter-cultural. To that I shall return. The immediate question, though, is what are the elements of tradition that are being affirmed and what are the elements of contemporary culture that are being resisted. The conservative reaction seems to purloin some modern technological spoils, musical fashions and styles of therapy in the service of the most absolutizing features of the tradition, asking worshippers to affirm what many people of faith cannot affirm. And the reason they cannot affirm it is not simply to do with cultural fashions or a kind of political liberalism or the sort of analysis of religion undertaken by scholars like Girard and Berger. No, the world of homage and of presence is more seriously and perhaps even permanently undermined by the more thoroughgoing scepticism arising from what is loosely called post-modern philosophy.

Much philosophy since Nietzsche has combined with technological and psychological developments to dissolve the confidence of

Plato, of the Enlightenment and of 'common sense' that language and image represent or refer to Reality. If 'reality' and even the experiencing subject are increasingly seen as a linguistic and therefore a human construct, what place is left for a 'real presence', whether out there or in here? If structure is inconstant, this involves not just the changing of liturgical forms or worshipping styles but the dissolution of any shape or direction to liturgical action. There is neither dialectical synthesis nor narrative closure, no Alpha or Omega, and the binary opposition of 'heaven' and 'earth' no longer has even metaphorical meaning. Suspicion of even the most apparently beneficent structures of power (Foucault) combines with the war on 'logocentricity' (Derrida) to undermine the metaphysical grounding of Reality and Presence which has been a presupposition of Christian worship.[3]

The logical outcome of this philosophical and cultural onslaught on the symbolic universe of homage and real presence would be to ditch the whole enterprise. The reference of liturgical language and gesture are dispersed, as are the very subjects and object of worship. The paying of homage has been unveiled as pathological or masochistic; even the melancholy, long, withdrawing roar that Matthew Arnold heard on Dover Beach has now become inaudible to people with any degree of self-consciousness or critical awareness. So if we still have a sense of gospel or Christian story let us forsake talk of any Transcendent Other, let alone any cult or sacrifice. These are irritating nostalgic remnants. The only kind of Christian worship which could survive such a reformation would be that of the Society of Friends.

The reason I do *not* take this line is that, examining myself and listening to others, I find that while the ultimate reference of religious language is indeed untraceable and the source of religious experience infinitely dispersed, nevertheless the *forms* of religion (ritual, sacraments, prayer and so on) are extremely persistent. With all the suspicion I can muster, I cannot reduce this persistence to the expression of nostalgia or masochism or alienation. I do not agree

3 For a sympathetic, attractive, but to my mind ultimately unconvincing response to this critique, see J. R. Middleton and B. J. Walsh, *Truth is Stranger than it Used to Be* (London: SPCK, 1995).

with traditional propositional or modern liberal theology in seeing religious language as having straightforward reference to metaphysical or experiential objects. Nor do I agree with Rudolf Otto and John of Patmos that abasement before the Supreme Being is the fulfilment of humanity. But dispensing with worship as homage, with God as Emperor, does not mean that nothing remains – far from it. There are huge tracts of what could broadly be called 'worship' which have nothing to do with homage but which have to varying degrees been suppressed by the politicization of liturgy. I am using *celebration* as a sort of conceptual focus for this terrain, examining it under five aspects.

Celebration as play

'Celebration' is a rather solemn-sounding Latin word, one which has a long history in the understanding of Christian liturgy. But its ordinary sense of playing, having fun, holding a party, should not be sublimated by priests or puritans. Play, which is almost universal in human societies and in many animal societies, can be spontaneous or ordered, highly creative or highly repetitive, yet it is something which in economic or scientific terms is completely pointless and useless. Despite this pointlessness, the child (or adult?) at play is likely to be completely absorbed in and completely serious about what she is doing.

Ronald Grimes has analysed different 'modes of ritual sensibility', most of which have certain social or religious or political objects such as healing or commemorating. But the mode he sees as in one sense 'the most relevant […] to liturgical rites' is that of celebration, which he defines as 'expressive play' or 'ritualized play'. Such rites, he says, 'are subjunctive, and their "as if" quality, like that of good fiction, must be at once convincing and specially framed'. Writing from a general, not a specifically theological or Christian stance, Grimes goes on to say that 'something is drastically wrong with an understanding of ritual which can only apprehend it in terms of work'

(Grimes, 42–9). To push his point a bit further, worship undertaken as a piece of work or service, with some worthy or unworthy ulterior motive – such as the deepening of spiritual awareness, the escaping of hell, a good harvest, evangelism, the forgiveness of sin – is not sufficiently single-minded or playful to qualify as celebration. So the steep decline of traditional protestant worship, which was low on ritual but high on seriousness and which inculcated understanding and moral purpose very effectively in the period of the Enlightenment and Industrial Revolution, need not be a matter for regret (cf. White, 96–9). The point of worship, the point of play, is that it is pointless. It is engaged in for sheer delight. It is the most immediate possible living of good news.

Interestingly, there was a strong case made against what might be called a 'liturgical work ethic' over seventy years ago by one of the pioneers of the Roman Catholic liturgical movement, Romano Guardini, who devoted a chapter of his influential little book *The Spirit of the Liturgy* to what he called 'the playfulness of the liturgy'. In it he stresses that, like the artist or the child at play, liturgical action is 'free from purpose'; he draws comparisons with the movement of the cherubim in Ezekiel's vision and with holy Wisdom (or the Son of God) 'playing' before the Father, while recognizing that 'grave and earnest people, who make the knowledge of truth their whole aim, see moral problems in everything, and seek for a definite purpose everywhere, tend to experience a peculiar difficulty where the liturgy is concerned' (Guardini, 85–106).[4] Indeed, this emphasis on actions (as opposed to words or texts) was characteristic of the liturgical movement of the middle part of the twentieth-century and of its sacramental theology, a point brought out well by John Robinson in his account of the experimental liturgy at his Cambridge college in the 1950s (Robinson, 14–20). As actors have always known, the playing is the doing is the telling is the knowing. It is not being naive or superstitious to claim with Theodore Jennings that liturgy provides a

4 Cf. the treatment of liturgy as 'holy games' in Kieran Flanagan, *Sociology and Liturgy: Re-presentations of the Holy* (London: Macmillan, 1991), pp. 292–300; of play as a 'signal of transcendence' in Peter Berger, *A Rumour of Angels* (London: Allen Lane, 1970), pp. 76–9.

'ritual knowledge', which is 'primarily corporeal rather than cerebral, primarily active rather than contemplative, primarily transformative rather than speculative', and that 'it is in and through the action [gesture, step, etc.] that ritual knowledge is gained, not in advance of it, nor after it' (Jennings, 111–27). Unravel this action, intellectualize this knowledge, and you destroy the play by purpose. One could conjecture that this is what happened to the creative work of the liturgical movement once it became institutionalised by forces such as the Second Vatican Council or the General Synod of the Church of England.

The so-called postmodern age takes play more seriously and learning more playfully than earlier generations – and could do so more effectively if greater imagination and bolder alternative communities could liberate both education and play from the late-capitalist growth-and-production ethic. But the Churches have a long way to go if they are to recover the sense of carnival, celebration and bodiliness within their worship. The twentieth century has seen signs of such a recovery in the spread of speaking in tongues and in the more relaxed attitude towards ritual, image and gesture in protestant worship; but generally in Europe it would be easy to agree with Frances Ward that '[o]ur liturgies are too sanitized, too beautiful, too boring to take us to the danger places where regeneration can begin' and to ask with her, 'Where is the subversion, the mockery of authority, the grotesque, the violent?' (Ward, 168). Ward points to that telling and moving parable of the recovery of life through feasting in the film *Babette's Feast*. But part of the point of that story is that the artistic, extravagant, playful and immensely serious redemption comes from outside the self-consciously Christian community. After all, the long history of protestant valuation of productive activity and the even longer history of Christian suspicion of the body are hardly likely to be overcome in a flash, despite the resources of feasting and parable within the Gospels and Christian tradition. Perhaps it will again be from outside the Church or from its fringes – from theatre and dance and music – that the recovery of worship as celebration and play will be completed. And then Guardini's 'grave and earnest people' may join in the Christian dancing of the new millennium.

Celebration as proclamation

I move now from celebration as play to celebration as proclamation. In many ways this is not a big move; but it is an important one to prevent worship and celebration from becoming confined to the rite, to the rules of play. Proclamation is an extension of what Grimes calls the 'as if' or 'subjunctive' quality of ritual. Grimes is building here on the important earlier work of Victor Turner, whose anthropological studies likewise drew on a very wide variety of rituals and lifestyles – African, Hindu, Catholic, hippy. Turner saw the 'liminality' or threshold character of religious rites as doing something more radical than the consolidation of social structures that previous anthropologists and sociologists had seen as their function. Rather, the structure is in tension with 'anti-structure', an alternative or utopian or carnivalesque social reality, to which the rite gives access and to which Turner gave the name *communitas*. *Communitas*, he wrote,

> has an existential quality [...] *Communitas* has also an aspect of potentiality; it is often in the subjunctive mood. Relations between total beings are generative of symbols and metaphors and comparisons; art and religion are their product rather than legal and political structures [...] Prophets and artists tend to be liminal and marginal people, 'edgemen' [...] In their productions we may catch glimpses of that unused evolutionary potential which has not yet been externalized and fixed in structure. (Turner, 127–8)

Ritual in this sense is neither an act of homage nor an affirmation of existing society. It is a performance of utopia or dream-time. That alternative reality, that experiencing of *communitas*, may be placed imaginatively in past or present or future. But if it is to be not just performance or play but also proclamation – and indeed, if it is to be faithful to the eschatological origins of Christianity – then the future dimension is essential. What is proclaimed in worship is what is yet to be.

Yet ours is an age which more than any previous one is entranced by the multiple and ephemeral experiences of the present, an age which, against the great weight of previous Western imagination, reckons seriously with 'the end of history'; and in such an age this proclamation of the future will be increasingly counter-cultural or 'anti-structural'. Unless such boldness is available within the Churches then the end of history will mean the end of the Eucharist. The reason I say this is to do with the 'if' and its expression through performance. As in their distant origins, ritual and theatre remain very close. Peter Brook ended his powerful apologia as a theatre director with a peroration on this 'if', and one could try substituting for 'theatre' the word 'church' and for 'play' the word 'worship':

> In everyday life 'if' is a fiction, in the theatre 'if' is an experiment.
> In everyday life 'if' is an evasion, in the theatre 'if' is the truth.
> When we are persuaded to believe in this truth, then the theatre and life are one.
> This is a high aim. It sounds like hard work.
> To play needs much work. But when we experience the work as play, then it is not work any more.
> A play is play. (Brook, 157)

Christian worship, and particularly the Eucharist, is then a great 'if', a play in the 'subjunctive' mood. Through the ritual of communion among equals, it enacts in the sacred space of the present the achievement of salvation in the past and proclaims the possibility of its fulness in the future – or, as St Paul rather more simply put it, 'when you eat this bread and drink the cup you proclaim the Lord's death until he comes' (1 Corinthians 11:26). The proclamation is ritual rather than verbal, playful rather than cultic. But, to adapt Peter Brook, when we are persuaded to believe in its truth then sanctuary and life are one. The Mass, like the theatre, is about conversion – conversion of the space, conversion of the material elements, conversion of the actors, but ultimately conversion of the world outside the sanctuary.

Without this final projection worship, as much as theatre, remains entertainment. With it, the performance of the Eucharist, like that of Shakespeare or Brecht, becomes inescapably political, transforming not just perception but praxis. I dare to suggest and I certainly hope that it will increasingly effect such transformation in the coming century, as dissatisfaction with existing political structures grows and as the necessity for human survival of dismantling the ruling military-economic-cultural empire becomes more apparent (an empire symbolically focused in the USA but more subtly and globally intertwined and subtlest of all in its proclamation of pluralism and the 'free market'). And eucharistic proclamation will do this not as some kind of prelude or visual aid to the real business of political action or alternative living, but as the actual celebration of it. It will do this as engagement with the powers, continuing Jesus' engagement with them in exorcism and parable, in argument and feasting. Ritual, says Tom Driver, 'is neither a detached contemplation of the world nor a passive symbolization of it, but is the performance of an act in which people confront one kind of power with another and rehearse their own future' (Driver, 188).

That confrontation of powers and rehearsal of the future may seem a far cry from the common British experience of worship, where the rehearsal is more often of the past and the confrontation is customarily focused on flower arrangements and hymn tunes. Beneath much church life lies a fearfulness of celebration and of the body, even a death wish; while Churches that are more flourishing and externally lively (I am thinking particularly of neo-pentecostal or 'charismatic' worship) are adept at wallowing in emotional experience of the present, with the future celebrated mainly as the growth of the Church and as escape into heaven. Either way there is not much proclamation going on. To keep these shows on the road requires a persistence in the sense of homage. It also requires in the first case a stream of recruits for nostalgia and in the second a frantic search for relevance and innovation. And it could well be that all three exercises can be maintained well into the new century before collapsing completely.

But despite these perhaps unfair pictures and predictions I am not despondent about the future of worship and even of worship as proclamation. This is partly because I believe it simply does not matter whether the Churches grow or not. More importantly, it is because there is something in the Christian sacramental signs and actions which is inherently subversive and which in the end will out so long as the sacraments are performed, despite the long history of the taming of baptism and eucharist by Church and State alike. Even the extremes of protestant verbosity and of catholic cult cannot permanently conceal the enactment of reversal, of conversion and of communion in both sacraments. It is significant that in the impressive sacramental revival in Anglicanism in the nineteenth and twentieth centuries – a movement which in many ways was deeply traditionalist – there was a close connection between sacramentalism and socialism, and in many cases with much more radical local or international politics (cf. Gray, part II). The connection has not died out, nor is it confined to Anglicanism; but it is highlighted by two contemporary Anglican socialist writers in particular, Kenneth Leech and Timothy Gorringe. Drawing examples from some local churches of the present and recent past, Leech writes of the liturgy as 'a counter-cultural activity, a prefiguring of the world as it could be [...] the heart of the protest against the disorder of the world', while Gorringe's 'reflections on the Eucharist' describe it as 'prayer for the coming of the peaceable kingdom, and a step on the road to its realization [...] the seedbed of political imagination and creativity' (Leech, 170, 186; Gorringe, 60, 72). In such worship, and I would say inherently in the eucharistic action, celebration and proclamation and praxis are inseparable – which suggests that the neglecting or perfunctory performance of the sacraments is not just bad liturgical practice but bad news for the world.

Celebration and immanence

I am not therefore envisaging and certainly not hoping for an abandonment of traditional form or sacramental ritual in the liturgies of the new century. But it does seem to me that if the Churches are to engage with postmodern culture in a way that is both open and critical, and if worship is to be celebration rather than homage, then a rewriting of liturgical language, gesture and story-telling is called for. This is something much more radical than the 'liturgical revision' that has been and has been undertaken by the 'mainstream Churches' in the twentieth century, good and necessary as much of that revision was. The inadequacy of official reforms lies not just in the bureaucratic and archaeological tendencies for which liturgists are notorious but in the very nature of the shift to celebration. You can order people to pay homage and prescribe how they are to do so, but you cannot order people to celebrate. And while no form of celebration is totally spontaneous or totally original, and while there will presumably remain for the Churches of the third millennium certain given factors in the biblical images and the story of Jesus, the creative and interpretative energy will come 'from below'. Perhaps it always has done; but technological and political developments that seem set to continue for the foreseeable future mean that corporate creativity is focused less and less on national or professional or denominational structures and more and more on local, often shifting communities on the one hand and on global networking on the other. Nearly all the more interesting recent developments in liturgy have come from small pentecostal Churches, from feminist groups or from communities like Iona and Taizé, as many more established liturgists will freely admit. At the same time there has been an increasing eclecticism in liturgical forms and language and especially music, with Western Christians both catholic and protestant freely surfing through Orthodox and Celtic and Jewish material and sometimes through forms lying well outside the biblical and monotheistic traditions.

The dangers for the tradition of Christian worship are obvious. For all its creative energy, the merely local celebration can become sectarian or solipsistic; the eclectic collage of liturgical clippings can become consumerist or no more than entertainment. In either case worship may be very playful but can cease to be proclamation. At the risk of becoming one of those who order people how to celebrate, I want to draw out three further directions or even principles which I think may or should apply to the development of Christian worship, beginning with *immanence.*

Traditional Christian worship has placed a premium on transcendence and verticality. The altar or the pulpit was set apart, raised up, and the enthroned priest or preacher who occupied this exalted space was the representative of the yet more transcendently enthroned God – the God of Patmos. In such a sanctuary the worshipper should stand back or kneel back, and her eyes, like those of the four living creatures, should be fixed on the throne, not on the neighbour. Now the twentieth century saw great changes to this spirituality in most Western Churches. The altar has usually moved to the centre of the assembly, the pulpit has often gone altogether. While the words of homage to the Transcendent Other have been barely altered, the ritual and architecture tell a different story, one which proclaims relationships which are primarily horizontal and neighbourly rather than vertical and submissive. There has sometimes been a cost to this, which much liturgical reform at the turn of the century is striving to redeem: some loss of poetry or mystery, some tendency to didacticism, above all a sometimes complacent locating of the holy presence within the assembly ('We are the Body of Christ ...'). But worship now takes much more seriously the terrestrial world in which its play and proclamation are performed and from which it draws its words and symbols.

There are certainly powerful resistances to this shift to immanence, principally in the very authoritarian and male-controlled cultures of the Vatican and of American fundamentalism. But the value of the shift seems to me great and for the foreseeable future irreversible. And there is no overriding reason why worship which celebrates horizontal and human and ecological relationships, worship which – like Don Cupitt's 'long-legged fly' – skates the surface rather than plumbs the depths, should not apprehend mystery and Spirit. The traditional prioritizing of depth over surface is in any case a misleading one, as 'postmodern' and feminist critiques have repeatedly emphasized: a priority founded variously on Platonic dualism, on scientific hubris, on patriarchy and hierarchical order. Relationship, sensation, friendship, forgiveness and love – the key elements celebrated by the Christian Gospel – are in the strict sense of the world superficial: that is, they consist in movement across the limitless surface of the world. That is furthermore the energetic movement of Ezekiel's cherubim or of the pentecostal Spirit. And both the syntax and the narrative of the Hebrew Bible are horizontal or 'paratactic'. Walter Brueggemann's impressive theological reading of the Old Testament stresses and celebrates this horizontal yet infinitely mysterious dimension, as Jewish interpretation always has done, and the contrast he draws is less between surface and depth than between 'density' and 'thinness' (Brueggeman, 205–12, 277–82). The density of encounter with the neighbour or the land or the text opens up a 'surplus of meaning', it is sufficient impetus to wonder and worship. So paradoxically the vertical language of transcendence, of ascending or descending to other realms, may now be the language or ritual that has become 'thin' in resonance and meaning; it engenders a ritual which Theodore Jennings might describe as solipsistic and 'falsified' by its lack of correspondence to the world of 'significant action outside the ritual' (Jennings, 119–20) At the beginning of the third millennium it seems that the Church is caught between the thinness of traditional depth language and the density of horizontal celebration. The former, pointing to cosmic hierarchy and progress to 'heaven', still calls the tune in liturgical texts and often in church order, while the latter is where the spiritual energy lies. And many Christians who instinctively sense the mismatch turn outside the Churches for spiritual sustenance and transforming praxis.

Apart from the purging of language, there seem to me to be two areas where the horizontal dimension may be made more explicit in future and actually contribute to the sense of mystery or density of Christian worship and so to its proclamatory power. The first is in a way the completion of work begun by the sixteenth-century Reformers, the clearer transformation of altar into table – the locus of communion between human equals rather than sacrifice to the God who craves blood and praise. This is not to abandon all sacrificial reading of the Eucharist, which in a way is written into its performance by the words of Jesus at the last supper. But it is to relate its performance more closely to the earlier meals of Jesus, where forgiveness and salvation are enacted simply by eating together; and to relate it more closely also to the ordinary meals of the world – their companionship, their economics, their hunger.

The second movement is more a reversal of the Reformers' work, or at any rate of the effect of their treatment of the Bible: namely, what could be called a move from creed to midrash. Reading of the biblical text has been a constant feature of Christian worship, and this is unlikely to change. But particularly since the Reformation, the text has become a kind of pretext for doctrine: the story or poem incomplete until it is turned into sermon, and the sermon one which will clarify meaning and affirm belief. The 'vertical' Christian tendency to distil biblical narrative into credal proposition contrasts with the Jewish midrashic tradition of simply setting texts alongside other texts and alongside opinions and arguments and jokes in an endless horizontal concatenation of meanings that are unexhausted by complete formulation. If Christianity were to learn again from its mother in the postmodern age, this could redeem the liturgical use of scripture from the woodenness of its performance and the thinness of its interpretation which are so prevalent today. With Bible as with Eucharist, the release from compulsion to define and to set boundaries could be the way to a celebration that is thoroughly this-worldly and endlessly mysterious.

Ambiguity – and silence

This leads from immanence to the subject of *ambiguity*, which I am relating to poetry. The authoritarian mind and the cravers of homage have little patience with either. Their lust for certitude and order are not fed by entertaining a multiplicity of meanings in Bible or sacrament, let alone by refraining from attributing meaning at all. But the comfort of univocal meaning can be won only at the cost of sacrificing the poetry of the Bible or the symbolism of the sacraments, each of which has the uncomfortable energy to generate new meaning and new praxis. The cost would also seem to entail sacrificing a lively apprehension of Spirit, which in the biblical and trinitarian traditions is the dynamic of relationship that cannot be confined to any one channel but blows where it will. So Harvey Cox, for all his sympathy with pentecostalism, is surely right to argue that if in the next century pentecostalists do not resist the fundamentalist tendencies within many of their Churches they will have betrayed their experiential rejoicing in the Spirit (Cox, 308–20). Pentecostalism and poetry should be and can be partners – on the one hand, brimming over with the experience and energy that cannot be formulated or have precise meaning attached to them, while on the other hand creative of new language, of absurd tongues.

Yet in the end human beings are not capable of a sustained expression of such experience and energy. That is why both pentecostal tongues and poetic liturgy are constantly subject to lapsing from their ambiguity into the security of definition – or alternatively into silence. The silence is the awareness that the Logos cannot be grasped, perhaps that the Logos does not exist, so that utterance is vain. But silence too is ambiguous. Ihab Hassan, in his subtle examination of modern and postmodern literature in *The Dismemberment of Orpheus*, speaks of the 'two accents' of silence arising from the breakdown of language and narrative in our century. One is 'the negative echo of language, autodestructive, demonic, nihilist'; the other 'its positive stillness, self-transcendent, sacramental, plenary' (Hassan, 248). The latter is clearly akin to the silence of traditional Christian negative theology or apophaticism, to the nada, nada, nada of St John of the Cross and the silence of R. S. Thomas's empty churches. And Hassan seems to suggest that the utterers of the postmodern silence have the choice between apophaticism and nihilism: 'Playing their stringless lyres, modern authors enchant us with their twin melodies, and we dream of bright life or unspeakable sleep' (4). The nihilist dream of unspeakable sleep may still leave space for stories and for play; it leaves none for proclamation and none therefore for worship that is recognizably Christian. But something of the apophatic dream of bright life I find expressed in the central section of Gillian Clarke's poem 'Mass of the Birds':

> [...] The mist is off the fields. Swifts
> spin their shrill litanies.
> Under the barn's beaten silver
> incense of cut grass, creosote,
> the sun's mat at the door.
> We bring our privacies.
>
> Rough table. Circle of chairs.
> A heel of granary loaf.
> Wine over from last night's supper.
> A leather book. Luke. Romans.
> Corinthians. Silences.
> A congregation of eight.

The lapsed, the doubting, those
here for the first time, others
regular at named churches
share the meaning of breaking bread,
of sipping from one glass,
of naming you.

Mass of the birds. A blackbird calls,
a wren responds, calling, answering
what we can only feel.
We offer this as the sun
raises its wafer too brilliant
to look at or understand. (Clarke, 89)[5]

In this poem full of liturgical tradition and imagery there is nevertheless an openness of meaning, a refraining from definition. And I am sure it is no coincidence that this poetic openness is matched by the openness of the table to unconventional worshippers and the openness of the doors to the natural world. The words trail away into the pentecostal language of birds and sun. And they trail away too into silence and into ritual action. So that in this unassuming congregation of eight, miles away from cathedrals and revival meetings, there is a coming together of pentecostal experience, apophatic silence and the deep structure of catholic ritual.

Such a fertile combination is more than adequate to nurture a creative development of Christian worship in the coming centuries. In its sacred spaces and sacred language there may, I conjecture, be a liberation from the pathologies of religion – from the lust for affirmation and exclusion and the paying of homage. And more positively, the spaces and languages may celebrate liberation into an infectious practice of forgiveness and justice: a genuine *koinonia*, deeply embedded in worldly experience, but playfully enacting the worldly and unworldly story of Jesus.

5 With this poetic density, contrast the thinness of Don Cupitt's imagination of the Eucharist of the future in his *Radicals and the Future of the Church* (London: SCM Press, 1989), pp. 170–2. On the relationship of apophatic theology to liturgy see further Flanagan, *Sociology and Liturgy*, pp. 310–20.

Bibliography

Berger, Peter. *The Sacred Canopy*. New York: Doubleday, 1967.

Brook, Peter, *The Empty Space* (1968). Harmondsworth: Penguin, 1972.

Brueggemann, Walter. *Theology of the Old Testament*. Minneapolis, MN: Fortress Press, 1997.

Clarke, Gillian. *Selected Poems*. Manchester: Carcanet, 1985.

Cox, Harvey. *Fire from Heaven: The Rise of Pentecostal Spirituality and the Reshaping of Religion in the Twenty-First Century*. London: Cassell, 1996.

Driver, Tom. *The Magic of Ritual*. San Francisco: Harper, 1991.

Girard, René. *The Scapegoat*. Baltimore, MD: Johns Hopkins UP, 1986.

Gorringe, Timothy. *The Sign of Love: Reflections on the Eucharist*. London: SPCK, 1997.

Gray, Donald. *Earth Altar: The Evolution of the Parish Communian in the Church of England to 1945*. Alcuin Club Collections, 68. London, 1986.

Grimes, Ronald. *Beginnings in Ritual Studies*. Lanham, MD: University Press of America, 1982.

Guardini, Romano. *The Spirit of the Liturgy*. London: Sheed & Ward, 1930.

Hassan, Ihab. *The Dismemberment of Orpheus: Toward a Postmodern Literature*, 2nd ed. Madison, WI: University of Wisconsin Press, 1982.

Jennings, Theodore. 'On Ritual Knowledge', *Journal of Religion*, 62 (1992).

Lawrence, D. H. *Apocalypse* (1931). Harmondsworth: Penguin, 1974.

Leech, Kenneth. *The Sky is Red: Discerning the Signs of the Times*. London: DLT, 1997.

Otto, Rudolph. *The Idea of the Holy*. Oxford: OUP, 1923.

Robinson, John. *Liturgy Coming to Life*. London: Mowbray, 1960.

Turner, Victor. *Ritual Process: Structure and Anti-Structure*. London: RKP, 1969.

Underhill, Evelyn. *Worship*. London: Nisbet, 1936.

Ward, Frances. 'Writing the Body of Christ', *Theology*, 100 (1997).

White, Susan. *Christian Worship and Technological Change*. Nashville, TN: Abindon Press, 1994.

ALISON JASPER

Word and Flesh: The Sign of Female Circumcision.[1]

Re-reading the incarnation

A central teaching of Christianity is the belief that God in Jesus Christ shared our embodied humanity. The Word became flesh. But teaching about 'flesh' (σάρξ) has always been problematic. Divine incarnation – commentators in the past have stressed – has nothing much to do with human fleshly desire, with embodied desire. Arguably, from the beginning, Christians have not really known what to do with the erotic force or power that comes from the depths of our bodily being, where, a modern feminist theorist like Audre Lorde might say, our sense of self begins, taking fully into consideration the 'chaos of our strongest feelings' (Lorde, 54). From early on, the incarnation of God has been presented to Christians more as the wonderful sacrifice of absolutely spiritual divinity than as the wonderful sanctification of embodied humanity with all its powerful drives, desires and needs. The human body with its rich and sometimes disturbing connections with both materiality and spirituality has frequently been reduced simply to the site of *concupiscentia*, of desire as sin. At the same time the embodiment of God has become defined largely as passibility – He suffered through his incarnation as, it seems, we do too.

The priority of divine Word over flesh, understood in this way, can also be interpreted as the fundamental characteristic of what Western feminism identifies as patriarchal. As feminist philosophers like Luce Irigaray have suggested, the ideal of masculinity in the West is not simply associated with the divine but has become the measure

1 This paper was first given as a contribution to a Day Conference entitled 'Deeply Material', held at Glasgow University, Department of Theology and Religious Studies, Saturday 6 May 2000.

of all human aspirations, a form of projection which disassociates human aspiration or desire almost entirely from the symbolism of the feminine including the material and fleshly (Irigaray, 58–72).

And yet, it does not have to be read in this way. Divine incarnation, Word as flesh, does not have to be interpreted in these terms. The priority of God's creative Word represents one interpretation of the Christian texts. Yet, and at the same time, without flesh there would be no Word as Christians have understood that. The twelfth-century theologian Hildegard of Bingen knew this when she conceived of the whole of the universe in terms of a human body and its humours. The material world is God's creation yet without that creation, the divine Word would be effectively an impotent silence, or at most a potential unexpressed. Many Christian theologians have sought to minimize the implication that Word without flesh is impotent, for example by distinguishing artificially between the body and the flesh or by emphasizing the sense in which Mary, the essentially human mother of Jesus, was a stranger to fleshly desire or the corruption of original sin, even to the extent of formulating the dogma of the immaculate conception – the teaching that the Virgin's parents conceived her without passing on original sin – in other words, separating her as far as was possible from the infection of bodily desire. Nevertheless, we can surely say that God is dependent upon our world of embodied desire continually to testify to the light – in other words to revision, to reimagine, to respond, to feel and to desire that light to shine in the world.

The inscription of female identified flesh

Taking rationality or reason as defined within the masculine traditions of Western philosophy as the nature and character of the divine Word, then those with the power to influence or teach have always sought to prove its superiority to body, seen as primarily the site of devalued fleshly motivation or desire. Embodied desire is silenced and the body is inscribed with the Word of reason, in some cases literally so. In

Toni Morrison's novel *Beloved*, Sethe bears on her back the marks of the whip cut into the skin and beaten into the flesh by violent men, the Word restricted to a singular powerful White definition of reason that, divinized, turns certain human beings and certain aspects of human subjectivity into objects of hatred and mistrust.

A new reading of the relationship between Word and flesh begins to loosen ties with the traditional hierarchy and provides a clear basis for opposing this kind of treatment meted out to the excluded and devalued. By implying that there might even be a degree of heterogeneity within the divine – both Word and flesh – this new reading of the incarnational text takes up common cause with feminist theory in the broadest sense in that it seeks to challenge the prevailing patriarchal singularity and exclusiveness that expresses itself through various forms of 'inscription'. It even offers, perhaps, coherent grounds for opposing the controversial practice of female circumcision (hereafter, FC) or female genital mutilation (hereafter, FGM) which, of course, usually occurs in cultures and countries that are largely non-Christian.

Male circumcision / female mutilation?

In the West we are familiar with male circumcision. In Genesis 17 God orders Abraham to circumcize his foreskin and do the same to all the males of his family and tribe, as a mark of the covenant between God and Abraham's (male) descendants. As a sign of this covenant with God, Jews continue the practice of circumcizing male infants to this day. And, although it is not mentioned in the Qur'an, many Muslims too practise male circumcision, on the grounds that it was a tradition instigated by Abraham and supported by Mohammed himself.[2]

2 See, for example, Sami Aldeeb, 'Jehovah, His cousin, Allah and Sexual Mutilations', in *Sexual Mutilations: A Human Tragedy* (New York: Plenum Press, 1997).

Female circumcision features in some Islamic cultures too. The practice does not necessarily begin with the introduction of the religion of Islam, nor is it limited to these Islamic cultures, but clearly it has been 'naturalized' there just as, for example, the subordination of women in general has been 'naturalized' within aspects of Christian culture. There are, then, classical Islamic extra-Qur'anic sources which explain the origins of female circumcision by suggesting, for example, that it was first performed on Hagar by Abraham at the instigation of Sarah, for reasons of jealousy.[3]

As this traditional reading of the practice itself suggests, there are significant differences between male and female circumcision, some of which might seem to justify the now common practice of renaming it female genital *mutilation*. One key difference between the two practices is that female circumcision routinely impairs sexual function. The majority of women who are circumcized, have undergone pharaonic circumcision which actually removes the clitoris, thereby making female orgasm impossible.[4] In the majority of cases female circumcision is also associated with the practice of infibulation (sewing up) of the vulva until marriage, leaving only a small opening about the size of a finger tip, which must be cut or forced open.

Again, male circumcision does not usually result in chronic discomfort or present major health risks whereas the very serious consequences of female circumcision and infibulation together are widely referred to in published work on the subject.[5] These include obstruction of the most basic functions of urinating and menstruating as well as an increased likelihood of painful sex, damage to the

3 Aldeeb, 1997. Also see Paul Jason Ford, 'Female Circumcision: Power/Alienation', 1996 (<www.vanderbilt.edu/AnS/philosophy/Students/FordPJ/POWER.HTM>).

4 An alternative 'Sunna' form of circumcision which involves removal of the prepuce of the clitoris is a less common alternative. This does not impair sexual function.

5 For example, Malik Stan Reaves, 'Alternative Rite to Female Circumcision Spreading in Kenya', Africa News Service, November 1997 (www.africanews.org/specials/19971119). See also Waris Dirie and Cathleen Miller, *Desert Flower: The Extraordinary Life of a Desert Nomad* (London: Virago, 1998).

urethra, infertility and childbirth complications. Finally, more subtly inscribing a difference between male and female forms of circumcision, is the fact that although male circumcision may be related to a clearer definition of gender – circumcision removes the foreskin which may be regarded, in some cases, as analogous to the vagina – it is not commonly defended by practitioners in terms of a need to control male sexuality. On the other hand, amongst those peoples who practise circumcision – the nomadic Darod of Somalia is one example – circumcision has been explicitly defended as a means of reducing female sexual desire[6] which is regarded as dangerous or potentially destructive of social order (Smith, 2449–2504). In general terms the procedure seems to reflect a male preoccupation with self-perpetuation and ownership (Abdalla, 35) that might appropriately be symbolized in terms taken from Christian culture as the inscription of the male Word on the female flesh.

Female circumcision as 'sign'

We are becoming aware of the story of female circumcision or mutilation in the West. We know that female circumcision is a practice affecting millions of women in Africa and parts of Asia. The World Health Organization estimated in 1988 that over 80 million women in more than 30 countries had undergone the procedure, and UN figures suggest that, averaging it out over a year, as many as 6,000 girls each day may be involved (Dirie/Miller, 230). As people move from one continent to another, they take their customs with them so

6 This does not in fact appear to be one of the consequences of FC/FGM. See Paul Jason Ford, 'Female Circumcision: Power/Alienation': 'The removal of the clitoris does not decrease sexual desire. It simply decreases the chance of the satiation of that desire.'

In Dirie/Miller, 1998, Dirie says: 'When I met Dana, I finally fell in love and wanted to experience the joys of sex with a man. But if you ask me today, "Do you enjoy sex?" I would say not in the traditional way. I simply enjoy being physically close to Dana because I love him' (Dirie/Miller, 227).

that there is now evidence of the practice taking place in the Western world.

We generally respond with horror and indignation. Although governments are still reluctant to intervene, Western-based organizations are getting involved (Seager). The issue begins to feature in magazine articles and books for the general reader. 1997, for example, saw the publication in the US of a book entitled *Desert Flower*, the ghost-written account[7] of a Somalian woman, Waris Dirie, who escaped from her nomadic life in the desert and eventually, after an extraordinary struggle, made a career as a model in London and the US. This book contains the most graphic account of Dirie's own circumcision. In this book we learn that circumcisions are carried out on very young girls without anaesthetic or sterile equipment by women who depend for their living on travelling from group to group to perform similar operations. In the deserts of Somalia, for example, where there is little or no healthcare available, there is always an increased risk of shock, infection and even death. Dirie recalls an older sister and a cousin (Dirie/Miller, 49), both of whom had died directly as a result of being circumcized. In one case the wound became gangrenous and in the other, the little girl bled to death. Dirie's book ends with an appeal to the reader to join the UN-based *Campaign to Eliminate FGM.*

But stories, like mutilated bodies, are always marked by excisions and alterations. The mutilated or altered shapes of our patriarchal stories in the West reveal the narrative process shaping women's lives and indeed their very identity in a way analogous to circumcision and infibulation carried out on so many women in Africa and Asia. And when we tell a story we are frequently doing something more than 'telling it how it is'.

For example, motivations in reading/publishing the story of FC/FGM may not be simply a matter of altruism. We may well be horrified by female circumcision in Africa, but for Western women

7 Dirie herself has had little formal education and so her story is actually written by a 'ghost writer', Cathleen Miller, working from tapes and published first in the US by William Morrow and Company Inc., New York, and then by Virago in the UK in 1998.

there are practices closer to hand which are regularly condoned that, arguably, are motivated by a similar body aesthetic or attempts to control sexuality. There are many common Western practices that inscribe the body, for example facelifts, breast implants or reductions, body – including genital – piercing and even shaving. People in the West who undergo these forms of mutilation/alteration do so in order to make themselves conform to a certain body image. Of course female circumcision is almost universal in parts of Africa (Seager, 52–3)[8] because it is linked to cultural expectations of marriage which is the mechanism of cultural and actual survival in many cases. But the motivations in and outside of the Western world in this respect represent different points on a continuum. In the West shaved legs, plucked facial hair, body piercings and breast implants or reductions are promoted as a way of making women feel more attractive and thus more confident about themselves. In parts of Africa, girls regard their appearance after circumcision as preferable and more attractive.[9] The point is, whether we are talking about a woman circumcising a child with a dirty razor blade or a woman paying for her breasts to be altered in a private hospital with anaesthetics and sterile equipment, we are talking about pressure to make bodies conform. The fact that the pressures are less intense and that the conditions are not usually life-threatening in the West does not in itself, I think, allow us to distinguish absolutely between 'us' and 'them' and thus justify 'our' demand for the elimination of FC/FGM. On these grounds alone, it might make sense to call for regulation of the practice, for sterile circumcision kits or a demand that only children over twelve be allowed to undergo the process if they choose. Otherwise perhaps our horrified reactions to FC/FGM could be put down more to the perception of circumcision as a custom belonging to the exotic,

8 The proportion of women and girls with genital excision or infibulation is 80–100 per cent in Somalia, Ethiopia and Sudan, Gambia and Sierra Leone. In all these cases, the government has a published policy of opposition to the practice (1995 figures). The percentage is 50–79 per cent in Egypt, Kenya, Chad, Nigeria, Benin, Togo, Côte d'Ivoire, Guinea, Guinea-Bissau, Mali and Burkina Faso.

9 See Paul Jason Ford, 'Female Circumcision: Aesthetics/Analogies in Western Culture', 1996 (www.vanderbilt.edu/AnS/philosophy/Students/FordPJ/ aesthet.htm).

racially different peoples of impoverished, and therefore uncivilized, third-world countries, by which exclusion we contribute to our own normative self-image.

The Jewish scholar Daniel Boyarin suggests, interestingly, in his book on the Christian apostle Paul, that the Christian aversion to Jewish circumcision of the male at the beginning of the Christian era may have itself been linked to the very processes that have caused women in the West at least to be devalued through the development of a gendered hierarchy that relegates that which is symbolically associated with the female – including the bodily – to the lower order (Boyarin, 36–8). In other words, he suggests that by devaluing the significance of physical circumcision, Paul and his followers also devalued the significance of the body, or at least, in this case, the male body! Perhaps we need to guard against the possibility that aversion to female circumcision has its roots in a similar perception, feeding a belief that what is done to the body is ultimately unimportant or insignificant in contrast to some aspect of our selves that is not implicated in the processes of embodied desire. It may be that such opposition to female circumcision effectively fails to see circumcision as a sign however perverse of the irreducible significance of what Christianity refers to as the flesh.

In the Western world we are certainly beginning to make changes in our attitudes towards the body and towards our embodied desires. In Morrison's novel *Beloved*, published in 1987, set in the American South in the middle of the nineteenth-century, the character, Baby Suggs, an unchurched black preacher tells her congregation of freed or escaped slaves to laugh and dance and cry and to love and cherish their bodies and their internal organs. She tells them that what is most important is the grace, the power of imagination, to recognize that they can love their own flesh whatever neglect and mistreatment it has received through the definition of worthlessness imposed on them by powerful white women and men (Morrison, 88). The prize is not the biblical crown of unfading laurels but, says Baby Suggs, the beat and beating heart, a reference which blurs the lines between literal and metaphorical, making the body a significant – even a holy – place. The African American writer bell hooks is another example of a writer who has tried to break down the barriers imposed in large part by

Christian-sponsored dualisms and hierarchies and proposed the term 'yearning' for the embodied human longing for all the true goods of life without misleading distinctions between materiality and spirituality (hooks, 2).

We read that Waris Dirie as an adult, now living and working in the West, views the practice of circumcision as a brutal and ungodly affront to the integrity of women. She is unequivocal on the subject:

> I feel that God made my body perfect the way I was born. Then man robbed me, took away my power and left me a cripple. My womanhood was stolen. If God had wanted those body parts missing, why did he create them? (Dirie/Miller, 238)

These published words can, of course, be seen as an expression of the erotic, that force or creative energy within us all that, according to Audre Lorde again, needs to find its outlet in satisfying our human capacity for joy (Lorde, 56–8) in all its forms without hierarchical distinctions between body and soul or flesh and spirit. In speaking publicly about her circumcision, initially to a reporter from the magazine *Marie Claire*, Dirie was breaking a silence of anger and helplessness that had been choking her, precisely by finding a way of representing her bodily suffering and anger in words. She was responding to an erotic impulse that drove her to recognize her own 'need for language and definition'. In other words, Dirie was enacting the reintegration of Word and flesh in that particularly Western definition of the problem. She was defining for herself and then repudiating a practice that spoke to her of oppression and pain.

But her book is a product of the Western world nevertheless, characterized by commercial currents that dictate how a story is told and the demand for some conformity to the underlying myths that structure our own culture. And so it seems to me that there is bound to be a clash at some point. Occasionally, Dirie does seem uncomfortable with the way in which the story she is telling seems to force her to choose between worlds. Other than the circumcision issue, she writes:

> I wouldn't trade with anyone the way I grew up. Living in New York, although everyone talks about family values, I've seen very little of them. I don't see families getting together like we did, singing, clapping, laughing. People here

> are disconnected from one another; there's no sense of belonging to a community. (Dirie/Miller, 234)

My intention is to find an approach to the distressing practice of FC/FGM which does not compound the problem by practising further excisions and mutilations in terms of any sort of naively racist conclusions. I have tried to use the tools of a basically feminist analysis to reveal that within the Western myth of the Divine Human there lies a genuine recognition of the multiple significance of embodied desire, however strongly it has sometimes been resisted within the patriarchal Christian Church. This multiplicity or even heterogeneity within what we vision or imagine as God, therefore implicitly suggests respect for whatever is symbolically associated with the feminine including the body, and in particular in this case the female genitalia as a site of feminine *jouissance*. This conclusion is clearly related to the practice of re/valorizing multiple and non-privileged perspectives – in this case a female perspective – that is an important theme across the whole field of modern feminism. A classic example relevant to this discussion is, of course, Luce Irigaray's use of the female labia as symbolic of a feminine multiplicity that challenge phallocentric singularity.[10] Irigaray's work continues to resist singularity in all its forms not least the male penetrative inscription on the body marking it as female in the view of the male.

Equally, it seems to me, we have to be prepared to apply the same principles to the undoubtedly non-privileged perspective of those cultures in which FC/FGM is practised. On the stage created by the multi-million-pound publishing and media industries of the West that process a homogenized morality, they are in danger of appearing like the bogeymen of Western fairy tale and nightmare, personifying

10 See, for example, Luce Irigaray, *This Sex which is Not One* (trans. Catherine Porter with Carolyn Burke, Ithaca: Cornell University Press, 1985), 24: 'In order to touch himself, man needs an instrument, his hand, a woman's body, language […] And this touching requires at least a minimum of activity. As for woman, she touches herself without any need for mediation and before there is any need to distinguish activity from passivity. Woman "touches herself" all the time […] for her genitals are formed of two-lips in continuous contact. Thus, within herself, she is two but not divisible into one(s) – that caress each other.'

our deepest fears and anxieties. We must surely continue to oppose the practice of FC/FGM as one exercise, amongst others, of power over women alienated in this case from their own sexuality and from the power to change the way in which their society operates, but we should also be prepared to admit that FC/FGM also represents a recognition of an ultimately irrepressible female potency. Female circumcision can be seen, perversely, as a genuine sign of the significance of embodied desire. The mutilation is at once an excision and a visible mark or sign of women's embodied fertility.

Christians and those of a Christian background, therefore, need to be absolutely clear that their motivations for opposing FC/FGM do not result from the view of cultures which practice FC/FGM as somehow Other in the exclusive sense that leads back into singularity and the gendered hierarchies of traditional Christian interpretations. Circumcision as a practice that takes 'flesh' seriously, then, should remain a 'sign' to us in order to prevent such oppressive practices being repeated.

Bibliography

Abdalla, Raquiya Haji Dualeh. *Sisters in Affliction.* 1982.

Boyovin, Daniel. *A Radical Jew: Paul and the Politics of Identity.* Berkeley, CA: University of California Press, 1994.

Dilie, Waris, and Cathleen Miller. *Desert Flower: The Extraordinary Life of a Desert Nomad.* London: Virago, 1998.

hooks, bell. *Yearning, Race, Gender and Cultural Politics.* Boston, MA: South End Press, 1990.

Irigaray, Luce. *Sexes and Genealogies*, translated by G. C. Gill. London: Routledge, 1993.

Lorde, Audre. *Sister Outsider: Essays and Speeches.* Freedon, CA: The Crossing Press, 1984.

Morrison, Toni. *Beloved.* London: Picador, 1988.

Seager, Joni. *The State of Women in the World Atlas.* Harmondsworth: Penguin, 1997.

Smith, Robyn Cerny. 'Female Circumcision: Bringing Women's Perspectives into the International Debate.' *Southern California Law Review,* 65 (1992).

Kiyoshi Tsuchiya

A Response to Postmodern Theology

'The Centre' in the University of Glasgow's Department of Theology and Religious Studies, now called the Centre for the Study of Literature, Theology and the Arts has been pursuing an alternative form of theology that is rooted in Christian theology and yet is more relevant to our secularized cultural life. This new theology is a direct result of a new way of reading the Bible that no longer assumes an essential difference between the sacred book and the rest of literature and the arts. It is necessarily interdisciplinary and open to insights from contemporary studies of literature and the arts called 'post-modern'. It in turn intends to find a 'theological' moment in literary and artistic creation and reception. Its goal is to liberate theology from its traditional confines to make it applicable to all of our cultural activities. In this essay I would like to examine whether this new theology merely retains the old theological premise and re-authorizes it in a new language. If that is the case we have a new theology that simply bypasses the scrutiny that the old theology had to go through.

If we examine this new theology in the light of the age-old question what religion is, that is, if we place it in the spectrum of the contending theistic and non-theistic views of religion, it appears non-theistic, certainly free of premises derived from traditional Christian doctrines. However, it remains distinctly Judaeo-Christian in its commitment to begin with the Bible. It is non-theistic so far as it assumes nothing prior to the written text, but it is firmly rooted in the Judaeo-Christian tradition of upholding the biblical narrative as the primary source of all theological discussion.

Theistic Christianity owes its origin to Greek philosophy. The constant exchange between the Platonic tradition and Christianity often took the form of a philosophical theology – as in mysticism – that provided a speculative framework within which the biblical narrative was told. Within this framework people could still work from and towards a unitive experience and see similar practices in other religious and philosophical traditions. In contrast, postmodern theology assumes nothing prior to the biblical narrative. Here the whole practice takes place between the text and interpretation. Interpretation is always a shift or drift from the text, and each deviation then becomes an added text that calls for interpretation. The text thus turns out to be 'intertext' that extends itself forward and backward indefinitely. Derrida's 'différance' explains this well. Here the notion 'origin' of the text is impossible, making any attempt at unitive experience meaningless. For a lack of origin means a lack of end. By assuming nothing other than the text and interpretation, and by placing the question concerning the origin and the conclusion out of interpretative reach, postmodern theology frees itself from any relevance to speculative practices. We can certainly restate this loss as 'liberation' and agree to celebrate rather than lament it. Even so, asking why the speculative framework and the biblical narrative began to fall apart or whether they were united in the first instance is important. Postmodern theology, however, begins with the recognition of their fundamental incongruity and of the priority of the biblical narrative over mystical speculation. It is an attempt at reinventing Christianity as a fully non-theistic religion, and along the way it rids itself of the last trace of Christian mysticism.

It therefore has nothing to do with transcendence. Previously, the biblical narrative, the incarnational theology, and even the ecclesiastic justification were supported by a transcendental argument and were comparable with other forms of transcendentalism. Christian transcendentalism was a guarded one, believed to be possible only through the divinely inspired text, the divine incarnation and the divinely sanctioned sect. It jealously protected the oneness and onceness of these textual, personal, and political revelations. Christian transcendentalism was thus strained from the beginning. It is its emphasis on the unretrievability and unrepeatability of these revelations that finally made it impracticable in the modern, 'secularized' society. For those who readily accept the bankruptcy of Christian transcendentalism there are two ways forward, either to look for another form of transcendentalism or to assume that the end of Christian transcendentalism is the end of any transcendentalism and see it as the beginning of a new theology. Postmodern theology is clearly the latter. It is rooted in a remnant of divine revelation, that is, a text, a person, and a community, that is no longer supported by divine authentication. In practice the biblical narrative still receives special attention not because it is proof of authentication but because it is the prime record of the loss. This primacy of the Bible appears accidental, but it is no longer a matter of dispute for the lack of a speculative framework that used to keep it in place. Being cleared of the need of divine authentication, the biblical narrative is no longer accountable to anything else than to itself. It is therefore autonomous. An interpreter of the biblical narrative has to work out damnation and salvation all from within the act of reading. Hence we hear in abundance confessions to 'the original sin of writing' or hopes for 'a redemptive reading'. Postmodern theology thus preserves a traditional Christian soteriology by restating it in literary and artistic terms.

Postmodern readers of the Bible maintain that the Bible matters. Yet they no longer see themselves as being responsible for explaining why. An explanation of this kind would inevitably require a form of transcendental argument. Postmodern theology, assuming no origin and expecting no conclusion, recognises no need or possibility of authentication other than the very act of writing and reading the text. This is why postmodern theologians are comfortable with the practice of reading the Bible as literature. In his *Book of God* Gabriel Josipovici asks 'whether we are fundamentalists or atheists', whether 'the difference [of the Bible is] absolute or relative, whether it is inherent in the Bible or merely the result of extrinsic cultural factors' (Josipovici, 3). This is the standard questioning that used to divide the believer from the non-believer. Yet instead of taking it on board he only promises that the whole book should be an answer. He acknowledges that the Bible 'has *mattered* in the past' and asks whether one could read the Bible 'if one's own stake were not correspondingly high' (xii). Again he only promises that his book is in itself an answer. The advantage of suspending these old questions is that he can claim equal seriousness in reading the Bible as any theologians of the past did and simultaneously exercise the freedom of a literary critic who has no commitment to the Bible. It is an attempt to strike a middle ground between theology and literary criticism. In this essay I would like to re-examine two pioneering attempts at reading the Bible in this manner, by Geoffrey Hartman and Gabriel Josipovici, and see how they maximize the benefit of this suspension while maintaining the fundaments of the Judaeo-Christian tradition, 'election' in the case of Hartman's 'The Struggle for the Text' and 'incarnation' in the case of Josipovici's 'Jesus: Narrative and Incarnation'.

It is not surprising, therefore, that postmodern readers of the Bible find their prime example in the midrashic reading of the Hebrew Bible. James L. Kugel explains on what basis the rabbis exercise their interpretative freedom:

> Divine words have an existence independent of circumstance and immediate intention, that, in short, a text is a text, and whatever hidden meaning one is able to reveal in it through 'searching' [possible original meaning of the word, 'midrash'] is *there*, part of the divine plan. (Kugel, 79)

Kugel provides a remarkable example of this sort of interpretation, remarkable both in the degree of the interpreter's dedication to the text and the level of manipulation he exercises in interpreting the text. Here is Amos' dire declaration 'She has fallen and will no more rise, the virgin of Israel'. One rabbi repunctuated it and read 'She had fallen and will no more rise, O virgin of Israel'. The point is that this obvious textual tampering is a faithful and serious and not at all ridiculous attitude towards what the rabbi and the whole nation regard as the sacred text. Only within the utter commitment to the Bible do rabbis exercise their interpretative freedom. Kugel says that this example 'is indeed amusing, the gallows humor of the prisoners of the Text; and it is the heartfelt hope of a people' (80). Mircea Eliade's and others' *Encyclopaedia of Religion* says:

> All Midrashic teaching undertakes two things (1) to explain opaque or ambiguous texts and their difficult vocabulary and syntax thus supplying us with what we would call literal or close-to-literal explanation or, for lack of that, purely homiletical guess; (2) to contemporize, that is, so to describe or treat biblical personalities and events as to make recognizable the immediate relevance of what might otherwise be regarded as only archaic.

The relevance between the archaic text and the contemporary interpreter is not self-evident; therefore it takes a full interpretative effort to recover the relevance. As to its origin, it says:

> A question when, precisely, the interpretation of the Torah began may never be answered satisfactorily. For from the moment any text is adopted as a rule or guide of life, some interpretation – added explanation, commentary – inevitably becomes necessary.

The claim that the Torah should have immediate relevance here and now is based upon, needless to say, the Jewish Covenant. The purpose of interpretation is to fill the gap between the text and the interpreter, and by doing so to re-establish the relevance between the text and the interpreter and finally to reconfirm the Covenant.

Thus for a Jewish interpreter the Hebrew Bible is both binding and liberating. It is by their Covenant, of which the Torah is the proof, that the Jews become the prisoners of the text. And in this prison they can exercise their interpretative freedom in the form of midrash. It is important to notice that the content of the Covenant, that is, the biblical text, is indeterminate in the sense that its meaning is never fully known to the interpreter. It remains blank and keeps demanding interpretation. And since no interpretation is final its demand for interpretation is endless. Here is an unbreakable circularity between the Covenant that demands interpretation and interpretation that in return reconfirms the Covenant. For Kugel and others this is the only reason why the Hebrew Bible is open to interpretation. The Covenant demands that it be trusted, be taken as a true promise and not a lie. Yet it is only a promise; that is, no one knows whether it is true until the last moment. The Covenant therefore demands the covenantee to maintain its truth-claim. Interpretation is an attempt at maintaining this assumption, without which the Covenant itself would become meaningless. In this sense, and in this sense alone, the Hebrew Bible is not literature.

A reader of the Hebrew Bible finds openness not only in the open-endedness of the Covenantal promise but also in its narrative style that contains many gaps and leaps. Erich Auerbach compares the Hebrew Bible with the Greek text and finds that these blanks are characteristic of the Hebrew accounts of persons and events. Its particular effect, according to Auerbach, is to create the sense of 'suspense':

> the externalization of only so much as is necessary for the purpose of the narrative, all else left in obscurity; the decisive points of the narrative alone are emphasized, what lies between is nonexistent; time and place are undefined and call for interpretation; thoughts and feeling remain unexpressed, are only suggested by the silence and the fragmentary speeches; the whole permeated with the most unrelieved suspense and directed towards a single goal, remains mysterious and 'fraught with background'. (Auerbach, 11–12)

It is not difficult to see why this suspense is inherent to the way the Covenant is understood and recorded. The Covenant is a promise that is in the process of fulfilment. As it is, it suggests the existence of the unknown purpose that rules over every account of persons and events. This purpose, although in itself hidden in the background, exercises its power in discerning what is meaningful and what is not, what events and people are to be considered or ignored. A reader is drawn into this suspense as soon as he or she becomes aware of this unexpressed purpose. That is, he becomes a reader of a hidden text, a searcher of a hidden meaning. He no longer reads the text as it is but plunges into the depth and darkness that the text now indicates behind itself. Frank Kermode uses the term 'secrecy' in the sense that a secret shows and hides itself simultaneously, so that a reader's attention is inevitably drawn to it in a desire to find it out. Following Schiller, Auerbach explains that suspense 'robs us of our emotional freedom, turns our intellectual and spiritual powers in one direction' (11). As Auerbach says, the Hebrew text contains 'a second, concealed meaning'. An ordinary reader of an ordinary text may also seek for a second meaning. But once under the Covenant, this second meaning, which remains concealed, becomes first, and whatever one sees on the surface of the text becomes secondary. With this shift, what used to be the background becomes the foreground. The point is that, in spite of this shift, the background does not become brighter, that this new foreground retains its darkness and obscurity just as it did before.

A gap, a lacuna, in the Hebrew text strikes suspense. That is, it is not neutral but laden with a hidden purpose; it is covenantal and binding, and not liberating. Geoffrey Hartman in his essay 'The Struggle for the Text' shows how a critic like Roland Barthes who sees this gap as a neutral opening misses this covenantal dimension. Barthes describes the gap in the Hebrew Bible as 'the discontinuities of readability, the juxtaposition of narrative entities which to some extent run free from an explicit logical articulation' and argues that one should resist an attempt of filling up this gap and 'hold its significance fully open' (quoted in Hartman, 14). Barthes sees the gap as a neutral opening, and, according to Hartman, fails to see that under the Covenant a gap is opened only to be fulfilled. A gap is there for the covenantee to find a fulfilment and not for a neutral interpreter to exercise his unrestrained freedom.

Having argued this far, however, Hartman does ask himself whether he can read the Hebrew Bible as literature, and whether he can read the Bible outside the Covenant. He asks this question as a literary critic, that is, placing himself outside the Covenant. This is how he justifies his trial. 'The only virtue I can claim for the literary study of the Bible is [...] that while it can hardly be more imaginative than the masters of old, *it can dare go wrong*' (Hartman, 9). What difference this makes in interpreting the text is unclear. I do not think that he becomes freer or more daring in discussing, for example, the dark side of the Jewish Covenant, as he does in the article. However, towards the end of his article he tentatively suggests what I would like to call 'the literary covenant'. This is a covenant that a reader makes every time he encounters a difficult, baffling text and tries to read it. The question is whether the literary covenant is the same as, or different from, the Jewish Covenant. The question reminds us of Auerbach's curious comment, 'The concept of God held by the Jews is less a cause than a symptom of their manner of comprehending and representing things' (Auerbach, 8). If this is the case, and if Hartman accepts this, what Hartman does by introducing the literary covenant is to suggest that the Jewish Covenant is the effect, and not the cause, of this literary covenant, that Jewish theology is the result of their biblical narrative. Thus he can argue that the Bible is primarily literature. Yet there is still another, obvious question, whether we need this covenant to read Homer. According to Auerbach, the answer is 'No'. Then we have two ways of reading, that is, two different attitudes towards texts. Do we choose one or the other attitude according to the material? The postmodern reader, however, cannot maintain this distinction between in the light of intertextuality that simply overrides such a distinction. Do we take two attitudes in one act of reading? This is unlikely. Are we, then, already chosen or condemned to a particular way of reading even before we start?

It is not difficult to see why Barthes's neutral reading of the Hebrew Bible appears ill applied. But it is difficult to find an essential difference between rabbinical midrash and Hartman's 'literary' reading of the Bible. The notion of the divine design looms equally over the rabbi's historical reading and Hartman's literary reading. In Hartman's practice it is no longer foundational but merely literary, that is, God manifests himself not in history but in a story. Hartman's attempt thus reminds us of an obvious etymology. The point is that Hartman will not decide whether the Bible is history or story, unlike critics such as Kugel and Barthes for whom the question is already decided one way or the other. As seen above, his 'literary' covenant is a way of retaining this uncertainty. It is difficult to say what this covenant precisely is, although it is not that difficult to say what it is not. It is neither a midrashic/covenantal one like Kugel's, nor a formalistic/non-covenantal one like Barthes's.

Gabriel Josipovici plays upon the same uncertainty in his presentation of an alternative, 'narrative', 'incarnation'. In his chapter entitled 'Narrative and Incarnation', he proposes to read the Gospel narrative as biography. According to him, the purpose of the Gospel narrative or any narrative is to give the reader a vivid impression of the subject figure. 'A biography is a narrative of the life and death of the subject' (Josipovici, 210). When successful it brings the subject to life. Its purpose is not to prove and preserve historical facts about the subject but to tell a good story. According to Josipovici, biography is more fictive than factual, and it is more effective when fictively vivid than when factually thorough. Once recorded, the fact about the subject's life and death gives way to a fiction, a biography. Josipovici repeatedly plays down the importance of fact over fiction on the ground that fact cannot but be represented fictively. To read the Gospel narrative as biography, therefore, is to disregard its claim to historical validity and to replace the notion of a historical incarnation with that of a 'narrative' incarnation. To accept that the Gospel narrative is a biography is to argue that we should find in the Gospel not the fact of historical incarnation but only the fictive account of the event and that we are after all only the reader of the narrative account and not the witness of the event itself for whom narrative a incarnation is the only accessible one.

Following Josipovici's argument, the distinction between fact and fiction ceases to serve as a reliable criterion of credibility. Instead, he presents the distinction between narration and persuasion: narration tells a story while persuasion asserts its factual truth and demands the reader's consent. Josipovici's point is that the reader can trust fictive narration while he may feel suspicious of persuasion that can only emphasize the factual credibility. In his words, 'we assent to narratives, as we do to people, to the degree that we grow to feel we can trust them' (Josipovici, 234). We find in the Gospel narrative both ordinary and extraordinary events. The ordinary events the Evangelists simply narrate, while they cannot but persuade when they present the extraordinary events. By the Gospel's 'ordinary' accounts he means Jesus' physical presence, that is, his anger, hunger and death. In terms of the fact–fiction distinction, he would argue that these accounts are fictive but ordinary and therefore powerfully indicative of the fact behind them, while the extraordinary accounts that have little fictive value need to be forced upon the reader as fact, only to raise the reader's suspicion. He simply declares: 'in biblical narratives [...] it is moments of ordinariness [...] which establish the grounds of our trust' (234). He would read these ordinary accounts in 'the simple and natural way in which they ask to be read, that is, as we read or listen to all narratives which engage our interest but about which we are not asked to hold particular views' (233). So far as ordinary events are concerned, the narrative incarnation is successful.

How successful is he, then, in separating the narration of ordinary moments from the extraordinary claims that the Gospels no doubt make? These claims are so extraordinary that even the ordinary minded Evangelists could not narrate them. Josipovici admits that the Gospel carries persuasion as well as narration, and that the persuasive parts are awkward. But he insists that these persuasions, 'these narrative flaws' in the canonical Gospels are relatively minor compared with the ones in the apocrypha, in which the reader encounters so many miracles at so many levels that he soon loses the sense of them. Josipovici presents the case as being a contrast between the canonical writers who narrate and the apocryphal ones who persuade. His observation, however, does not explain why the canonical writers also persuade or why the extraordinary persuasion in the canonical Gospels is so significant. Moreover, the comparison between the canonical and apocryphal writers allows another reading. While the canonical writers are well aware of the distinction between the ordinary and extraordinary events, the apocryphal writers have only a vague distinction between them even to the extent of placing them side by side with no tension. The apocryphal writers use as many miracles as they please not because they try hard to authenticate their narratives by them as Josipovici suggests, but because they simply have no reason to restrain themselves from them. It is the canonical writers who exhibit their keen sensitivity to the distinction between the ordinary and the extraordinary. In telling their story they select the few but most extraordinary events and place them in between the ordinary narratives. The purpose is to emphasize their extra-ordinariness and show how powerfully and decisively the extra-ordinary takes over the ordinary. It seems to me that the narration of these ordinary moments is there only to enhance by contrast the effect of their extraordinary persuasion. In reading the Gospels, we are made aware of the ordinary moments, but they are there to be broken for the sake of achieving the maximum emphasis upon the extraordinary moments.

Contrary to Josipovici's argument, the canonical writers appear to be keener and subtler persuaders than the apocryphal ones. We can support this view by examining their two different ways of presenting the incarnation. To use Josipovici's distinction they are either apocalyptic or gnostic. They either see it as a once-for-all historical event or the knowledge that is accessible everywhere anytime. Here the distinction between history and story reappears. The canonical writers are anxious to convey this extraordinary yet historical, apocalyptic event and to persuade the world of its validity. It is this urgent anxiety in them that sensitizes them to the sharp distinction between the ordinary and the extraordinary and leads them to the tensioned contrast of the two to the extent of overriding one by the other. That is to say, this urgent need of persuasion is what distinguishes the canonical writers from their apocryphal counterparts. At this point Josipovici resorts to the initial indeterminacy that characterizes his and other similar approaches and says: 'if all is fairy tale as in the apocryphal Gospels, then Incarnation and Resurrection are without meaning, but if all is the harsh reality of the world then they are also without meaning' (255). The point, however, is that this 'meaning' cannot but be apocalyptic and demand ultimate persuasion. This apocalyptic message is not an accidental addition to the biographical accounts as Josipovici's initial discussion may seem to imply, but it is the central message that runs through the Gospel narrative and controls these biographical accounts from behind. Here is an irony. Josipovici picks up the moments in the Gospel narrative when persuasion recedes to the background and praises them as a great narrative achievement, while the Evangelists' primary concern is not to narrate but to persuade. If he is to argue that narration is a better form of persuasion, he has to admit that the whole Gospel is ultimately a persuasion and that as a persuasion it increases both the believer's conviction and the non-believer's suspicion.

Josipovici's treatment of the biblical parables appears to fall into a similar irony. Taking up the parable of the prodigal son he tries hard to establish that this is primarily a narration and not persuasion, that is, it is a story of a father and two sons, the eldest and the youngest, not an allegorical account of God, the Jews and the Christians. He says: 'We may start to read this with the firm notion that the elder son "stands for" this or that, but once we enter the narrative we have to abandon our preconceptions and surrender ourselves to it' (227). He quotes from Bernard Harrison and insists that the Gospel parables are open ended. However, there is at least one parable in the Gospel narrative that seems to work in the opposite direction, that is, to force and reinforce a particular point of view and a particular message.

Josipovici mentions the parable of the fig tree only briefly, saying it is there 'to make a symbolic point' (220). My question is whether this 'symbolic point' and the way it is presented in the Gospel narrative is at odds with Josipovici's argument that the parables are open ended. This parable appears in every synoptic Gospel with different emphases as to what it means. Assuming Mark's account is the oldest, we can trace how the original account was worked into a parable that is charged with a specific symbolic point.

> And on the morrow, when they were come from Bethany, he was hungry: and seeing a fig tree afar off having leaves, he came, if haply he might find any thing thereon: and when he came to it, he found nothing but leaves; for the time of figs was not yet. And Jesus answered and said unto it, No man eat fruit of thee hereafter for ever, and his disciples heard it. (Mark 11:12–14; KJV)

Here is no conclusion, no comment; therefore no forced interpretation. We are not told even what happened to the tree. The narrative thus appears to retain a parabolic openness. However, we need to remember that this openness is not neutral but binding. If we examine what is told in the parable and what is left open, we see how limited as against free, and how charged as against neutral, this apparent openness is. We are told of Jesus' displeasure and his following curse on the fig tree. What we are not told is why he was displeased and what happened to the tree. That is, whatever interpretation we are to make from his hasty and unnatural (or supernatural) demand on the tree and the subsequent curse, and whatever level of freedom we are to exercise in dealing with these questions, our interpretations are bound to the parable's central theme, demand and curse. Interpreters are here only to make sense of them. A parable of this sort inevitably gathers interpretative layers almost immediately. We can see the process in the recantation of the same story in the other Gospels.

> And when he saw a fig tree in the way, he came to it, and found nothing thereon, but leaves only, and said unto it, Let no fruit grow on thee henceforward for ever. And presently the fig tree withered away. And when the disciples saw it, they marvelled, saying, How soon is the fig tree withered away! (Matthew 21:19–20)

Here the Evangelist gives the consequence of the curse, and this allows him to add an extra layer of interpretation:

> Jesus answered and said unto them, Verily I say unto you, If ye have faith, and doubt not, ye shall not only do this which is done to the fig tree, but also if ye

> shall say unto this mountain, Be thou removed, and be thou cast into the sea; it shall be done. (v. 21)

This layer of interpretation aims at what Josipovici calls 'a symbolic meaning'. But it still gives an impression of being arbitrary and accidental. That is, it is not generated symbolically from within the story but forced upon it from without. Matthew's attempt at conveying the message therefore remains unconvincing. Finally, this is from Luke:

> He spake also this parable: A certain man had a fig tree planted in his vineyard; and he came and sought fruit thereon, and found none. Then said he unto the dresser of his vineyard, Behold, these three years I come seeking fruit on this fig tree, and find none: cut it down; why cumbereth it the ground? And he answering said unto him, Lord, let it alone this year also, till I shall dig about it, and dung it: And if it bear fruit, well: and if not, then after that thou shalt cut it down. (Luke 13:6–9)

Here the message is unmistakably clear. The symbolic meaning turns out to be the ultimatum 'Except ye repent, ye shall all likewise perish'. The parable of the fig tree is a parable so far as it invites interpretation. However, its openness is a false openness that catches the reader's mind and deprives him of free engagement. The irony is that Mark's account, the oldest and the least elaborate, is the most parabolic, and that when it is made into a parable it no longer narrates but just persuades.

Considering how Josipovici presents the parable of the Prodigal Son and how we read that of the fig tree, it seems fair to say that opening is only one of the two functions of the biblical parables. The other function is to send a clear and uncompromising message.

Seeing the two literary projects, by Hartman to read the Hebrew Bible as literature, and by Josipovici to read the Gospel as biography, it is clear that they have to override the distinction between the Bible and literature. They play with the idea that by their attempt the Bible may resolve itself into the mass of literature. However, they do not come clean as to whether their attempt strikes at the possibility of the Bible absorbing the rest of literature, and whether they are in the end arguing that the ultimate task of literature is to narrate the biblical soteriology as well as or even better than traditional theology did. Their advantage is that the key concepts they use, literary covenant and narrative incarnation, are applicable beyond the traditional confines of 'election' and 'incarnation'. In fact they are applicable indefinitely. Following their argument we might as well accept that a reader, as soon as he or she reads anything, cannot but re-enact Judaeo-Christian soteriology.

Postmodern theology thus shifts the playground of Christian soteriology. Yet it still retains the notion of election and incarnation and their oneness and onceness, if no longer in principle then still in practice. Moreover, by suspending any foundational argument these notions are freed from any geographical and historical confines and through the web of intertextuality they become universally applicable. The question is whether this practice still partakes of the salvation of Israel. The Judaeo-Christian practice, as well as other religious practice, begins with openness. Yet there is clearly an anomaly in fundamentally curtailing that original openness. The difficulty is that those who are outside the tradition do not understand the oneness and onceness of election and incarnation, and those who are inside the tradition either refuse to explain why or, when they try, end up giving a passionate apology that explains nothing. Both Hartman and Josipovici intend to begin their reading of the Bible without preconceptions, yet have their indeterminacy curtailed from the start. It is possible that the postmodern theologian would still defend this curtailment, often uncritically, and refuse to see beyond the text in much the same way as those who refused to see beyond their election or their salvation. We still need to ask whether that is the goal of this new theology, that is, whether we can accept a religion without transcendence.

Bibliography

Auerbach, Erich. *Mimesis: The Representation of Reality in Western Literature* (1946), translated by Willard Trask. Princeton, NJ: Princeton UP, 1968.

Hartman, Geoffrey H. 'The Struggle for the Text', in Geoffrey H. Hartman and Sanford Budick (eds.), *Midrash and Literature*. New Haven and London: Yale UP, 1986.

Josipovici, Gabriel. *The Book of God: A Response to the Bible*. New Haven and London: Yale UP, 1988.

Kugel, James L. 'Two Introductions to Midrash', in Geoffrey H. Hartman and Sanford Budick (eds.), *Midrash and Literature*. New Haven and London: Yale UP, 1988.

List of Contributors

DAVID JASPER is Professor of Literature and Theology at the University of Glasgow and was Director of the Centre for the Study of Literature, Theology and the Arts from 1991 to 1998.

S. BRENT PLATE is a graduate of the Centre and holds a Ph.D. from Emory University, Atlanta. He is Assistant Professor of Religion and the Visual Arts at Texas Christian University.

STEPHEN FOUNTAIN holds a Ph.D. from the Centre. Having taught Religion and Literature for a number of years he is now studying to become a medical doctor.

ANDREW W. HASS holds a Ph.D. from the Centre, and is Visiting Professor of Religion and Literature in the Honours College at the University of Houston, Texas.

ELIZABETH PHILPOT holds an M.Litt. in Art History and Biblical Studies from the Centre. She is currently completing her doctoral studies in Art History at the University of Göteborg, Sweden.

PETER STILES holds a Ph.D. from the Centre and teaches at Trinity Grammar School, Sidney, Australia.

JEFFREY F. KEUSS holds a Ph.D. from the Centre and is a Lecturer in Practical Theology at the University of Glasgow, and currently co-Director of the Centre.

CATHERINE RAINE holds a Ph.D. from the Centre, and having taught for a number of years in Glasgow, now lives in Canada.

DAVID E. KLEMM is Professor in the Department of Religious Studies at the University of Iowa. He was Visiting Professor at the Centre in 1999.

DARREN J. N. MIDDLETON holds a Ph.D. from the Centre and is Assistant Professor of Literature and Religion at Texas Christian University.

GEORGE NEWLANDS is Professor of Divinity at the University of Glasgow, and was Director of the Centre from 1998 to 2002.

CHRISTOPHER BURDON holds a Ph.D. from the Centre and is Principal of the Church of England Northern Ordination Course, Manchester.

ALISON JASPER holds a Ph.D. from the Department of Theology and Religious Studies, the University of Glasgow, and is a Lecturer in Religious Studies at the University of Stirling.

KIYOSHI TSUCHIYA holds a Ph.D. from the Centre and is a Lecturer in Eastern Religions at the University of Glasgow. He was for many years the Deputy Director of the Centre.

DARLENE BIRD is currently completing a Ph.D. at the Centre, having previously gained an M.Phil. with Distinction in Literature and Theology at the University of Glasgow.

Religions and Discourse

Edited by James M. M. Francis

Religions and Discourse explores religious language in the major world faiths from various viewpoints, including semiotics, pragmatics and cognitive linguistics, and reflects on how it is situated within wider intellectual and cultural contexts. In particular a key issue is the role of figurative speech. Many fascinating metaphors originate in religion e.g. revelation as a 'garment', apostasy as 'adultery', loving kindness as the 'circumcision of the heart'. Every religion rests its specific orientations upon symbols such as these, to name but a few. The series strives after the interdisciplinary approach that brings together such diverse disciplines as religious studies, theology, sociology, philosophy, linguistics and literature, guided by an international editorial board of scholars representative of the aforementioned disciplines. Though scholarly in its scope, the series also seeks to facilitate discussions pertaining to central religious issues in contemporary contexts.

The series will publish monographs and collected essays of a high scholarly standard.

Volume 6 Stuart Sim and David Walker: *Bunyan and Authority.* 239 pages. 2000. ISBN 3-906764-44-3 / US-ISBN 0-8204-4634-3

Volume 7 Simon Harrison: *Conceptions of Unity in Recent Ecumenical Discussion.* 282 pages. 2000. ISBN 3-906758-51-6 / US-ISBN 0-8204-5073-1

Volume 8 Gill Goulding: *On the Edge of Mystery.* 256 pages. 2000. ISBN 3-906758-80-X / US-ISBN 0-8204-5087-1

Volume 9 Kune Biezeveld and Anne-Claire Mulder (eds.): *Towards a Different Transcendence.* 358 pages. 2001. ISBN 3-906765-66-0 / US-ISBN 0-8204-5303-X

Volume 10 George Newlands: *John and Donald Baillie: Transatlantic Theology.* 451 pages. 2002. ISBN 3-906768-41-4 / US-ISBN 0-8204-5853-8

Volume 11 Kenneth Fleming: *Asian Christian Theologians in Dialogue with Buddhism.* 388 pages. 2002. ISBN 3-906768-42-2 / US-ISBN 0-8204-5854-6

Volume 12 N. H. Keeble (ed.): *John Bunyan: Reading Dissenting Writing.* 277 pages. 2002. ISBN 3-906768-52-X / US-ISBN 0-8204-5864-3

Volume 13 Robert L. Platzner (ed.): *Gender, Tradition and Renewal.* Forthcoming. ISBN 3-906769-64-X / US-ISBN 0-8204-5901-1

Volume 14 Michael Ipgrave: *Trinity and Inter Faith Dialogue: Plenitude and Plurality.* 397 pages. 2003. ISBN 3-906769-77-1 / US-ISBN 0-8204-5914-3

Volume 15 Kurt Feyaerts (ed.): *The Bible through Metaphor and Translation: A Cognitive Semantic Perspective.* 298 pages. 2003. ISBN 3-906769-82-8 / US-ISBN 0-8204-5919-4

Volume 16 Andrew Britton and Peter Sedgwick: *Economic Theory and Christian Belief.* 310 pages. 2003. ISBN 3-03910-015-7 / US-ISBN 0-8204-6284-5

Volume 17 James M. M. Francis: *Adults as Children: Images of Childhood in the Ancient World and the New Testament.* Forthcoming. ISBN 3-03910-020-3 / US-ISBN 0-8204-6289-6

Volume 18 David Jasper and George Newlands (eds): *Believing in the Text: Essays from the Centre for the Study of Literature, Theology and the Arts, University of Glasgow* 248 pages. 2004. ISBN 3-03910-076-9 / US-ISBN 0-8204-6892-4

Volume 19 Leonardo De Chirico: *Evangelical Theological Perspectives on post-Vatican II Roman Catholicism.* 337 pages. 2003. ISBN 3-03910-145-5 / US-ISBN 0-8204-6955-6

Volume 20 Heather Ingman: *Women's Spirituality in the Twentieth Century: An Exploration through Fiction.* 232 pages. 2004. ISBN 3-03910-149-8 / US-ISBN 0-8204-6959-9

Volume 21 Ian R. Boyd: *Dogmatics among the Ruins: German Expressionism and the Enlightenment as Contexts for Karl Barth's Theological Development.* 349 pages. 2004. ISBN 3-03910-147-1 / US-ISBN 0-8204-6957-2

Volume 22 Forthcoming.

Volume 23 Malcolm Brown: *After the Market: Economics, Moral Agreement and the Churches' Mission.* 321 pages. 2004. ISBN 3-03910-154-4 / US-ISBN 0-8204-6964-5